THE MINDFUL SCHOOL

The Mindful School

Transforming School Culture
through Mindfulness
and Compassion

edited by
Patricia A. Jennings

associate editors
Anthony A. DeMauro
Polina P. Mischenko

THE GUILFORD PRESS
New York   London

Library of Congress Cataloging-in-Publication Data

Names: Jennings, Patricia A., editor. | DeMauro, Anthony A., editor. |
   Mischenko, Polina P., editor.
Title: The mindful school : transforming school culture through mindfulness
   and compassion / edited by Patricia A. Jennings ; associate editors
   Anthony A. DeMauro, Polina P. Mischenko.
Description: New York, NY : The Guilford Press, 2019. | Includes
   bibliographical references and index.
Identifiers: LCCN 2019009869 | ISBN 9781462540020 (hardback) | ISBN
   9781462539987 (paperback)
Subjects: LCSH: Affective education. | Reflective teaching. |
   Mindfulness-based cognitive therapy. | Stress management for children. |
   School environment--Psychological aspects. | BISAC: EDUCATION /
   Educational Psychology. | PSYCHOLOGY / Psychotherapy / Child & Adolescent.
   | SOCIAL SCIENCE / Social Work.
Classification: LCC LB1072 .M56 2019 | DDC 370.15/34--dc23
LC record available at *https://lccn.loc.gov/2019009869*

About the Editor

Patricia A. Jennings, PhD, is Professor of Education in the Curry School of Education and Human Development at the University of Virginia. She is an internationally recognized leader in the fields of social–emotional learning and mindfulness in education. Dr. Jennings received the Cathy Kerr Award for Courageous and Compassionate Science from the Mind and Life Institute and has been cited by *Mindful* magazine as one of "Ten Mindfulness Researchers You Should Know." She has published on topics including mindfulness for teachers and compassionate teaching. She spent over 22 years as a teacher, school director, and teacher educator.

Associate Editors

Anthony A. DeMauro, PhD, is Associate Director of Dalai Lama Fellows and Assistant Director of Student Initiatives at the Contemplative Sciences Center of the University of Virginia. In these roles, he works with young leaders around the world and university students to deepen connections to themselves and others through contemplation and holistic approaches to well-being. Dr. DeMauro's scholarly work, emerging from years of experience in K–12 schools, focuses on how teachers' personal mindfulness practices influence their teaching practices. He has taught courses in classroom management and mindfulness for preservice and inservice teachers. Additionally, Dr. DeMauro delivers professional development programs to educators through Cultivating Awareness and Resilience in Education and cofacilitates mindfulness retreats for teenagers with Inward Bound Mindfulness Education.

Polina P. Mischenko, EdM, is a doctoral candidate in the Curry School of Education and Human Development at the University of Virginia. She conducts research on the experiences of teachers delivering mindfulness-based curricula and on approaches to teaching mindfulness in elementary school settings. She also facilitates mindfulness-based programs and workshops for school faculty and students, and assists local organizations and school districts with their mindfulness-based initiatives. Ms. Mischenko has worked in school settings and education organizations in the United States, Russia, Spain, and Switzerland.

Contributors

Rebecca N. Baelen, MSEd, Education Policy Division, Graduate School of Education, University of Pennsylvania, Philadelphia, Pennsylvania

Jessica Blum-DeStefano, PhD, Education Leadership, Bank Street Graduate School of Education, New York, New York

Richard C. Brown, MA, Contemplative Education Department, Naropa University, Boulder, Colorado

J. Douglas Coatsworth, PhD, Department of Human Development and Family Studies, Colorado State University, Fort Collins, Colorado

Velma L. Cobb, EdD, Lander Center for Educational Research, Graduate School of Education, Touro College, New York, New York

Meghan Damler, MS, Crestwood School, Paris Community Unit School District 4, Paris, Illinois

Anthony A. DeMauro, PhD, Contemplative Sciences Center, University of Virginia, Charlottesville, Virginia

Eleanor Drago-Severson, EdD, Education Leadership and Adult Learning and Leadership, Teachers College, Columbia University, New York, New York

Michael V. Esposito, MA, Department of Psychology, University of Pittsburgh, Pittsburgh, Pennsylvania

Brian M. Galla, PhD, Department of Psychology, University of Pittsburgh, Pittsburgh, Pennsylvania

Melissa W. George, PhD, Department of Human Development and Family Studies, Colorado State University, Fort Collins, Colorado

Elizabeth Grassi, PhD, Department of Education, Regis University, Denver, Colorado

Alexis Harris, PhD, Youth-Nex Center, Research Faculty, Curry School of Education and Human Development, University of Virginia, Charlottesville, Virginia

Patricia A. Jennings, PhD, Department of Curriculum, Instruction, and Special Education, Curry School of Education and Human Development, University of Virginia, Charlottesville, Virginia

Polina P. Mischenko, EdM, Department of Curriculum, Instruction, and Special Education, Curry School of Education and Human Development, University of Virginia, Charlottesville, Virginia

Robert W. Roeser, PhD, Department of Human Development and Family Studies, College of Health and Human Development, The Pennsylvania State University, University Park, Pennsylvania

Lisa Sankowski, EdM, Center for Courage and Renewal Northeast, Wellesley College, Wellesley, Massachusetts

Deborah L. Schussler, PhD, Department of Education Policy Studies, College of Education, The Pennsylvania State University, University Park, Pennsylvania

Pamela Seigle, MS, Center for Courage and Renewal Northeast, Wellesley College, Wellesley, Massachusetts

Rebecca L. Tadlock-Marlo, PhD, Department of Counseling and Higher Education, Eastern Illinois University, Charleston, Illinois

Cynthia Taylor, PhD, Department of Psychology, Portland State University, Portland, Oregon

Aimee Kleisner Walker, PhD, Department of Human Development and Family Studies, Colorado State University, Fort Collins, Colorado

Chip Wood, MSW, Center for Courage and Renewal Northeast, Wellesley College, Wellesley, Massachusetts

Contents

Contents

Contents

PART III. LOOKING TO THE FUTURE

PART I

INTRODUCTION

CHAPTER 1

Where Are We Now?
Where Are We Going?

Preparing Our Students
for an Uncertain Future

PATRICIA A. JENNINGS
ANTHONY A. DEMAURO
POLINA P. MISCHENKO

A conundrum in education today is how to prepare our students for the future. This task, which education has always faced, has become a challenge because we can no longer predict what our children's future will hold. Consider this: could you have predicted our lives as they are today even a decade ago? The rate of change has accelerated to the point that we don't really know what to expect. This uncertainty creates an unparalleled level of stress among educators, students, and their parents, triggering a mental health crisis and interfering with learning. It is more evident than ever that we must prioritize resilience and adaptability so we can cope with these rapid social changes. We need to learn ways to calm our anxious nervous systems and tackle change and the challenges that accompany change with mental clarity, emotional calm, and kindness to others—other human beings, animals, and our environment. The growing popularity of mindfulness- and compassion-based practices in schools suggests that many of us are beginning to recognize these practices as potential approaches to cultivate these strengths. This handbook is intended to provide educators with the most current research

3

and evidence-based practices and approaches to transform our schools with mindfulness and compassion.

Mindfulness and Its Place in 21st-Century Schools

Mindfulness is commonly defined as "the awareness that emerges through paying attention on purpose, in the present moment, and nonjudgmentally to the unfolding of experience moment by moment" (Kabat-Zinn, 2003, p. 145), and is developed through mindful awareness practices, such as meditation and yoga. Continual engagement with mindful awareness practices cultivates a state of mindfulness in one's everyday life, which involves a greater awareness of one's inner mental and emotional processes, as well as a deepened contact with the outer world through heightened sensory experiences and greater attunement in interpersonal interactions. The state of mindful awareness has also been described as "open-hearted" (Kabat-Zinn, 2005, p. 24), where one is not simply more attentive to life's experiences, but is also more accepting and nonjudgmental toward the inner and outer happenings of life. Thus, individuals experience a deeper and more caring sense of connection to themselves, others, and the world around them when they bring mindful awareness into their daily lives. Mindfulness has gained increasing popularity in the West over the last 15 years, and research has shown mindfulness-based programs to be beneficial for adults' psychological health (Khoury et al., 2013), stress management (Chisea & Serretti, 2009), attentional abilities, and maintaining emotional balance (Sedlmeier et al., 2012).

Considering the attentional and emotional demands of teaching, many mindfulness-based programs have been developed specifically for teachers. Such programs aim to provide teachers with the "habits of mind" (Roeser, Skinner, Beers, & Jennings, 2012, p. 167) to create emotionally supportive learning environments while maintaining their own well-being and motivation to teach. Understanding that teachers are a foundational part of any educational endeavor and also that teachers' own social and emotional competence is necessary for any student growth in this domain (Jennings & Greenberg, 2009), many mindfulness-based educational initiatives have been started by working with teachers. The programs for teachers, highlighted by Cynthia Taylor, Patricia A. Jennings, Alexis Harris, Deborah L. Schussler, and Robert W. Roeser (Chapter 5, this volume), have demonstrated early success in impacting teachers' well-being and their abilities to manage occupational stressors (Benn, Akiva, Arel, & Roeser, 2012; Jennings, Frank, Snowberg, Coccia, & Greenberg, 2013; Roeser et al., 2013), while also improving the quality of their interactions with students (Jennings et al., 2017) and student engagement (Brown et al., 2017).

Additionally, many scholars have identified how mindfulness can cultivate essential skills for students' success (Meikeljohn et al., 2012; Mind and Life Education Research Network, 2012). Helping students pay attention in school, providing them with skills to manage stress and navigate emotional challenges, and learning ways to cooperatively interact with others are some of the primary goals of mindfulness-based programs for students. Many of these programs have also demonstrated success in these areas and are reviewed by Rebecca N. Baelen, Michael V. Exposito, and Brian M. Galla (Chapter 2, this volume). Although interest in mindfulness-based programs for students is rapidly growing, the research on their efficacy and ideal structural components (i.e., program length and format, delivery approach) is still very nascent. Therefore, schools must be deliberate and intentional in implementing such programs to ensure they meet each school's unique culture and needs. Chapter 2 offers some important considerations in regard to this decision-making process.

While the research on mindfulness-based programs for teachers and students is promising yet still burgeoning, there is also a great need for understanding how other educational stakeholders play a role in adopting and implementing mindfulness in schools. Engaging school administrators, mental health workers, and parents will also be vital in making mindfulness initiatives cohesive and sustainable. Therefore, in the current handbook we included the experiences and scholarship of these stakeholders to offer a comprehensive perspective of how mindfulness can be infused into schools.

Compassion

As mentioned earlier, mindfulness involves an awareness and acceptance of internal and external experience. These factors are prerequisites of compassion, defined as "the process of recognizing suffering and the motivation to relieve suffering" (Jennings, 2019, p. 131). First one must recognize the suffering of another by becoming aware and noticing the signs of suffering. These signs can be obvious, such as seeing a student crying, or subtle, such as a student quietly tensing up in anticipation of an unexpected exam. Signs of suffering can also be confusing. For example, often when a person is deeply suffering, he can attempt to hide his condition by acting defiant, angry, or aloof. The awareness cultivated by practicing mindfulness can help us recognize these behaviors as symptoms of suffering, rather than automatically judging them as bad behavior. Next, the openness and non-judgmental acceptance of what is occurring is necessary to attune with the other. If we are judging him, it may be difficult to empathize, to understand how he is feeling and feel *with* him. These initial steps in the cultivation of compassion are critical. However, they are not enough. The next step is to regulate the strong emotions that often accompany empathy. If I feel with his suffering but become overwhelmed by his pain, I won't be able to help him. So, I must also calm the strong feelings that can arise in the face of such suffering and consider what he needs and how I best can help, which may involve creating space for the answer to unfold, rather than a knee-jerk impulse to "fix." Finally, I must express my intention to help, which may be simply being present for his suffering and listening. We cannot always solve others' problems and eliminate their suffering, but our calm, open-hearted, mindful presence can make a huge difference to their healing. In this way, mindfulness can help us build compassion and provide our students with models of compassion.

Compassion is not simply an interpersonal process; it involves an expansion of our sense of connection to others in society. It broadens our connection to the whole of humanity. By recognizing our common humanity, we open our inner circles to include all humans regardless of race, ethnicity, gender, ethnicity, sexual identity and preference, national origin, or religion. It expands further to encompass our care for other species of animals and plants and the whole of life on our planet. Finally, it can expand to include those living things yet unborn, our future generations. In the school setting, compassion is a powerful catalyst for building strong and supportive school communities that are diverse, equitable, and resilient.

School Transformation

We are not merely calling for another educational reform effort. There have been enough failed educational reforms in recent decades that have only resulted in disrupting schools' abilities to serve the needs of students, while perpetuating many of the educational inequities that plague our schools. What we are calling for is a complete transformation of the educational system. While reforms attempt to improve the condition of an existing system, transformation involves changing the very nature of the system itself. We do not hold that mindfulness and compassion alone are enough to fully transform schools, nor do we claim to possess the blueprint for the transformation we are seeking. However, we do feel that mindfulness and compassion can serve as an essential vision and framework for the transformation we seek.

Just as mindfulness helps us more clearly see and understand our internal processes and their impact on the outer world, mindfulness can also help us collectively see the internal and external workings of our school systems and its impacts on children, adults, and the larger society. Seeing these relationships more clearly, we can then identify what is needed most and respond to the challenges in an intentional and skillful way. Compassion provides the necessary framework for grounding the change in an ethics of care and attending to the needs of the most vulnerable. Mindfulness and compassion also provide the patience and constant critical reflection required to guide the unfolding transformation.

Transformation will likely not result from the continual striving for a "silver bullet" solution to our educational issues, as has been the case with previous educational reforms. When pressured to solve a problem, our egos, anxieties, and perhaps even hurt and anger can prevent us from seeing clearly and responding skillfully. Yet, mindfulness allows us to fully behold and experience the present moment for all that it brings and helps us see the situation from an entirely new perspective. Such a widening of our viewpoint can allow for a multitude of new connections to be made and brand new possibilities to arise.

While mindfulness orients us to the present moment, we do not simply ignore the past and how it has brought us here. This is particularly important for work in educational systems in which the historical structures and relationships with other systems (cultural, political, economic, etc.) will continue to impact the current state of education. Much of the needed healing and transformational work will have to be informed by our past failures and constantly renewed systems of oppression. By fully inhabiting the present moment, we must also contemplate where the present moment is taking us and keep an eye on the future. Transformation will not occur overnight, so we must consistently align our decisions and actions toward the future we envision.

When we inhabit the present moment with clarity, no longer driven by our past hurts or fears about the future, we create a space for insight, wisdom, creativity, and innovation to arise. Constantly grounded in an ethics of care and understanding of our interdependence, we ensure that our movement is meeting the needs of all and shares a commitment to our shared humanity. Then we begin to generate the personal and collective energy to fuel the transformation, all the while staying open to new insights and voices to inform the movement so that it is responsive to change and does not become stagnant.

The school transformation we are calling for will not be accomplished quickly, easily, or by a single group of educational stakeholders. Transformation will require a sustained and collaborative effort among practitioners working within schools (teachers, administrators, mental health workers, etc.), students, their parents, researchers, policymakers, and even the larger general public who shape schools through their political decisions. Schools operate as systems with numerous interrelated and interdependent elements. All parts, both human and inanimate (i.e., physical spaces and resources), work together and influence one another, such that all must contribute to the comprehensive, cohesive, and sustainable transformation we advocate. Not only must all stakeholders' perspectives and experiences be valued and infused into the work of transformation, but a broader understanding of systems is also needed to plan for both the bottom-up and top-down work needed to create a full transformation.

Understanding the need for a collaborative and cohesive effort, we have assembled as many different perspectives as possible and made the content accessible to all who are looking to contribute to this transformation. We have gathered the authentic voices and experiences of various educational stakeholders to contribute to this work by highlighting successes, learning from past failures, and creating a vision for what is possible with continued commitment to mindfulness and compassion in schools.

Important Considerations

Meta-analyses examining data from numerous studies have found that mindfulness-based programs for students and teachers show promise for improving well-being (Carsley, Khoury, & Heath, 2018; Klingbeil et al., 2017; Klingbeil & Renshaw, 2018; Rawana, Diplock, & Chan, 2018; Zoogman, Goldberg, Hoyt, & Miller, 2015). However, research involving adults has occasionally found increases in psychological distress as a result of participation in MBIs (Van Dam et al., 2018). Among healthy adults, this may be a transitory effect as participants become more aware of emotions resulting in increased perceived stress (Hayes & Feldman, 2004). More research is required to determine the best approach for at-risk populations. To be on the safe side, educators should proceed with caution and consideration for individuals with trauma and other mental health issues (see Jennings, 2019, for specific recommendations). This volume offers years of collective wisdom regarding how to successfully introduce mindfulness and compassion practices in schools settings. Two important considerations: (1) educators must cultivate their own mindfulness and compassion first before introducing activities to students, and (2) practices should be presented as invitational and program participants should be allowed to opt out of activities if they so choose.

Overview of This Volume

In Chapter 2, Rebecca N. Baelen, Michael V. Esposito, and Brian M. Galla review the most rigorous research to date on mindfulness programs for PreK–12 students. They first provide an overview of the various ways that programs have been structured and delivered in schools, including detailed descriptions of some of the most widely used and evidenced-based programs. Then they summarize the current body of research on these programs and evaluate the strength of the evidence on the impact of mindfulness programs on students' mental health and psychological well-being, self-regulation, physical health, and academic functioning. The authors then provide some lessons learned from the research and recommendations for educators, administrators, and policymakers interested in implementing mindfulness programs in schools. Also included in the chapter is a case study of the implementation process of one mindfulness program and the insights gained from the various successes and challenges experienced in different school contexts.

This chapter is followed by a case study (Appendix 2.1) about the integration of mindfulness at the International School of Geneva. Edmundo Timm, the mindfulness coordinator and drama teacher, shares his experience coordinating and implementing mindfulness programs and innovative initiatives at the secondary school. He describes the mixed student perceptions that were encountered in delivering a mindfulness-based program to adolescents, and how important it is to be flexible, creative, and responsive in order to successfully share the benefits of mindfulness with students.

In Chapter 3, Pamela Seigle, Chip Wood, and Lisa Sankowski share how mindful awareness and compassionate practices can be thoughtfully integrated into the work of the adult community in schools. They emphasize the importance of creating school cultures based on relational trust, and outline the components for a healthy school community (the four R's): respectful relationships, space for reflection, models of resilience, and time for renewal. They propose that listening to self and others is "the indispensable foundational skill" for adults to effectively engage in the four R's. The authors describe several practical ideas, simple approaches, and vivid case studies that bring this work to life.

In Chapter 4, Eleanor Drago-Severson and Jessica Blum-DeStefano explore the key role that school principals play in supporting mindfulness in themselves and in their schools. Working through a constructive–developmental lens, the authors highlight the qualitatively different orientations (or developmental ways of knowing) adults bring to teaching, learning, and leading. They provide a novel exploration of the parallels between mindfulness and adult development in relation to the school context, and describe how mindfulness and developing greater internal capacities can help principals encourage growth within themselves and others and work more effectively with their school communities to lead meaningful change. Not only do the authors explain the benefits of this approach, but they also describe useful strategies for principals to promote greater mindfulness in themselves and others, while considering the developmental diversity that exists in their adult school community.

This chapter is followed by a case study (Appendix 4.1) by former principal Linda Rosenbury, who has spent time implementing schoolwide mindfulness programming at the Brooklyn Urban Garden Charter School in New York.

In Chapter 5, Cynthia Taylor, Patricia A. Jennings, Alexis Harris, Deborah L. Schussler, and Robert W. Roeser draw on the results of their research and work on teacher dispositions to present a conceptual framework of the "mindful teacher": The Calm, Clear, Kind Framework. They review both qualitative and quantitative research that show how these qualities can be developed through mindfulness and compassion training programs for teachers. Additionally, their chapter includes descriptions of the core program practices of Mindfulness-Based Emotional Balance (MBEB), Cultivating Awareness and Resilience in Education (CARE), and Community Approach to Learning Mindfully (CALM for Educators) programs, as well as rich anecdotes from teachers who have participated in these programs that illustrate the three dimensions of the mindful teacher framework.

In Chapter 6, Polina P. Mischenko and Patricia A. Jennings present a multiple-case study of how three elementary school teachers, delivering a

mindfulness-based social–emotional learning curriculum with high implementation fidelity, cultivated a passion (or a high level of buy-in) for practicing and teaching mindfulness. The authors first explore the role of buy-in
and passion in effective teaching, especially as it relates to mindfulness, and
review relevant literature on the mechanisms and conditions that may foster buy-in. Then the authors provide narrative accounts of how three teachers with no formal experience in mindfulness (including one teacher who
was initially resistant to delivering the curriculum) developed a passion for
practicing and teaching mindfulness. The mechanisms and conditions that
promoted the development of their passion are discussed and presented in
a preliminary conceptual framework.

In Chapter 7, Rebecca L. Tadlock-Marlo and Meghan Damler describe
how school counselors are positioned to be key change agents for integrating mindfulness into schools and transforming school culture. The authors
highlight the ways that school counselors can teach students mindfulness
exercises and the applications of the exercises to personal, social, academic,
and college and career readiness domains. They also discuss the various
opportunities school counselors have to collaborate with administrators,
teachers, and parents to create a cohesive and comprehensive support system
for students' holistic well-being. The chapter includes several case examples
from one school counselor's experiences using mindfulness to help students
navigate challenges related to managing stress, regulating attention and
hyperactivity, and working through exposure to trauma.

In Chapter 8, J. Douglas Coatsworth, Melissa Ward George, and
Aimee Kleisner Walker advocate for the inclusion of parents as partners in
creating mindful and compassionate schools. They review the theoretical
background and conceptual model of the Mindfulness-enhanced Strengthening Family Program 10–14 (MSFP), a school–family partnership training program developed around mindfulness concepts and practices. They
describe the five dimensions characteristic of mindful parenting, which
they use within their program as foundational mindfulness skills: listening
with full attention, nonjudgmental acceptance of self and child, emotional
awareness of self and child, self-regulation in the parenting relationship,
and compassion for self and child. This chapter also includes case study
examples from research on MSFP and argues for the importance of teacher
mindfulness in parent–teacher interactions. Finally, the authors identify the
barriers to engaging parents in school–family partnerships and how mindfulness and compassion skills can help facilitate collaboration.

Chapter 9 addresses the role of teacher education in school transformation. Richard C. Brown and Elizabeth Grassi share the story of how Naropa
University's state-approved teacher licensure program was founded. This
program integrates elements of mindfulness, awareness, compassion, sensory
embodiment, and artistic expression to prepare contemplatively competent
teachers. The authors discuss how they developed a vision for contemplative
teaching into a comprehensive teacher education program now recognized

by the State of Colorado for teacher certification. Brown and Grassi describe the process of aligning the curriculum with state standards of teacher quality, intentionally sequencing learning experiences, and providing faculty and instructors with the specialized skills needed to deliver this type of curriculum. They also provide curricular artifacts from this one-of-a-kind program to clearly illustrate the major components of such an undertaking.

In Chapter 10, Velma L. Cobb reminds us that any school transformation must operate with an equity lens if it is to truly meet the needs of all students. Attending to the historical structures that have brought the U.S. educational system to its current state, Cobb provides a vision for how we need to move forward and repair the harm that has been inflicted and continues to affect our most vulnerable students, families, and communities. She also outlines the fullness of the challenge we face, requiring both internal and external work to create the individual and collective transformation we seek.

Conclusion

We recognize that the transformational process we propose in this book is a tall order. It will not happen overnight. It will take many years to turn our huge educational bureaucracies toward a more equitable and just system that effectively prepares our children and youth to make valuable contributions to our rapidly changing society. In the words of W. H. Murray:

> Until one is committed, there is hesitancy, the chance to draw back, always ineffectiveness. Concerning all acts of initiative and creation, there is one elementary truth the ignorance of which kills countless ideas and splendid plans: that the moment one definitely commits oneself, then providence moves too. All sorts of things occur to help one that would never otherwise have occurred.
>
> A whole stream of events issues from the decision, raising in one's favor all manner of unforeseen incidents, meetings and material assistance which no man [or woman] could have dreamed would have come his [or her] way. (Murray, 1951, p. 6)

As stated by Goethe (1835/1902):

> Whatever you can do or dream you can, begin it. Boldness has genius, power and magic in it. Begin it now. (Goethe, 1835/1902, p.15)

References

Benn, R., Akiva, T., Arel, S., & Roeser, R. W. (2012). Mindfulness training effects for parents and educators of children with special needs. *Developmental Psychology, 48*, 1476–1487.

Brown, J. L., Jennings, P. A., Cham, H., Rasheed, D., Frank, J. L., Doyle, S., . . . Greenberg, M. T. (2017, March). *CARE for Teachers: Direct and mediated effects of a mindfulness-based professional development program for teachers on teachers' and students' social and emotional competencies.* Presented at the Society for Research on Educational Effectiveness Annual Conference, Washington, DC.

Carsley, D., Khoury, B., & Heath, N. L. (2018). Effectiveness of mindfulness interventions for mental health in schools: A comprehensive meta-analysis. *Mindfulness, 9,* 693–707.

Chiesa, A., & Serretti, A. (2009). Mindfulness-based stress reduction for stress management in healthy people: A review and meta-analysis. *Journal of Alternative and Complementary Medicine, 15,* 593–600.

Goethe, J. W. (1902). *Faustus: A dramatic mystery* (J. Aster, Trans.). London: Longman, Rees, Orme, Brown, Green & Longman. (Original work published 1835)

Hayes, A., & Feldman, G. (2004). Clarifying the construct of mindfulness in the context of emotion regulation and the process of change in therapy. *Clinical Psychology: Science and Practice, 11,* 255–262.

Jennings, P. A. (2019). *The trauma-sensitive school: Building resilience with compassionate teaching.* New York: Norton.

Jennings, P. A. (2019). *The trauma-sensitive classroom: Building resilience with compassionate teaching..* New York: Norton.

Jennings, P. A., Brown, J. L., Frank, J. L., Doyle, S., Oh, Y., Tanler, R., . . . Greenberg, M. T. (2017). Impacts of the CARE for Teachers program on teachers' social and emotional competence and classroom interactions. *Journal of Educational Psychology, 109,* 1010–1028.

Jennings, P. A., Frank, J. L., Snowberg, K. E., Coccia, M. A., & Greenberg, M. T. (2013). Improving classroom learning environments by cultivating awareness and resilience in education (CARE): Results of a randomized controlled trial. *School Psychology Quarterly, 28,* 374–390.

Jennings, P. A., & Greenberg, M. T. (2009). The prosocial classroom: Teacher social and emotional competence in relation to student and classroom outcomes. *Review of Educational Research, 79,* 491–525.

Kabat-Zinn, J. (2003). Mindfulness-based interventions in context: Past, present, and future. *Clinical Psychology: Science and Practice, 10,* 144–156.

Kabat-Zinn, J. (2005). *Coming to our senses: Healing ourselves and the world through mindfulness.* New York: Hachette.

Khoury, B., Lecomte, T., Fortin, G., Masse, M., Therien, P., Bouchard, V., . . . Hofmann, S. G. (2013). Mindfulness-based therapy: A comprehensive meta-analysis. *Clinical Psychology Review, 33,* 763–771.

Klingbeil, D. A., Renshaw, T. L., Willenbrink, J. B., Copek, R. A., Kai, T. C., Haddock, A., Yassine, J., & Clifton, J. (2017). Mindfulness-based interventions with youth: A comprehensive meta-analysis of group-design studies. *Journal of School Psychology, 63,* 77–103.

Klingbeil, D. A., & Renshaw, T. L. (2018). Mindfulness-based interventions for teachers: A meta-analysis of the emerging evidence base. *School Psychology Quarterly, 33,* 501–511.

Meiklejohn, J., Phillips, C., Freedman, M. L., Griffin, M. L., Biegel, G., Roach, A.,

... Isberg, R. (2012). Integrating mindfulness training into K–12 education: Fostering the resilience of teachers and students. *Mindfulness, 3,* 291–307.

Mind and Life Education Research Network (MLERN). (2012). Contemplative practices and mental training: Prospects for American education. *Child Development Perspectives, 6,* 146–153.

Murray, W. H. (1951). *The Scottish Himalayan expedition.* London: J. M. Dent & Co.

Rawana J. S., Diplock, B. D., & Chan, S. (2018). Mindfulness-based programs in school settings: Current state of the research. In A. Leschied, D. Saklofske, & G. Flett (Eds.), *The handbook of school-based mental health promotion: An evidence informed framework for implementation* (pp. 323–356). New York: Springer.

Roeser, R. W., Schonert-Reichl, K., Jha, A., Cullen, M., Wallace, L., Wilensky, R., ... Harrison, J. (2013). Mindfulness training and reductions in teacher stress and burnout: Results from two randomized, waitlist control field trials. *Journal of Educational Psychology, 105,* 787–804.

Roeser, R. W., Skinner, E., Beers, J., & Jennings, P. A. (2012). Mindfulness training and teachers' professional development: An emerging area of research and practice. *Child Development Perspectives, 6,* 167–173.

Sedlmeier, P., Eberth, J., Schwarz, M., Zimmermann, D., Haarig, F., Jaeger, S., & Kunze, S. (2012). The psychological effects of meditation: A meta-analysis. *Psychological Bulletin, 138,* 1139–1171.

Van Dam, N. T., van Vugt, M. K., Vago, D. R., Schmalzl, L., Saron, C., Olendzki, A., ... Meyer, D. E. (2018). Mind the hype: A critical evaluation and prescriptive agenda for research on mindfulness and meditation. *Perspectives on Psychological Science, 13,* 66–69.

Zoogman, S., Goldberg, S. B., Hoyt, W. T., & Miller, L. (2015). Mindfulness interventions with youth: A meta-analysis. *Mindfulness, 6,* 290–302.

CHAPTER 2

A Selective Review of Mindfulness Training Programs for Children and Adolescents in School Settings

REBECCA N. BAELEN
MICHAEL V. ESPOSITO
BRIAN M. GALLA

Mindfulness training has rapidly grown into a billion-dollar industry (Wieczner, 2016). Businesses, clinics, and hospitals around the country regularly offer mindfulness training programs to adults. In 2015, over 80% of medical schools provided mindfulness training as part of their curriculum (Black & Slavich, 2016); in 2016, 22% of employers nationwide offered some form of mindfulness training to their employees (Taylor, 2016). The growing popularity of mindfulness with adults has some evidentiary support: Comprehensive reviews of the scientific literature suggest that mindfulness training can help lower anxiety, depression, and pain (Goyal et al., 2014; Hofmann, Sawyer, Witt, & Oh, 2010).

As the effort to introduce mindfulness to adults has grown, so too has the movement to share these trainings with children and adolescents, particularly in school settings. Studies show that boosting social and emotional attitudes and skills—including self-regulation, stress management, emotional awareness, conflict resolution, prosocial behaviors, and positive self-views—through school-based interventions can improve mental health, reduce conduct problems, and enhance academic performance (Durlak,

Weissberg, Dymnicki, Taylor, & Schellinger, 2011; Taylor, Oberle, Durlak, & Weissberg, 2017). School-based mindfulness training programs may be one way to promote these positive social and emotional competencies and enhance success both in the classroom and beyond (Davidson et al., 2012).

Over the past two decades, a wide variety of programs have been developed to teach the skills and practices of mindfulness to youth. The majority of these programs derive from existing programs for adults (e.g., mindfulness-based stress reduction [MBSR], Kabat-Zinn, 1990) but have been adapted to match the developmental needs of children and adolescents (e.g., using shorter, but more frequent periods of mindfulness practice). Mindfulness training programs in the school setting are delivered in a variety of ways, from those that replace traditional classes or curricula (e.g., physical education or health class), to those that attempt a seamless integration with existing instructional time. A nonexhaustive list of well-known programs includes MindUP (Schonert-Reichl et al., 2015), the Holistic Life Foundation's Stress Reduction & Mindfulness Curriculum (Holistic Life Foundation, 2016), and the Mindfulness in Schools Project (Kuyken et al., 2013). We highlight these programs in greater detail in the boxed features throughout this chapter.

Given the rapid advances in the field of mindfulness training with youth, the current chapter is intended to provide educators, school administrators, and policymakers with an accessible, but selective, overview of mindfulness training programs that are being tried in school settings and a summary of the evidence regarding their efficacy for promoting social, emotional, and academic competencies.

Scope of the Review

What is the evidence to date for mindfulness training programs delivered in school settings? We want to make clear that it was not our intention to review *all* the scientific literature to answer this question. Rather, for our purposes here, we have limited our review to studies that met certain criteria. First, we only reviewed studies of mindfulness training programs conducted during the regular school day with preschool to 12th-grade students; we excluded studies of after-school, clinical, or community-based programs. Second, we focused our review on studies that met a minimum level of scientific rigor. Specifically, we only included peer-reviewed studies using randomized controlled designs (where one group of students is randomly selected to participate in a mindfulness training program and is compared to another group that is randomly selected to participate in business-as-usual practices or another program that does not contain mindfulness training) or studies using matched-comparison group designs (in which one group of students participates in a mindfulness training program and is compared to a group of equivalent students who do not participate in the program). In addition, we excluded studies with fewer than 30 total participants. Our intention in reviewing only the most rigorous quantitative studies of school-based mindfulness training programs was to provide educators, school administrators, and policymakers with a knowledge base informed by the best science to date.

Overall Study Characteristics

In total, 34 studies, involving 6,271 youth, met our inclusion criteria (as of February 2018). We briefly describe key characteristics of the included studies. For an extensive description of each study, please refer to Table 2.1.

Student Characteristics

Age

The age of students ranged from 3 to 18 years old. Eleven studies (32% of all reviewed studies) were conducted with high school students (grades 9–12), six (18%) with middle school students (grades 6–8), nine (26%) with elementary school students (grades K–5), four (12%) with both elementary and middle school students, one (3%) with both middle and high school students, and three (9%) with preschool students.

Student Populations

Six studies (18% of all reviewed studies) examined programs that targeted a specific subgroup of the student population (e.g., students exhibiting certain academic, behavioral, or emotional problems). Three studies assessed the impact of a targeted Breathing Awareness Meditation program for African American youth with high blood pressure or at risk for developing hypertension (Barnes, Pendergrast, Harshfield, & Treiber, 2008; Gregoski, Barnes, Tingen, Harshfield, & Treiber, 2011; Wright, Gregoski, Tingen, Barnes, & Treiber, 2011); another study looked at the effects of an adapted Mindfulness-Based Cognitive Therapy (MBCT) program for high school girls (Atkinson & Wade, 2015); and two studies evaluated yoga programs for students with academic, behavioral, or emotional issues (Fishbein et al., 2016; Powell, Gilchrist, & Stapley, 2008). The other 28 studies focused on universally delivered programs—intended for the general population of students. Of these "universal intervention" studies, 10 (29% of all reviewed studies) looked at programs delivered in schools, in which the majority of students were ethnic/racial minorities, immigrants, or economically disadvantaged. The remaining studies evaluated programs administered in a range of suburban and rural public and private schools.

Program Characteristics

Program Descriptions

Studies varied widely based on the types of programs evaluated. Five studies (15%) assessed programs consisting of brief mindfulness practice sessions—10 minutes of mindfulness exercises daily (e.g., Breathing Awareness Meditation program). Twelve studies (35%) looked at programs that were adapted from curricula and programming used with adults (e.g., Mindfulness in Schools Project). Six studies (18%) examined the outcomes of yoga-based programs (e.g., Kripalu-based Yoga). The remaining 11 studies (32% of all studies reviewed) evaluated novel programs that emphasized different elements of mindfulness, social–emotional learning, neuroscience, or kindness practices (e.g., Kindness Curriculum).

Program Length and Format

Programs ranged from 3 to 12 minutes of mindfulness practice daily for 12 weeks (Britton et al., 2014) to 100-minute curricular lessons delivered once a week for 8 weeks (Raes, Griffith, Van der Gucht, & Williams, 2014). In many of the programs, lessons began with a short mindfulness exercise intended for students to calm themselves. Then, students engaged in an experiential activity (e.g., a game, discussion, or physical movement) or learned about a key mindfulness component (e.g., awareness of self or attention regulation). Lessons often closed with another brief, guided mindfulness exercise (e.g., body scan, breathing exercise).

Programs differed with regard to encouraging or requiring students to carry out a home mindfulness practice. In 5 studies (15%) engaging in home practice was a program requirement, while in 10 studies (29%) it was encouraged but not required. Interestingly, only 2 studies assessed the effects of home practice on program outcomes and found that the amount of time spent practicing at home was related to improvements in mindfulness and psychological well-being (Huppert & Johnson, 2010), as well as reductions in stress (Kuyken et al., 2013). Future research might do well to explore the impact of out-of-school practice, as well as practice time more generally on youth outcomes (e.g., Galla, Baelen, Duckworth, & Baime, 2016a).

Programs were also designed with the cognitive, emotional, and social development of the youth participants in mind. For instance, some programs incorporated experiential learning activities and games in order to provide play-based and interactive exposure to mindfulness (e.g., Attention

TABLE 2.1. Studies Reviewed

Reference	Sample size	Target population	Average age (grade)	Program name	Program components
Atkinson & Wade (2015)**	217	All-girls' schools in Australia; *Targeted:* Females	15.7 (9–12)	Adapted MBCT	Mindfulness- and acceptance-based exercises (specifically related to body image), exercises adapted from MBCT, interactive activities
Bakosh et al. (2016)*	191	Suburban public schools (Chicago, IL)	*nr* (3)	Mindfulness-Based Social Emotional Learning Program	Audio recordings based on MBSR practices
Barnes et al. (2008)**	66	High schools; *Targeted:* African American adolescents with high blood pressure	15.2 (9–12)	Breathing Awareness Meditation (BAM)	Primary practice of MBSR
Bergen-Cico et al. (2016)**	144	Public school (Greater Boston, MA)	11.3 (6)	Mindful Yoga (inspired by YogaKids)	Brief mindful practices and yoga poses
Britton et al. (2014)**	101	Private Quaker school (Providence, RI)	11.8 (6)	Integrative Contemplative Pedagogy (ICP)	Mindfulness meditation practices
Fishbein et al. (2016)**	85	Nontraditional public school; *Targeted:* Students with academic and behavioral problems	16.7 (9–12)	Mindful Yoga Curriculum	Meditation practices, yoga, mindfulness concepts
Flook et al. (2010)**	64	On-campus elementary school (UCLA)	8.2 (2–3)	Mindful Awareness Practices	Sitting meditation, body scans, activities, and games

Program length	Outcome measures	Reported findings	Follow-up	Program facilitator	Implementation measures
90 min 3×/ week for 1 week; home practice encouraged	Student self-reports of weight and shape concerns, psychosocial impairment, eating disorder symptoms, dietary restraint, attitudes toward appearance, negative affect, mindfulness, body mass index (MH, PWB, BSR, PH)	No main effects found at 1- or 6-month follow-up	1 and 6 months	External facilitator: *First author and graduate students; each graduate student received 2-hr individual training from first author*	Student and teacher reports of program acceptability
10 min 5×/ week for 8 weeks	Student grades; teacher reports of student classroom behavior (AF)	Improved reading and science grades; reduced disruptive classroom behavior; no effects on math, spelling, writing or social studies grades	None	Classroom teacher: *Participated in 60-min training on program content, structure, and classroom tools*	Logs of teachers' daily activities; teachers completed feedback surveys about program feasibility
10 min 5×/ week for 12 weeks; home practice required (10 min 7×/ week)	Blood pressure, heart rate, and overnight sodium excretion (PH)	Reduced blood pressure, heart rate, and overnight sodium excretion	None	Classroom teacher: *Training not specified*	External evaluation of implementation quality
4 min 3×/ week for entire school year	Student self-reports of short- and long-term self-regulation (BSR)	Improved total and long-term regulation; no effect on short-term regulation	None	Classroom teacher: *Completed 30-hr training in Yoga Kids program; certified through Yoga Alliance*	Logs of teachers' daily activities; comments on program feasibility; parent and student feedback
3–12 min 5×/ week for 6 weeks	Student self-reports of clinical and subclinical symptoms, positive/ negative affect and mindfulness (MH, PWB)	Reduced suicidal ideation; no effects on internalizing or externalizing symptoms, affect, attention, or mindfulness	None	Classroom teacher: *Completed mindfulness training (ICP or MBSR)*	Student journals about acceptability of meditation practices
50 min 3×/ week (20 sessions total)	Student self-reports of emotional, behavioral, and cognitive dysregulation, impulse control, negative mood, mindfulness, drug use; teacher reports of student behavioral and social competencies; performance tasks of impulse control (PWB, BSR, ER, AF)	Reduced alcohol use; improved social competency behaviors; no effects on self-regulation, mood, mindfulness, emotion regulation, or involuntary engagement coping	None	External facilitator: *Yoga instructors; certified through Yoga Alliance*	Not specified
30 min 2×/ week for 8 weeks	Teacher and parent reports of student executive functioning (EF)	Improved executive functioning for children with low executive functioning at baseline	None	External facilitator: *Not specified*	Not specified

(continued)

19

TABLE 2.1. (*continued*)

Reference	Sample size	Target population	Average age (grade)	Program name	Program components
Flook et al. (2015)**	66	Urban public schools (Midwest, US)	4.7 (PreK)	Kindness Curriculum	Mindfulness-based prosocial skills training
Gregoski et al. (2011)**	166	High schools; *Targeted:* African American adolescents with high blood pressure	15.0 (9)	Breathing Awareness Meditation	Primary practice of MBSR
Huppert & Johnson (2010)*	155	Private boys' schools (UK)	14 and 15 *(nr)*	Adapted MBSR	Adapted MBSR: Lessons on mindfulness principles, mindfulness practices, and CD for guided home practices
Johnson et al. (2016)**	308	One private and three public schools (Australia)	13.63 (7–8)	Mindfulness in Schools Project (.b)	Adapted MBSR and MBCT: Lessons on mindfulness principles, mindfulness exercises
Johnson et al. (2017)	555	One private and three public schools (Australia)	13.44 *(nr)*	Mindfulness in Schools Project (.b)	Adapted MBSR and MBCT: Lessons on mindfulness principles, mindfulness exercises
Kuyken et al. (2013)*	522	Secondary schools (UK)	14.8 *(nr)*	Mindfulness in Schools Project	Adapted MBSR and MBCT: Lessons on mindfulness principles, mindfulness exercises

Program length	Outcome measures	Reported findings	Follow-up	Program facilitator	Implementation measures
20–30 min 2×/week for 12 weeks	Teacher reports of students' social competence, student grades, behavioral tasks of executive functioning, self-control, and prosocial behavior (PWB, BSR, EF, ER, AF)	Improved prosocial behavior, report card grades, and teacher-reported social competence; no effects on executive functioning or self-control	None	External facilitator: *Experienced mindfulness instructor*	Not specified
10 min 5×/week for 12 weeks; home practice required (10 min daily and 20 min daily on weekends)	Student self-reports of stress; blood pressure, heart rate, and overnight sodium excretion (MH, PH)	Reduced blood pressure and heart rate; no effects on overnight sodium excretion or stress	None	Classroom teacher: *Attended supervised training by program instructors*	Observations of session quality and implementation fidelity
40 min 1×/week for 4 weeks; home practice encouraged	Student self-reports of mindfulness, resilience, and well-being (PWB)	No effects on mindfulness, resilience, or well-being; home practice associated with improvements in mindfulness and well-being	None	Classroom teacher: *Training not specified; longstanding mindfulness practitioners*	Not specified
35–60 minutes 1×/week for 8 weeks; home practice encouraged	Student self-reports of anxiety, depression, weight and shape concerns, well-being, mindfulness, self-compassion, and emotion regulation (MH, PWB, ER)	No effects on anxiety, depression, weight, and shape concerns, emotion regulation, mindfulness, self-compassion, or well-being at 3-month follow-up	3 months	External facilitator: *First author; experienced mindfulness practitioner and certified in .b*	Teacher and student feedback on program acceptability; student home practice surveys
40–60 min 1×/week for 9 weeks; brief practices led by classroom teachers at beginning of lessons; home practice encouraged	Student self-reports of depression, anxiety, weight and shape concerns, well-being, and mindfulness (MH, PWB)	No effects on depression, anxiety, weight and shape concerns, mindfulness, or well-being at 6- or 12-month follow-up	6 and 12 months	External facilitator: *First author; experienced mindfulness practitioner and certified in .b* Classroom teacher: *Used a script/audio files to lead brief practices*	Competence of instructor and fidelity of program lessons assessed; home practice surveys; parent and student feedback surveys
1×/week for 9 weeks (total minutes not recorded)	Student self-reports of depression, stress, and well-being (MH, PWB)	Reduced depression, stress, and improved well-being at 3-month follow-up; home practice associated with improvements in well-being and reductions in stress	2–3 months	External facilitator and Classroom teacher: *Curriculum developers or teachers trained and approved by developers to deliver program*	Student surveys; teacher ratings of experience delivering the program

(continued)

21

TABLE 2.1. (*continued*)

Reference	Sample size	Target population	Average age (grade)	Program name	Program components
Mendelson et al. (2010)**	97	Urban public schools; majority African American (Baltimore, MD)	10.1 (4–5)	Stress Reduction and Mindfulness Curriculum (Holistic Life Foundation)	Yoga, guided breathing practices, discussions of mindfulness principles
Metz et al. (2013)*	216	Suburban public schools	16.5 (10–12)	Learning to BREATHE (Broderick, 2013)	Adapted MBSR: Lessons on core mindfulness principles, discussions, and mindfulness practices
Napoli et al. (2005)**	194	Urban public schools (Southwest, US)	*nr* (1–3)	Attention Academy Program (Napoli et al., 2005)	Breathing practices, body scans, mindful movement, and sensorimotor awareness activities
Noggle et al. (2012)**	51	Public school (rural MA)	*nr* (11–12)	Kripalu-based yoga	Yoga, breathing practices, relaxation techniques, and mindfulness practices
Parker et al. (2014)**	111	Public schools (Southeast, US)	10.09 (4–5)	Master Mind	Mindful breathing, mindful movement, real-world applications of mindfulness principles, and daily mindfulness practices
Powell et al. (2008)*	107	Primary schools; *Targeted:* Students with emotional and behavioral difficulties at risk for exclusion (UK)	8–11 (*nr*)	Self-Discovery Programme	Yoga, massage, and relaxation techniques

Program length	Outcome measures	Reported findings	Follow-up	Program facilitator	Implementation measures
45 min 4×/week for 12 weeks	Student self-reports of depression, involuntary response to stress, positive/negative emotions, and relationships with teachers and peers (MH, PWB, ER)	Reduced involuntary response to stress, rumination, intrusive thoughts, and emotional arousal: no effects on depression, positive affect, or relationships with teachers or peers	None	External facilitator: *Males of similar racial and economic background as students; trained in Holistic Life Foundation Curriculum*	Qualitative feedback from students and teachers about program acceptability and feasibility
15–25 min 1–2×/week for 16 weeks (18 sessions); home practice encouraged	Student self-reports of emotion regulation, efficacy of emotion regulation, psychosomatic complaints, and stress (MH, ER)	Improved emotion regulation and efficacy of emotion regulation; reduced psychosomatic symptoms and stress	None	Classroom teacher: *Attended 8-wk MBSR course and 2-day inservice for Learning to BREATHE*	Teacher feedback and fidelity logs; student feedback on satisfaction with program; classroom observations
45 min 2×/month for 24 weeks (12 total sessions)	Student self-reports of test anxiety; teacher reports of student attention and social skills; behavioral measures of attention (MH, EF, AF)	Improved attention and social skills (teacher report), improved selective attention; reduced test anxiety; no effect on sustained attention	None	External facilitator: *Trained mindfulness instructors with 10 and 20 years of teaching experience*	Not specified
30 min 2–3×/week for 10 weeks	Student self-reports of stress, resilience, mood disturbance, positive/negative affect, mindfulness, positive psychology, and anger expression (MH, PWB, ER)	Improved mood disturbance and negative affect; no effect on positive affect, stress, positive psychology, resilience, anger expression, or mindfulness	None	External facilitator: *Certified yoga instructors at Kripalu Center for Yoga and Health; attended yoga ed training program*	Student program evaluations
15 min 5×/week for 4 weeks (20 total sessions)	Student self-reports of intention to use substances; teacher reports of student behavior, emotion regulation, and self-control; behavioral task of executive functioning (BSR, EF, ER, AF)	Improved executive functioning, self-control (boys only), behavior and emotion regulation; reduced aggression, social problems, and anxiety (girls only); no effect on intentions to use substances or teacher-rated attention problems	None	Classroom teacher: *Participated in 8-hr training with the program developer*	Observations of implementation fidelity; teacher interviews and surveys about program feasibility and acceptability
45 min 1×/week for 12 weeks	Teacher reports of student behavior (AF)	Improved self-confidence, social confidence, communication with peers and teachers, contribution in class and reductions in total difficulties at 7-month follow-up	7 months	External facilitator: *1-day training with program developer; one massage therapist and one certified yoga teacher*	Not specified

(continued)

TABLE 2.1. (*continued*)

Reference	Sample size	Target population	Average age (grade)	Program name	Program components
Quach et al. (2016)**	198	Large public school; majority low-income, Hispanic (Southwest, US)	13.18 (7–9)	Adapted MBSR	Adapted MBSR: Breathing techniques, mindfulness meditation, and group discussion
Raes et al. (2014)*	408	Secondary schools (Belgium)	15.4 *(nr)*	Mindfulness Group Program	Components of MBSR and MBCT: Mindfulness practices, group discussions, and lessons on mindfulness principles
Ramadoss & Bose (2010)* (Study 2)	557	Large urban public school; majority African American and Hispanic (California)	High school students *(nr)*	Transformative Life Skills	Focused breathing, sitting meditation, and yoga
Raveepatarakul et al. (2014)**	82	Thailand	8–11 *(nr)*	Mindfulness Enhancement Program	Sitting meditation, games, and group discussion
Schonert-Reichl & Lawlor (2010)*	246	Urban public schools (Western Canada)	11.4 (4–7)	Mindful Education	Lessons to teach mindfulness skills and principles, mindful attention training practices
Schonert-Reichl et al. (2015)**	99	Urban public Schools (Western Canada)	10.24 (4–5)	MindUP	Mindfulness practices, lessons on mindfulness principles and social–emotional understanding, performing acts of kindness

Program length	Outcome measures	Reported findings	Follow-up	Program facilitator	Implementation measures
45 min 2×/ week for 4 weeks; home practice encouraged (15–30 min daily)	Student self-reports of stress, anxiety, and mindfulness; behavioral task of working memory capacity (MH, PWB, EF)	Improved working memory; no effects on stress or anxiety	None	External facilitator: *Yoga instructors; experienced meditators*	Observations of program fidelity and consistency of implementation; home practice logs
100 min 1×/ week for 8 weeks; home practice required (15 min daily)	Student self-reports of depression, anxiety, and stress (MH)	Reduced depression at 6-month follow-up; did not report outcomes for stress or anxiety	6 months	External facilitator: *Trained mindfulness instructors; trained and experienced in teaching curriculum*	Instructors met 8 times to discuss their experience and adherence to the protocol
15 min 5×/ week for 18 weeks	Student self-reports of self-control and stress (MH, BSR)	Reduced stress; no effect on self-control	None	External facilitator: *Certified yoga teachers with additional training in Yoga Corps to serve vulnerable populations*	Qualitative teacher and student feedback about program acceptability and feasibility
45–60 min 1×/week for 6 weeks; home practice required (10–15 min 6×/week)	Student self-reports of depression and mindfulness (MH, PWB)	Improved mindfulness and reduced depression at 2-week follow-up	2 weeks	External facilitator: *Study researcher; training not specified*	Not specified
40–50 min 1×/week and 3 min mindfulness practices 3×/ day for 10 weeks	Student self-reports of optimism, school and self-concept, positive/ negative affect; teacher reports of student social and emotional competence (PWB, ER, AF)	Improved social–emotional competence, (teacher report); improved optimism; improved self-concept for preadolescents, but not early adolescents	None	Classroom teacher: *Intensive 1-day training*	Biweekly consultations with program developers; teacher logs of implementation and surveys about program feasibility and acceptability
40–50 min 1×/week and 3 min mindfulness practices 3×/ day for 12 weeks	Student self-reports of emotional control, empathy, perspective taking, optimism, mindfulness, social responsibility, school and self-concept, depression; peer nominations of prosociality, aggressiveness, and popularity; student math achievement; behavioral tasks of executive functioning and working memory; cortisol (MH, PWB, EF, ER, PH, AF)	Improved executive functioning, math achievement, empathy, perspective taking, emotional control, optimism, school self-concept, mindfulness, peer-rated prosocial behavior and popularity; reduced depression and peer-rated aggressive behavior; higher levels of morning cortisol secretion	None	Classroom teacher: *Not specified*	Teacher surveys about implementation quality and frequency; daily logs of program implementation

(continued)

TABLE 2.1. (*continued*)

Reference	Sample size	Target population	Average age (grade)	Program name	Program components
Sibinga et al. (2013)**	41	School for low-income urban boys; majority African American (Baltimore, MD)	12.5 (7–8)	Adaptation of MBSR for urban youth	Components of MBSR: Lessons on mindfulness concepts, mindfulness practices, and group discussion
Sibinga et al. (2016)**	300	Urban public schools; majority low-income African American (Baltimore, MD)	12.0 (5–8)	Adaptation of MBSR for urban youth	Components of MBSR: Lessons on mindfulness concepts, mindfulness practices, and group discussion
Thierry et al. (2016)*	47	Urban elementary school; majority low-income Hispanic (Southwest, US)	4.55 (PreK)	MindUP	Mindfulness practices, lessons on mindfulness principles and social–emotional understanding, performing acts of kindness
Thierry et al. (2018)*	296	Urban public schools; majority low-income African American and Hispanic (Southwest, US)	4.5 (PreK)	Adaptation of MindUP	Lessons to teach about the brain, labeling feelings, impulse control, deep breathing, and body awareness practices

Program length	Outcome measures	Reported findings	Follow-up	Program facilitator	Implementation measures
50 min 1×/ week for 12 weeks	Student self-reports of psychological functioning, mindfulness, and coping; sleep monitoring and cortisol (MH, PWB, ER, PH)	Improved psychological functioning (reduced anxiety) and reduced rumination at 3-month follow-up; stress remained level for mindfulness group but increased for control group at 3-month follow-up; no effect on sleep or mindfulness	3 months	External facilitator: *Trained mindfulness instructor; 10 years of experience teaching mindfulness to youth*	Not specified
50 min 1×/ week for 12 weeks; home practice encouraged	Student self-reports of mindfulness, positive/ negative affect, mood, anger, posttraumatic symptoms, stress, depression, paranoid ideation, anxiety, self-hostility, somatization, coping, and coping self-efficacy (MH, PWB, ER)	Reduced somatization, depression, rumination, negative coping, self-hostility, negative affect, and posttraumatic symptoms; no effects on mindfulness, anger, anxiety, paranoid ideation, hostility, aggression, stress, coping, coping self-efficacy, positive affect, or positive coping	None	External facilitator: *Trained mindfulness instructors; more than 10 years of experience teaching mindfulness*	Program instructors met regularly to ensure consistency of implementation
20–30 min lessons (15 total) over entire school year (2–3 weeks for each concept), 1 min mindfulness practice 3× daily	Teacher and parent reports of executive functioning; test of receptive vocabulary and computer-based assessment of reading skills (EF, AF)	Improved executive functioning (teacher report, not parent report); improved vocabulary and reading scores at 1-year follow-up	1 year	Classroom teacher: *Trained in full-day training*	Teachers completed surveys about lessons, breathing practices, and student engagement
18 lessons (2 weeks for each concept) from October to March, breathing practice 3× daily	Behavioral tasks of executive functioning; teacher reports of student prosocial behavior; observer ratings of classroom quality; test of student academic skills (PWB, EF, AF)	Increased executive functioning; no effects on prosocial behavior or academic skills	None	Classroom teacher: *Intensive professional development training; five full days and one half-day*	2×/month teachers were observed by outside educator and mental health consultants; rated on lesson completion and student engagement

(continued)

TABLE 2.1. (*continued*)

Reference	Sample size	Target population	Average age (grade)	Program name	Program components
van de Weijer-Bergsma et al. (2014)**	199	Schools with majority immigrant youth (Netherlands)	9.3 (3–5)	Mindful Kids	Components of MBSR and MBCT: Inspired by Mindful Schools Program
Viafora et al. (2015)**	63	Charter schools; one serving homeless youth; majority Hispanic (California)	11–13 (6–8)	*nr*	Mindfulness activities, mindfulness practices, and discussions
Vickery & Dorjee (2016)*	71	Primary schools (North Wales)	7.9 (3–4)	Mindfulness in Schools Project (Paws b)	Adapted from .b program, formal and informal mindfulness practices
Viglas & Perlman (2017)**	127	Public schools; identified as serving populations with high external challenges (Toronto, Canada)	5.15 (kinder-garten)	Mindful Schools	Lessons on mindful breathing and moving, kindness and caring, mindful awareness practices
Wright et al. (2011)**	121	Public schools; *Targeted:* African American students at risk for developing essential hypertension	15.0 (9)	Breathing Awareness Meditation (BAM)	Primary practice of MBSR

Note: *Matched comparison group design; **Randomized Controlled trial design; *nr*, not reported in study; MH, mental health; PWB, psychological well-being; ER, emotion regulation; BSR, behavioral self-regulation; EF, executive functioning. PH, physical health; AF, academic functioning.

Program length	Outcome measures	Reported findings	Follow-up	Program facilitator	Implementation measures
30 min 2×/ week for 6 weeks; home practice encouraged	Parent reports of student anxiety, anger and social competence, sleep; student self-reports of rumination, emotional awareness, subjective happiness and sense of coherence; teacher reports of classroom climate (MH, PWB, ER, PH, AF)	Improved facets of emotional awareness and sense of coherence at 2-month follow-up; reduced rumination, parent-reported anxiety and aggressive behaviors at 2-month follow-up; no effects on sleep, happiness or parent-reported social competence	2 months	External facilitator: *Study author; experienced mindfulness trainer for adult groups* Classroom teacher: *Led daily mindfulness exercises*	Not specified
45 min 1×/ week for 8 weeks; home practice encouraged	Student self-reports of mindfulness, self-compassion, and psychological inflexibility (MH, PWB)	Improved mindfulness; no effects on psychological inflexibility or self-compassion	None	External facilitator: *Graduate student; 10 years of mindfulness practice and experience working with youth; participated in 10-week web-based training*	Not specified
30 min (12 total sessions) for 8 weeks; home practice encouraged	Student self-reports of mindfulness, positive/ negative affect, positive well-being, emotional awareness and expression; parent and teacher reports of students' executive functioning (PWB, EF, ER)	Reduced negative affect and improved meta-cognition (teacher report) at 3-month follow-up; no effects on mindfulness, parent-reported metacognition, positive affect, positive well-being, emotional awareness, or expression	3 months	Classroom teacher: *Trained in .b Foundations, later trained in delivery of Paws b curriculum*	Not specified
20 min 3×/ week for 6 weeks	Behavioral task of self-regulation; teacher reports of prosocial and maladaptive behaviors (PWB, BSR, AF)	Improved self-regulation and prosocial behavior; reduced hyperactivity; no effects on conduct problems, emotional symptoms, or peer problems	None	External facilitator: *Trained and certified to implement Mindful Schools Program*	Not specified
10 min 5×/ week for 12 weeks; home practice required (10 min/day and 20 min/day on weekends)	Blood pressure and heart rate; student self-reports of hostility (ER, PH)	Reduced blood pressure and hostility post-program (not at 3-month follow-up); no significant effects on heart rate reported	3 months	Classroom teacher: *Trained by program instructors; deemed certified to teach*	Weekly observations and qualitative assessments of teachers' implementation and student engagement

---

MindUP

MindUP is a universal, mindfulness-based, social–emotional learning (SEL) program that consists of 12 weekly 40–50 minute lessons and frequent brief mindfulness practices. The program includes interactive activities designed with the intention of developing core SEL competencies—self-awareness, self-management, social awareness, relationship skills, and responsible decision making—and promoting executive functioning, well-being, and prosociality (Maloney, Lawlor, Schonert-Reichl, & Whitehead, 2016, p. 315).

The brief mindfulness practices consist of focusing on breathing or listening to resonant sounds. These practices and the daily lessons are taught by a classroom teacher, who uses a standardized manual written and adapted for the age of students in the program. The manual includes teaching scripts, worksheets, and extension activities, all of which can be incorporated into classroom instruction (Maloney et al., 2016). The initial lessons aim to foster self-regulation through different activities (e.g., paying attention to physical sensations like smell and taste). The lessons then evolve into an emphasis on social–emotional understanding, in which students take on the perspective of others while reading literature or learn to practice gratitude with classmates. The lessons culminate with performing acts of kindness in the classroom and in the local community. Throughout the program, teachers are encouraged to incorporate these approaches into their overall instructional practice to ensure the greatest retention of program concepts (Schonert-Reichl et al., 2015).

Academy). Others, like MindUP, aimed to captivate student attention and interest by sharing the latest research from psychology and neuroscience. In programs adapted from traditional adult programming, lessons were shortened from 2–3 hours to 15–30 minutes (for younger students) or to 45–100 minutes (for high school students). The length of mindfulness practices also varied by program, but were shorter than the practices in adult programs, which last typically 45 minutes. In some cases, mindfulness practices were as short as 3 minutes (Britton et al., 2014; Schonert-Reichl et al., 2015).

Program Facilitation

Program delivery varied widely across studies (i.e., external facilitator, classroom teacher). Over half of the studies reviewed for this chapter (19 of 34) examined programs delivered by external facilitators. Eight of these studies (24%) assessed programs conducted by trained mindfulness instructors with experience teaching and practicing mindfulness. Four studies (12%) evaluated programs led by certified yoga instructors, and 7 studies (21%) assessed programs delivered by either study authors or program developers with multiple years of experience teaching and practicing mindfulness. For 2 of these studies, programs were codelivered by external facilitators and classroom teachers (i.e., external facilitators delivered the curriculum, and classroom teachers led daily guided mindfulness practices). In one study, a mix of classroom teachers and external facilitators delivered the program.

Fourteen studies (41%) examined programs administered entirely by trained classroom teachers. In eight of these studies (24%), teachers either attended an inservice training or were trained by the program supervisor, while in another three studies (9%), classroom teachers completed more extensive training (e.g., participated in an 8-week mindfulness program). Three studies (9%) did not specify how teachers were trained. In the case of some programs (e.g., Mindful Schools) teachers were paired with a mentor who provided feedback and support, as well as resources to aid with program implementation.

Program Implementation

Program implementation refers to what takes place when a program is delivered. To know if a program is implemented with fidelity, researchers conduct an evaluation of program quality and assess whether the program was delivered as intended (Domitrovich & Greenberg, 2000). Of the studies reviewed, 13 (38%) assessed program implementation either through classroom observations to rate facilitator competency and quality of instruction or with teacher logs for tracking daily activities and instructional time. In addition, 2 other studies noted that teachers met regularly to discuss and ensure adherence to the program, but there was no assessment of implementation in the classroom.

Program Feasibility, Acceptability, and Follow-Up

To evaluate program acceptability, or stakeholders' satisfaction with the program, 13 studies (38%) collected informal and formal feedback from teachers, students, and parents. Ten of the 13 studies collected feedback from teachers (e.g., surveys and interviews) to learn about program feasibility and acceptability. Nine gathered student feedback to gauge their perceptions of the programs, while 2 collected parent feedback. In addition, 12 of the 34 studies (35%) included in this review conducted a follow-up assessment with students intended to discern whether program effects endured for longer periods of time. Administration of follow-up assessments ranged from 2 weeks after program completion to an entire year later.

Studies that tracked implementation found programs to be delivered with fidelity and consistency; none reported major issues. Observers of classroom teachers reported varying instructional quality and competency of core program principles. Most teachers found that programs were easy to implement, and the vast majority reported that they were still able to complete their regular instructional goals. Students were resoundingly positive in their perceptions of the programs.

Summarizing the Evidence for School-Based Mindfulness Training Programs

We categorized the main outcomes from the studies reviewed into four categories: (1) mental health and psychological well-being, (2) self-regulation, (3) physical health, and (4) academic functioning. We provide a selective overview of the studies that examined each of these four outcome categories, highlighting some of the most noteworthy findings in each category.

Mental Health and Psychological Well-Being

Nineteen studies (56% of all reviewed) examined the effects of mindfulness training on mental health problems, such as reductions in symptoms of anxiety and depression, negative mood, and perceptions of stress, among others. In one study, 300 fifth- through eighth-grade students from a socioeconomically disadvantaged urban environment were randomized into a mindfulness group or a control group (Sibinga, Webb, Ghazarian, & Ellen, 2016). Those in the mindfulness group completed a 12-week mindfulness program adapted from MBSR. The mindfulness training program consisted of weekly 50-minute lessons taught by an experienced, certified MBSR instructor. Each lesson involved learning from didactic materials, engaging in mindfulness practices, yoga, and group discussions. Students in the control group completed a 12-week "Healthy Topics" course, in which they learned about nutrition, exercise, and other health behaviors. Results showed that, compared to students in the control group, those in the mindfulness group reported significantly fewer depressive and posttraumatic symptoms. However, there were no effects on anxiety, stress, or paranoid ideation. Other studies of mindfulness training programs with adolescents have found reductions in depressive symptoms that have lasted up to 2 weeks (Raveepatarakul, Suttiwan, Iamsupasit, & Mikulas, 2014), 3 months (Kuyken et al., 2013) and 6 months (Raes et al., 2014) after program completion.

In addition to reducing mental health problems, 21 studies (62%) examined the effects of mindfulness training for boosting psychological well-being, including increases in positive emotion, optimism, prosocial behavior, self-compassion, mindfulness, and resilience. In a study of 99 fourth- and fifth-graders, students were randomized to either the MindUP program or a "social responsibility" program (similar to a typical social–emotional learning (SEL) program) (Schonert-Reichl et al., 2015). Those in the MindUP program engaged in three breathing practices each day—each lasting 3 minutes—for 12 weeks, and participated in 45-minute lessons once a week. In the weekly lessons, classroom teachers delivered activities designed to promote different social–emotional skills (e.g., perspective taking and empathy), as well as kindness and prosocial behaviors (e.g., sharing and cooperation). At the end of the study, students who participated in the MindUP program demonstrated greater levels of self-reported empathy, perspective taking, and optimism compared to those who received the "social responsibility" program. This study also included peer nomination measures (the only study to use such measures)—whereby students rated their peers on prosociality, aggressiveness, and popularity. Students rated their peers in the MindUP program as more prosocial, trustworthy, and helpful than peers in the control group. In addition, students in the MindUP program were liked more by their peers and rated as less aggressive compared to peers in the control group. Similarly, two studies, one of preschoolers randomly assigned to participate in a mindfulness-based Kindness Curriculum (Flook, Goldberg, Pinger, & Davidson, 2015) and one of kindergarteners randomly assigned to participate in the Mindful Schools program (Viglas & Perlman, 2017), found significant improvements in prosocial behavior (e.g., showing empathy and compassion for others' feelings) for students in the mindfulness training programs based on teacher ratings. However, one adaptation of the MindUP program with preschoolers found no effects on prosocial behavior (Thierry, Vincent, Bryant, Kinder, & Wise, 2018).

Not all studies demonstrated improvements in mental health and psychological well-being. For instance, in one study with Australian middle schoolers, 550 students were randomized into one of three groups: a mindfulness training group with parental involvement, a mindfulness training group without parental involvement, or a control group (Johnson, Burke, Brinkman, & Wade, 2017). Those in the mindfulness groups completed the 9-week .b program (pronounced "dot b") developed by the Mindfulness in Schools Project. Each weekly lesson was taught by an external facilitator with a teaching certification in .b and 10 years of experience teaching and practicing mindfulness. The weekly lessons consisted of teaching core mindfulness principles and engaging in guided mindfulness practices (e.g., breath counting, body scans, open awareness). Classroom teachers also led brief mindfulness practices (using scripts) at the start of every lesson with these students. Finally, students were encouraged to practice at home using prerecorded audio files. The only difference between the two mindfulness groups was that, in one group, students' parents were involved. Parents were encouraged to discuss mindfulness at home and remind students to engage in home practices. Parents also received information about the program through an in-person meeting and weekly emails. Students completed self-report surveys about their depression, anxiety, weight, and shape concerns, mindfulness, and general well-being at three time points: immediately following the program, 6 months after the program, and 12 months after the program. At all three time points, the two groups who received the mindfulness training showed no difference from those in the control group. Similarly, another study of middle schoolers in a large public school found no effect of mindfulness training on stress or anxiety, but found effects on executive function (see the subsequent discussion) (Quach, Mano, & Alexander, 2016).

Overall, evidence from randomized controlled and matched-comparison studies suggests that school-based mindfulness training programs show promise in reducing mental health problems and promoting psychological well-being (including prosocial behaviors) in children and adolescents. Not all programs, however, have demonstrated effectiveness in generating these salutary effects. It is important to note that certain mindfulness training programs may not work for all populations or in all contexts, and that programs may work best when targeting the social and emotional needs of a specific population. For example, Sibinga et al. (2016) found reductions in depression among socioeconomically disadvantaged African American adolescents, whereas Johnson et al. (2016) and Johnson et al. (2017) found no improvements in depression in a universally administered mindfulness training program for Australian middle schoolers. That said, programs need not be targeted to be effective. Universally delivered programs have demonstrated evidence of effectiveness at improving a host of psychological well-being outcomes, including prosocial behavior, optimism, and positive mood (e.g., Flook et al., 2015; Schonert-Reichl & Lawlor, 2010; Schonert-Reichl et al., 2015; Viglas & Perlman, 2017).

Self-Regulation

Self-regulation refers to the voluntary direction of attention, emotions, and behavior in the service of a valued goal (Galla, Kaiser-Greenland, & Black, 2016b). Beyond intelligence and socioeconomic status, self-regulation is among the most robust predictors of academic achievement. Students who are better able to control attention, manage emotions, resist temptations, and work productively toward long-term goals are more prepared to learn when they enter kindergarten (Blair & Razza, 2007); earn higher grades in elementary, middle, and high school (Duckworth & Carlson, 2013; Poropat, 2009); are more likely to graduate from high school on time (Galla et al., 2014); and are more likely to earn a college degree (McClelland, Acock, Piccinin, Rhea, & Stallings, 2012). Given its relation to success in school and beyond (Duckworth & Carlson, 2013; Moffitt et al., 2011), self-regulation is considered a core competency targeted by SEL programs (Collaborative for Academic, Social, and Emotional Learning, 2017). Recent research suggests that mindfulness training programs may offer a unique

Mindfulness in Schools Project (.b and Paws b)

The Mindfulness in Schools Project (MiSP) was the first mindfulness-based curricular program to be implemented in schools in the United Kingdom. The program, referred to as .b (meaning "stop and be"), is designed for youth ages 11–18 years and is based on traditional adult mindfulness programs (e.g., MBSR and MBCT). To adapt these programs for youth, the program developers sought to teach the core mindfulness principles and skills more explicitly. They designed experiential and student-based activities, shortened the length of practice time, and adapted the course resources to be more appropriate for adolescents. The program went through several iterations over its first 4 years, whereby developers incorporated feedback from nearly 200 teachers and 2,000 students who went through the program (Kuyken et al., 2013).

The program is manualized and is made up of nine weekly lessons (40–60 minutes each) usually taught by an external facilitator trained in the .b curriculum (classroom teachers may also be trained to administer the program). Each lesson is designed to teach a unique mindfulness skill (e.g., paying attention, moving mindfully). Students are also taught short, unguided mindfulness practices (e.g., breath counting, watching thoughts) and are encouraged to listen to guided audio files at home (Johnson et al., 2017). In addition to .b, MiSP has expanded to include a curriculum for younger children, ages 7–11. This program—Paws b—builds upon .b and Susan Kaiser-Greenland's *Inner Kids* (Kaiser-Greenland, 2010). The lessons are either administered as six 1-hour lessons or 12 half-hour lessons. The lessons cover six themes (e.g., learning to train attention). Students are also encouraged, but not required, to do mindfulness practices at home using practice sheets called "Give It a Go" (Vickery & Dorjee, 2016).

and effective approach for promoting different facets of self-regulation, including executive function, behavioral self-regulation, and emotion regulation (Galla et al., 2016b). In total, 23 of the 34 studies (68%) reviewed in this chapter evaluated self-regulation outcomes related to either executive functioning, behavioral self-regulation, or emotion regulation.

Executive Functioning

Executive functioning refers to a set of interrelated cognitive abilities that enable goal-directed behavior, and is often considered the foundation of effective self-regulation (Diamond, 2013). Examples of executive functioning include the ability to shift attention from one thing to another (attention shifting), inhibit maladaptive impulses (inhibitory control), and hold information in mind despite distractions (working memory). Nine studies

(27% of all reviewed) examined the effects of mindfulness training on children's and adolescents' executive functioning.

In one notable study, researchers randomized 200 junior high school students (seventh to ninth graders) into one of three groups: a mindfulness group, a yoga group, or a wait-list control group (Quach et al., 2016). Each group met separately for 45 minutes, twice a week for 4 weeks during physical education class. The mindfulness and yoga programs were taught by external facilitators who were trained mindfulness and yoga instructors. Students in the mindfulness group practiced breathing techniques and formal mindfulness meditation (e.g., loving-kindness and awareness practices), and engaged in group discussions. Students in the yoga group practiced various breathing techniques, yoga poses, and also engaged in group discussions. Both groups were encouraged to practice at home daily for 15–30 minutes and record details about their practice in home practice logs. Results showed that those in the mindfulness group outperformed those in the yoga and control groups on a computerized working memory task. Similarly, studies with preschoolers (Thierry et al., 2018), elementary schoolers (Schonert-Reichl et al., 2015), and middle schoolers (Parker, Kupersmidt, Mathis, Scull, & Sims, 2014) have found improvements in executive functioning for those in the mindfulness training group based on computerized performance tasks, although one study with preschoolers did not (Flook et al., 2015).

Other studies relied on teacher and parent reports to assess changes in students' executive functioning. In one study, 64 second and third graders were randomized into either a mindfulness group or a control group. In the mindfulness group, students met twice a week over an 8-week period and engaged in a number of mindful awareness practices (e.g., sitting meditation), as well as activities and games (Flook et al., 2010). Study results indicated that students who were lower in executive functioning at the study outset and who participated in the mindfulness group showed greater improvement in executive functioning when compared to their counterparts in the control group, as indicated by teacher and parent reports. Other studies have also found that, based on teacher ratings, students who completed a mindfulness training program demonstrated better attention skills than those who did not (Napoli, Krech, & Holley, 2005); however, two studies found that, while teachers reported improved executive functioning, parents did not report these improvements (Thierry, Bryant, Nobles, & Norris, 2016; Vickery & Dorjee, 2016). Teacher-report outcomes are important to consider, but they should be interpreted with caution, as they may be susceptible to bias (e.g., the teacher knows which students have received the mindfulness training).

Taken together, these studies suggest that mindfulness training may promote executive functioning in youth. More research is needed to investigate which practices (e.g., mindfulness, yoga) are better for promoting executive functioning, and whether mindfulness training with youth can lead to long-term changes in executive functioning. Only one of the studies reviewed included a follow-up assessment, which found long-term improvements in students' executive functioning as reported by teachers, but not by parents (Vickery & Dorjee, 2016).

Behavioral Self-Regulation

Behavioral self-regulation refers generally to the ability to control behavior in the service of long-term goals. In total, seven studies (21%) measured some form of behavioral self-regulation (e.g., dietary restraint, self-control, intention to use substances). For example, in a study of 127 kindergarten students, researchers randomized classrooms into either a mindfulness group or a control group (Viglas & Perlman, 2017). The mindfulness group completed a 6-week Mindful Schools program. The program consisted of three 20-minute lessons per week (18 total), in which students engaged in mindful awareness practices (e.g., developing kind thoughts toward others) and mindful breathing practices. The program was delivered by a trained and certified teacher from the Mindful Schools organization. The control group carried on business as usual. At the end of 6 weeks, all students were asked to complete the Head–Toes–Knees–Shoulders (HTKS) task. The HTKS, presented as a fun game to students, is a validated measure of behavioral self-regulation in which students are instructed to touch their head, toes, knees, and shoulders in varying combinations (McClelland & Cameron, 2012). The study found that students in the mindfulness group performed better on the HTKS than those in the control group, indicating that the mindfulness program improved behavioral self-regulation (Viglas & Perlman, 2017). Another study with preschoolers found no effects of mindfulness training on behavioral self-regulation when using a delay of gratification task (Flook et al., 2015).

Emotion Regulation

Emotion regulation is defined broadly as the "processes by which individuals influence which emotions they have, when they have them, and how they experience and express these emotions" (Gross, 1998, p. 275). In total, 14 studies (41%) measured emotion regulation outcomes.

In a study of disadvantaged youth in Baltimore, researchers randomized 97 fourth and fifth graders into either a mindfulness group or a wait-list control group (Mendelson et al., 2010). The mindfulness group participated in the Holistic Life Foundation's Stress Reduction & Mindfulness Curriculum, which consisted of forty-eight 45-minute lessons over 12 weeks (four lessons per week). Each lesson involved yoga poses, breathing techniques, group discussions, and mindfulness practices (e.g., body scans, seated mindfulness exercises). The lessons were led by several instructors who had years of experience practicing mindfulness and who came from similar racial/ethnic and economic backgrounds as the students. The control group had an open "resource time," in which students engaged in non-academic activities. At the end of 12 weeks, students in the mindfulness group reported fewer "reactive" or involuntary responses to stress, including less rumination, less intrusive thoughts, and less emotional arousal, compared to those in the control group. However, these students did not experience improvements in well-being or reductions in depression above and beyond those in the control group.

Another study that also targeted disadvantaged urban youth found that the mindfulness group reported significantly lower rumination and use of negative coping strategies (e.g., self-blame) when compared to the control group (Sibinga et al., 2016). Other studies with elementary schoolers (Schonert-Reichl et al., 2015), middle schoolers (Sibinga et al., 2013), and high schoolers (Metz et al., 2013) have found that mindfulness training programs improve different facets of emotion regulation, including emotional arousal, coping strategies, and hostility; with respect to the latter, students were less hostile and better able to deal with difficult emotions.

Overall, evidence from this review suggests that school-based mindfulness training programs show promise for promoting emotion regulation. Moreover, and consistent with current thinking (Creswell & Lindsay, 2014), our review suggests that these programs may be especially beneficial for promoting emotion regulation among youth dealing with higher stress burdens (e.g., due to socioeconomic disadvantage).

Physical Health

Although it has been studied less often than mental health and self-regulation, researchers have also examined whether mindfulness training can promote aspects of physical health. Some indicators of physical health include blood pressure, cortisol levels, resting heart rate, body mass index, and sleep. Seven (21%) studies in our review examined the effects of mindfulness training programs on physical health. School-based efforts to promote physical health are one approach to prevent negative long-term health outcomes (e.g., cardiovascular morbidity and mortality) (Barnes et al., 2008).

Three studies assessed a Breathing Awareness Meditation program for African American students with high systolic blood pressure and/or at risk for developing hypertension (Barnes et al., 2008; Gregoski et al., 2011; Wright et al., 2011). Researchers collected measures of systolic and diastolic blood pressure, heart rate and, in the case of two studies, overnight sodium excretion, which is a measure of chronic stress. In one of these studies, African American high school students at risk for developing hypertension

Holistic Life Foundation:
Stress Reduction and Mindfulness Curriculum

Another program that has received attention in the media for its work with disadvantaged youth in Baltimore is the Stress Reduction and Mindfulness Curriculum developed by the Holistic Life Foundation. The program is focused on bringing mindfulness-based practices and yoga to urban youth living in poverty. The program aims to target youth populations experiencing the psychological effects of chronic stress (Mendelson et al., 2010). Currently, the Holistic Life Foundation serves 7,500 students per week in over 42 schools in the Baltimore area. The organization has trained and employs over 30 Baltimore youth to administer the program to students (Holistic Life Foundation, 2016).

The curriculum spans 24 weeks and consists of two 45-minute lessons per week. The lessons are taught by external facilitators who have been trained in the program curriculum and typically come from the same high-poverty neighborhoods as the students they work with (Mendelson et al., 2010). Each lesson starts with a centering practice, then transitions into a mindful movement activity (i.e., yoga or tai-chi). This activity is followed by a discussion on a mindfulness-related topic (e.g., using mindfulness techniques to respond to stressors) and ends with a guided breathing practice, in which students are taught to attend to certain foci (Holistic Life Foundation, 2016). All curricular components have been designed to cultivate capacities for sustained attention and greater awareness of thoughts, emotions, and physical states, as well as greater regulation of these states (Mendelson et al., 2010).

were randomized into a mindfulness group, a life skills group, or a no treatment control group (Gregoski et al., 2011). Those in the mindfulness group engaged in two 10-minute mindfulness practices each day of the school week (once during health class and once at home), and twice daily at home over the weekend. Those in the life skills group received training in life skills, such as conflict resolution, reflective listening, and anger management. Students in the control group attended the standard health education class. Each group participated in these activities for 3 months. Compared to students in both the life skills and control group, those in the mindfulness group experienced greater reductions in blood pressure and average daytime heart rate over the course of the 3 months. Two additional studies of African American adolescents found greater reductions in blood pressure for students in the mindfulness group (Barnes et al., 2008; Wright et al., 2011), and one study reported reductions in average schooltime heart rate for the mindfulness group compared to the control group (Barnes et al., 2008). Finally, one study found reductions in a measure of chronic stress (Barnes et al., 2008), while another study did not find a significant effect on this outcome (Gregoski et al., 2011).

Two other studies measured cortisol levels—a physiological indicator of stress. Of these two, one study found no effect of mindfulness training on cortisol levels (Sibinga et al., 2013), while the other study showed mindfulness training led to higher cortisol levels in the morning compared to students who did not receive this training (Schonert-Reichl et al., 2015). With such few studies, the effects of mindfulness training on cortisol levels in youth are inconclusive. Similarly, two studies looked at the impact of mindfulness training on sleep and neither found significant effects (Sibinga et al., 2013; van de Weijer-Bergsma, Langenberg, Brandsma, Oort, & Bögels, 2014).

Overall, evidence for the positive effects of mindfulness training on physical health outcomes in youth is still preliminary, but it does suggest that this training may be especially beneficial for youth at high risk for developing more serious health issues (Barnes et al., 2008; Gregoski et al., 2011; Wright et al., 2011).

Academic Functioning

Studies are beginning to examine whether mindfulness training programs can support academic performance (e.g., report card grades and tests of academic skills), positive academic behaviors (e.g., classroom engagement, participation, and cooperation), or both. Next, we highlight a few studies that examined outcomes related to academic functioning. Five (15%) studies assessed academic performance, and eight (24%) assessed academic behaviors, including maladaptive behaviors and social–emotional competencies.

In a study of 191 third graders, teachers who volunteered for the study were given a series of prerecorded audiotapes, each with a 10-minute mindfulness practice (Bakosh, Snow, Tobias, Houlihan, & Barbosa-Leiker, 2016). The audiotapes included a wide range of mindfulness practices derived from MBSR (e.g., body scans, breathing practices) and provided guidance on how to sit, as well as expectations for the practice. Teachers were asked to play one 10-minute audio exercise each day for 8 weeks. At the end of the 8 weeks, students who completed the mindfulness training showed significant improvements on teacher-reported reading and science grades, compared to those who did not complete the mindfulness training; however, there were no significant differences between groups on teacher-reported math, spelling, writing, or social studies grades. Teachers did report a significant decrease in classroom behavioral problems for students who received the mindfulness training, which may have contributed to the improvement in science and reading grades. It is important to note that teachers knew which students were receiving the mindfulness training and were also the ones assigning grades and reporting behavioral problems.

This type of reporting introduces bias and should be taken into consideration when interpreting results.

Other studies have found that mindfulness training improves academic behaviors in the classroom. In a study of 246 middle schoolers, students were nonrandomly assigned to a Mindful Education program or a wait-list control group (Schonert-Reichl & Lawlor, 2010). The program was delivered by classroom teachers, who completed a 1-day training and received biweekly consultation from program developers. The program consisted of ten weekly 45-minute lessons that each emphasized different social and emotional skills (e.g., teamwork). Additionally, students engaged in 3-minute mindfulness practices (e.g., focusing on the breath) three times throughout each school day. At the end of the study, teachers reported that students in the mindfulness group were more attentive and emotionally regulated and showed higher levels of social–emotional competence compared to students in the control group. As in the study of third graders just discussed, the teachers who provided these reports knew which students had participated in the mindfulness training—again limiting our interpretation of these findings to some degree. Other studies conducted with kindergarteners (Viglas & Perlman, 2017), middle schoolers (Napoli et al., 2005; Powell et al., 2008), and high schoolers (Fishbein et al., 2016) have found similar results with regard to academic behaviors, including reductions in hyperactivity and improvements in attention, social skills, and contributions during class time.

Studies that measure academic performance have found mixed results. One study of preschoolers found that children who participated in a mindfulness training program received better grades for approaches to learning, social and emotional development, and health and physical development compared to a control group (Flook et al., 2015); however, there were no significant differences between groups on grades for cognition and general knowledge or language development and communication. Another study of preschoolers, which used an adaptation of MindUP, found no differences between the mindfulness group and the business-as-usual group on vocabulary and reading scores at the end of preschool. However, the study did find significant differences on these measures at the end of kindergarten (1 year after the program ended), which may suggest that these effects manifest over time (Thierry et al., 2016).

Although research linking mindfulness training to academic outcomes is relatively sparse, the evidence to date indicates that this type of training may contribute to greater academic functioning, likely through classroom behaviors that promote student learning. However, with only five studies to draw upon, and the limited rigor of these studies, more research is needed before any definitive conclusions can be reached about whether mindfulness training directly or indirectly improves academic functioning.

Minds Over Matter: A Case Study

The Minds Over Matter program began with six women in Delaware who were inspired to share mindfulness practices with youth, particularly those experiencing trauma or dysregulation issues. We had the opportunity to speak with Karen Barwick, one of the founders of Minds Over Matter, to learn about the program and gain insights about implementing this type of program in schools (K. Barwick, personal communication, November 9, 2017).

The program started with two groups of adolescent girls who were being treated for anxiety at their school wellness center. With the first group of girls, Karen and her team used the .b curriculum (MiSP), which involved delivering the course content in 45-minute lessons and instructing the girls in mindfulness practices. For the second group, they tried the Mindful Schools program, which consists of breath awareness; walking, eating, and seeing practices; and lessons on kindness and caring. In the end, the Mindful Schools program was a better fit for Karen and her team's facilitation style as well as for the school contexts in which they were working. Karen noted that she was drawn to Mindful Schools because of its adaptability. In the end, Karen and her team developed Minds Over Matter as an adaptation of the Mindful Schools curriculum.

Since this first experience, Minds Over Matter has been administered to over 300 children, and Karen has gleaned many insights in the process. One insight has to do with the age of students receiving the program. Karen shared that it has been challenging to deliver the program to middle school students. "I experienced the middle school students as a little more confrontational. Some of the kids either didn't like the word *mindfulness* or found the practices 'boring.'" Her experience with elementary school students has been different. "I find the third and fourth graders to be a kind of sweet spot." In her view, these students tend to be more open to the practices and concepts of mindfulness compared to middle school students.

Karen shared that it is important to take the developmental stage of the child into consideration when implementing these types of programs in schools. Making the curriculum relevant to the students' lives (e.g., in sports and in the classroom) has worked especially well with middle schoolers, who are more inclined to challenge the material being offered. In contrast, Karen has found that elementary school students benefit from a creative approach—finding that fun, playful games or "hands-on" props help to communicate the concepts in ways that are more accessible for the younger students. Because classroom contexts differ, Karen feels it is up to the facilitator to develop his or her own approach for teaching the principles to the children.

Another insight has to do with time. Karen stressed that time is of the essence when it comes to implementing these types of programs in schools. She prefers the Mindful Schools approach not only because it is adaptable, but because the lessons are short (15–30 minutes once a week) and can be easily incorporated into regular class time.

Karen continued to share three more insights about implementation based on her recent experience working with a private school in Delaware. First, she said it has been crucial to have strong support from the school and/or district leadership. The head of this private school has been very supportive of the team's efforts and has been open to collaboration. With administrative support, the school decided to launch a second year of the program. This outcome leads into the second insight: for the best results, implement the program over multiple years. In the second year, the school is "marinating a bit more" on the core mindfulness principles, and the program is really starting to take hold, which has also encouraged teachers to take ownership. Karen's third insight is that teacher buy-in is essential. She mentioned that it has taken time, but teachers are now weaving elements of the program curriculum and practices into their transitions and rituals. Even more, a common mindfulness language has begun to emerge in classrooms throughout the school. In Karen's view, the second year marks immense progress compared to the first year, when the program seemed to be just one more thing teachers and students had to do. Now, with strong support from the head of school, another year of program delivery, and increased teacher buy-in, the program has become embedded into the fabric of the school and informs the way teachers are interacting with students.

On the flip side, when the program was administered to students in four public elementary schools in another district, it met several challenges and barriers. Minds Over Matter provided a 3-hour faculty in-service training to all teachers participating in the program. Because of a last-minute administration change, a few classrooms were added after the in-service training. As a result, the teachers in these classrooms did not have a clear understanding of their role in the program implementation (e.g., how to guide daily practices). At the end of the program, Karen and her team found that the classrooms that benefited most from the program were those with fully invested teachers who engaged in mindfulness practices on their own and with the children. These teachers integrated mindfulness into their daily routine, which made it a true collaboration between them and the external facilitators.

After program completion, the district held a parent information meeting about Minds Over Matter. Some parents who attended this meeting questioned the secularity of mindfulness practices and were upset that they had not had the opportunity to ask questions prior to the program's adoption. From Karen's perspective, the meeting provided the space for dispelling false beliefs about mindfulness and religiosity as well as addressing other concerns. In the end, the district decided not to bring the program back. Whether or not the decision was a result of parental concerns, lack of support from the district leadership, and/or teacher buy-in is unclear; however, when these elements have been in place, the program has been largely successful from Karen's perspective.

Karen proposed some final suggestions for implementing these types of programs in schools. For one, she said to start small. It can be great to have a big vision for change, but implementation and integration into a school setting takes time. She encouraged schools to find ways to "weave in" short practices

(continued)

throughout the week, so they become routinized and normalized. Second, she suggested that the program be contextualized to meet the needs of the school setting and/or student population. Third, she said it can be helpful to hold a parent meeting at the program outset to allay any concerns about religiosity and mindfulness by describing the secular nature of the practices and/or sharing research evidence. Finally, she urged educators to take up these practice themselves, so they can embody the core principles of mindfulness and become leaders within their schools.

Summary

The studies reviewed in this chapter suggest that school-based mindfulness training programs show promise for promoting mental health and psychological well-being, self-regulation (including executive function, behavioral self-regulation, and emotion regulation), physical health, and academic functioning in students. However, results from these studies were often inconsistent or nuanced. For instance, several studies (12 in total) found mindfulness training boosted mental health outcomes (e.g., reduced depression, stress, and anxiety), but these studies, when considered individually, often reported varying and sometimes inconsistent effects across measures of mental health. For example, Sibinga et al. (2016) found significant reductions in depression and posttraumatic symptoms for students in the mindfulness training group compared to those in the control group, but found no effects on anxiety, paranoid ideation, hostility, or stress. Along these lines, studies that reported beneficial outcomes for one domain (e.g., executive functioning) did not necessarily find salutary effects for other domains (e.g., mental health). For example, Quach et al. (2016) found significant improvements in working memory for students in the mindfulness training group compared to those in the yoga and control groups, but did not observe improvements in mental health outcomes (e.g., stress or anxiety).

We share this evidence to make the point that although mindfulness training programs can be effective in generating positive outcomes for youth in school settings, their effectiveness is not uniform for each measure within a domain or across domains (i.e., the four domains outlined in this chapter). The evidence for mindfulness training in schools is still nascent and tentative, especially with regard to academic performance (e.g., report card grades and tests of academic skills). Findings across the four domains reviewed in this chapter tended to vary, as programs and school contexts differed considerably. With that in mind, it is important to consider sociocultural and contextual factors when interpreting and generalizing these findings.

Lessons Learned

For educators, school administrators, and policymakers interested in the implementation of mindfulness training programs in schools, we highlight a few areas for consideration based on our review of the literature: (1) targeting programs for specific populations of students, (2) program facilitation, and (3) program structure and time.

Targeting Programs

When a school or organization decides to implement a mindfulness training program, the first step is to determine the primary outcomes of interest (e.g., mental health). Next, it is important to examine the evidence for programs that target both the outcomes and specific age and/or target group of interest. For example, a mindfulness training program that has been shown to produce improvements in mental health and psychological well-being for middle schoolers may not yield the same effects for elementary schoolers. Likewise, the program may have generated positive outcomes for one domain (e.g., executive functioning), but not for another domain (e.g., psychological well-being). In addition, the program may have been conducted and studied in a particular school setting where certain social and/or cultural factors affected students' perceptions of and engagement with program materials. We suggest that educators consider programs that have been evaluated with a similar population of students (i.e., age, race, economic background) and ideally in a similar school context.

It is also important to determine whether the program will be administered universally to all students or targeted toward a subgroup of students (e.g., higher risk or lower-performing students). On the one hand, targeted programs allow for intentional program design and implementation, which may serve to strengthen the program's overall impact. On the other hand, universally administered programs have the potential to benefit a broader range of students. In the studies reviewed for this chapter, we observed that the positive effects generated from universally administered programs were often due to significant gains among the lowest-performing or highest-risk students. This is consistent with a recent review of school-based mental health programs, which found universal approaches to be generally effective, but effects were often larger for higher-risk students (Weare & Nind, 2011). It appears that whether the program is targeted for a specific subgroup or administered universally, high-need students tend to benefit the most. Therefore, targeted programs may be the most cost-effective and time-efficient approach for closing gaps between high- and low-need students.

When selecting a targeted or universally administered program, we recommend that educators and administrators consider factors like financial capacity and other issues associated with targeted programming. Targeting a specific subgroup of students may be more cost-effective than administering a program universally to all students—a practical consideration. That said, there can be downsides to targeted programming, such as the stigma associated with being targeted, concerns about denying services to students in the nontargeted group, or difficulties determining a cutoff point for program entry. Since the evidence on school-based mindfulness training programs is still emerging, schools and policymakers should exercise caution when identifying programs, consider practical implementation issues, and understand the limitations of generalizing study findings to different school settings.

Program Facilitation

When selecting a school-based mindfulness training program, it is useful to consider who will be delivering the program (i.e., trained classroom teachers or external facilitators). In the studies we reviewed for this chapter, external facilitators who conducted mindfulness training usually had extensive experience practicing and teaching mindfulness. They were trained in administering the program curriculum and highly competent in their delivery of program materials. From the standpoint of program outcomes, this may mean that external facilitators promote deeper student understanding of core mindfulness principles and therefore foster more enduring effects.

On the other hand, relying on an external facilitator may pose problems for program sustainability. For one, it can be cost prohibitive for schools to hire an external provider, and it can be challenging for teachers to continue imparting program concepts and facilitating guided practices once the program ends. Instead, if a classroom teacher delivers the program, she learns the program concepts and is able to model mindfulness principles throughout the school day. Since teachers have more contact with students, there are also more opportunities to reinforce these concepts, which potentially promotes lasting change in students and program sustainability. These teachers might even begin to embody these principles, transforming their approach to instruction and, subsequently, the classroom environment.

In sum, there are benefits to having classroom teachers be the ones to administer mindfulness training programs (i.e., sustainability, reinforcement, and feasibility), but the success of this approach seems to depend on access to high-level, effective trainings to promote teacher competency. Based on the studies reviewed here, it remains unclear whether external facilitators generate better outcomes than classroom teachers. One possible path forward would be to pursue a "co-teaching" model, in which external facilitators administer the program in collaboration with classroom teachers. At the end of one study, several teachers advocated for this model, proposing it could leverage the expert knowledge and experience of the facilitator, as well as the expert classroom management skills of the teacher

(Johnson et al., 2016). Regardless, schools should consider factors like cost and sustainability when determining who will carry out the program.

Program Structure and Time

Finally, it is important to consider program structure and time when implementing mindfulness training programs in schools, especially given the demands placed on teachers and students throughout the school day. Programs that are more time intensive may come at the expense of regular classroom instruction, yet promote the greatest understanding and retention of program concepts and, subsequently, generate more enduring effects. On the other hand, programs that are brief, but frequent (e.g., 10 minutes of mindful breathing each day), can be fluidly integrated into class time, allowing teachers to attend to and attain other instructional goals. However, these programs may lack substantive and comprehensive attention to core mindfulness principles, which serve to support and justify continued practice after the program is finished.

Schools should weigh the costs and benefits associated with these different program structures, while considering the evidence highlighted in this chapter. For instance, programs that require minimal time (e.g., 10 minutes of mindfulness practice per day) still show positive effects on outcomes like self-regulation, physical health, and academic functioning. It may not be necessary to implement a time-intensive program to see results. It may be just as effective to seamlessly embed brief and frequent practices into the school day. Both approaches may allow for continual reinforcement, but less time-intensive programs may feel more feasible for teachers and more acceptable to students. That said, research on program structure and time is very much lacking. No studies to our knowledge compare mindfulness training programs that are administered using different structural and time formats. Therefore, more research is needed to determine which program formats are most effective and practical given the nature of school-based contexts.

Conclusion

Interest in and use of school-based mindfulness training programs will undoubtedly continue to grow. Our review shows that there is already an array of programs which vary widely in their approach to delivery (e.g., targeted or universal), structure (e.g., length, curricular format), and facilitation (e.g., trained classroom teacher or external facilitator). Our review also suggests that these programs are feasible, acceptable, and can be delivered with fidelity in a range of school settings. They hold promise for supporting multiple aspects of mental health and psychological well-being, self-regulation, physical health, and academic functioning. Still, caution should be exercised when it comes to selecting these programs as a means for boosting academic performance. Instead, they should be viewed as one approach for cultivating social and emotional capacities, which are important ends in themselves.

Finally, there is no definitive evidence regarding the type of program delivery, structure, and facilitation that promotes the greatest outcomes. Continued high-quality research in the years ahead will offer more clarity on the effectiveness of different programs as well as provide a clearer picture of the type of mindfulness practices that work best to support youth of different ages, backgrounds, and abilities. In the meantime, if a school or school district chooses to implement a mindfulness training program, it will be important to consider the outcomes of interest, the context, the school or school district's capacity, the program cost, and the sociocultural factors that might influence program acceptability and feasibility.

APPENDIX 2.1. Case Study of the International School of Geneva Secondary School Campus— Flexibility, Creativity, and Innovations

EDMUNDO TIMM
drama teacher and mindfulness coordinator,
International School of Geneva, La Grande Boissière Campus

I was born in Brazil and have been working at the International School of Geneva since 1998. The school is a large private foundation founded by civil servants from the International Labor Organization and the League of Nations (the precursor to the United Nations) in 1924 as the world's first international school and the birthplace of the International Baccalaureate Diploma Program. With 140 nationalities and 80 mother tongues, we remain the most diverse school in the world. The school consists of three campuses offering primary, middle, and secondary education to over 4,000 students in Geneva and the surrounding areas.

For 20 years I have been teaching theater in the secondary school and, since 2015, I have been involved in the implementation of the Mindfulness Program at the La Grande Boissière Campus (LGB), which is the largest and oldest campus, with 1,900 students.

Mindfulness and the Universal Learning Programme

The principal for the secondary school and LGB Campus Director, Dr. Conrad Hughes, explains:

Our curriculum, the Universal Learning Programme, is universal in its reach and addresses timeless areas of human activity. Our cohesive programmes focus on the process of learning in the broadest sense—covering intellectual, creative, social, ethical and physical development.

Mindfulness is a core expression of our desire to see learners approach knowledge, other people, themselves and the world around them through the dynamic matrix of these competencies. We are living in a world of volatility, uncertainty, complexity and ambiguity and in order to approach it serenely and with confidence, learners must have a grounded self-awareness.

Mindfulness, if practiced well, reinforces metacognition, wellness, concentration, inner-harmony and active listening, all critical elements of what it means to be a deep thinker.

This is why we are supporting the development of mindfulness for students, teachers and parents and feel that all 3.0 schools should be doing the same.

In 2015, as part of the school's Universal Learning Programme staff development, I had the opportunity to attend mindfulness workshops with Françoise Stuckelberger, a clinical psychologist, mindfulness-based stress reduction (MBSR) instructor, and mindfulness practitioner for children and teenagers. These introductory workshops included 3 full-day sessions followed by an adapted MBSR training (six sessions of 2 hours each and shorter home meditation practices). Even though I had been involved with different types of meditation for approximately 30 years, the workshops were a great opportunity to receive support from the school and to learn how to apply mindfulness in my professional field. Together with a small group of enthusiastic and engaged staff we attended the 6-week MBSR course and decided to implement some of the mindfulness techniques slowly in the school daily routine.

This first pilot project was presented to Year 11 students (15–16 years old) in two sessions of 45 minutes led by teachers who had attended the MBSR course. This was the first time the secondary students had been offered such an opportunity, and they received it well. In 2016, with the support of our principal, Dr. Hughes, and along with a group of staff members, we decided to give more teachers as well as students the opportunity to learn about mindfulness and benefit from the practices. This project came to comprise the following strategy.

Phase 1: Staff Training and Year 11 Mentor Program (2015–2017)

In 2015, I was working as a Head of Year 11 (pre-IB year–U.S. grade 10) and coordinating the general education program for 160 students and 10 mentors. Mentors are mostly subject-area teachers who will be the first contact if parents have a concern about their child. Mentors are not only responsible for students' academic progress, but also develop a relationship with the student as a person, getting to know the interests, skills, and ambitions of each member of the mentor group.

In September 2016 all mentors in Year 11 were invited to first attend the 8-week MBSR course and, upon successful completion, to follow up with a 6-week course on how to teach mindfulness to teenagers (45-minute classes for 6 weeks). These courses were part of the mentor training for the Year 11 Mentor Program and were led by MBSR instructor, Françoise Stuckelberger. Mentors were invited to attend the course; however, one refused to participate due to his personal religious convictions. I also accepted three staff members (one being the school nurse) who were not mentors to attend the courses because of their motivation to learn.

Mentors were generally interested and very enthusiastic to learn a new skill. The challenge was huge since it did add some extra work to their already busy teacher schedules. However, it also created a greater group spirit, because the quality of shared experience was excellent and the level of honesty and openness was higher than in typical faculty meetings.

From January to June 2017, we started offering mindfulness classes (six sessions of 45 minutes each) to all the students as part of the Year 11 mentor program. This course was obligatory; however, students had the right to not engage in the mindfulness practices if they did not wish to (although this was rare). Thus, the pilot project consisted of basic introduction exercises, such as mindful eating, body scan, discussion about stressful situations in the school environment, and mindfulness soundscape meditation (e.g., exploring sounds, silence, and sensations). This pilot course was created by Françoise Stuckelberger based on MBSR and taught by the mentors, in one case with the support of the school nurse.

From my perspective, and from hearing about the research results, the experience was very interesting. There were certainly some anecdotal success stories, such as the student who later in the year came to thank me for having the opportunity to practice mindfulness in the school, as she felt it helped her to relax and have more control over her emotions during the exam period.

In fact, student feedback from the first year showed that most students were receptive to the idea of having mindfulness classes. However, there were several things they did not like. For one, they found the physical environment was not conducive to mindfulness practice. For example, they mentioned that they heard noise from nearby classes and that the small and uncomfortable chairs did not allow students and teachers to have productive and enjoyable classes. Some students also mentioned that they did not engage with the activity because it felt like just another obligatory subject class. In general, the student perceptions of the program were mixed. Although there were some success stories, we decided to modify the program in response to this feedback.

Phase 2: The Mindfulness Silent Room (2016–present)

Taking into consideration feedback from the students and mentors, we decided to create a separate space to facilitate this new experience, and named it the

Mindfulness Silent Room. Using my knowledge and experience as a drama teacher, I helped to design a room that would be comfortable for students and would enable them to have a deeper mindfulness experience. It is a black-box installation, an immersive theater experience with lights, sounds, and projections in which students are invited to do one of three optional activities: (1) relax in silence, (2) meditate, and (3) sleep or dream. They are not allowed to read, draw, or have conversations with each other. They also must turn off their phones.

The Mindfulness Silent Room is always supervised by a staff member who has attended the MBSR course. Individual students can come to the silent room at any time. Last year, mentors for all grades were invited to reserve the Silent Room in order to bring their groups in for a mindfulness class. Students were also free to attend during their free periods. We are currently considering creating a pass, like that used for the nurse's office, so students can have access during class time.

Classes with the mentor groups are scheduled for Tuesdays mornings. The Silent Room mindfulness classes are led by me or one of the mindfulness-trained mentors. We run two 45-minute sessions for each mentor group, which provides a short introduction to mindfulness techniques and concepts. Before students enter the Silent Room for their session, we make sure to remind them what it means to respect the space. I explain the rules and how we should be attentive to the silence. I explain that it is like going to a ritual, a special environment that it is unique, and I have found that the students understand it is a privilege.

From my perspective, The Mindfulness Silent Room has been a great way to reach out to students in an open and appealing manner. First of all, they are more likely to join in and learn practices when they are not forced and when they find the environment relaxing and comfortable. Second of all, having worked as Head of Year 11 for about 17 years, I can confirm that The Silent Room has opened a door for students to initiate a conversation and talk about themselves, instead of being questioned by adults. While before (within Phase 1) we worked hard to engage students in talking about their experiences, thoughts, and feelings, now students are more likely to take the initiative and share some of their more honest and sincere concerns or questions after being exposed to the Silent Room.

Talking in the Silent Room might be perceived as a paradox, but it has been a productive one. As we grow older we will realize that life and mindfulness are full of inseparable opposites. I believe that in a school environment it is important to find this flexibility within ourselves to work with reality as it is, and to do what we can to offer students a variety of experiences and help them to find their own equilibrium and make their own choices that resonate with their hearts, emotions, and souls.

The following phase is a reflection of the flexibility, responsiveness, and commitment to sharing mindfulness with students in different and creative ways.

Phase 3: Mobile Soundscape Mindfulness Surprise Intervention (2017–present)

The Mindfulness Silent Room is located in the LGB Art Center, which is at a distance from the other subject departments. Given the large size of the campus, some teachers who are located in these departments asked me to bring a brief, unannounced intervention to their classrooms.

Following an agreement on timing with the teachers, I made a surprise visit to a subject class with my meditation instruments: a liquid light acoustic drum, Japanese Koshi, and Tibetan bowls. Students are invited to stop what they are doing for about 7 minutes. Typically, they are first invited to bring their attention to their breath, and then to listen to the sounds of the instruments. Finally, in between the sounds, they are invited to observe the silence.

This unexpected intervention has proven to be extremely well received by students and teachers. It does cause a short disruption to the dynamic of the class. However, the teachers and students have told me that the level of focus and concentration is higher after the intervention than before it. This of course remains to be empirically verified.

Conclusions and Lessons Learned

I believe that the Mindfulness Program has been very successful since more and more students are attending the Silent Room sessions. Students are grateful for the experience of discovering new possibilities for dealing with daily school routines, concerns, pressures, and expectations with less stress and anxiety. The Soundscape Mindfulness Surprise Intervention is also one that I plan to continue in the upcoming year. Fortunately, we have a very supportive staff and administration, which has proven very important in this work.

Also, I have found that although there are challenges with sharing mindfulness with adolescents, the newness of these interventions provides room for creativity. I truly believe that we should not force teenagers to meditate. However, we should allow them to have access to pleasant situations that will help them to develop their personal and emotional skills to face the challenges of this new era.

References

Atkinson, M. J., & Wade, T. D. (2015). Mindfulness-based prevention for eating disorders: A school-based cluster randomized controlled study. *International Journal of Eating Disorders, 48*, 1024–1037.

Bakosh, L. S., Snow, R. M., Tobias, J. M., Houlihan, J. L., & Barbosa-Leiker, C. (2016). Maximizing mindful learning: Mindful awareness intervention improves elementary school students' quarterly grades. *Mindfulness, 7*, 59–67.

Barnes, V. A., Pendergrast, R. A., Harshfield, G. A., & Treiber, F. A. (2008).

Impact of breathing awareness meditation on ambulatory blood pressure and sodium handling in pre-hypertensive African American adolescents. *Ethnicity and Disease, 18,* 1–5.

Bergen-Cico, D., Razza, R., & Timmins, A. (2015). Fostering self-regulation through curriculum infusion of mindful yoga: A pilot study of efficacy and feasibility. *Journal of Child and Family Studies, 24,* 3448–3461.

Black, D. S., & Slavich, G. M. (2016). Mindfulness meditation and the immune system: A systematic review of randomized controlled trials. *Annals of the New York Academy of Sciences, 1373,* 13–24.

Blair, C., & Razza, R. P. (2007). Relating effortful control, executive function, and false belief understanding to emerging math and literacy ability in kindergarten. *Child Development, 78,* 647–663.

Britton, W. B., Lepp, N. E., Niles, H. F., Rocha, T., Fisher, N. E., & Gold, J. S. (2014). A randomized controlled pilot trial of classroom-based mindfulness meditation compared to an active control condition in sixth-grade children. *Journal of School Psychology, 52,* 263–278.

Broderick, P. C. (2013). *Learning to BREATHE: A mindfulness curriculum for adolescents.* Oakland, CA: New Harbinger.

Collaborative for Academic, Social, and Emotional Learning. (2017). What is SEL? Retrieved from *www.casel.org/what-is-sel.*

Creswell, J. D., & Lindsay, E. K. (2014). How does mindfulness training affect health?: A mindfulness stress buffering account. *Current Directions in Psychological Science, 23,* 401–407.

Davidson, R. J., Dunne, J., Eccles, J. S., Engle, A., Greenberg, M., Jennings, P., . . . Vago, D. (2012). Contemplative practices and mental training: Prospects for American education. *Child Development Perspectives, 6,* 146–153.

Diamond, A. (2013). Executive functions. *Annual Review of Psychology, 64,* 135–168.

Domitrovich, C. E., & Greenberg, M. T. (2000). The study of implementation: Current findings from effective programs that prevent mental disorders in school-aged children. *Journal of Educational and Psychological Consultation, 11,* 193–221.

Duckworth, A. L., & Carlson, S. M. (2013). Self-regulation and school success. In B. W. Sokol, F. M. E. Grouzet, & U. Muller (Eds.), *Self-regulation and autonomy: Social and developmental dimensions of human conduct* (pp. 208–230). New York: Cambridge University Press.

Durlak, J. A., Weissberg, R. P., Dymnicki, A. B., Taylor, R. D., & Schellinger, K. B. (2011). The impact of enhancing students' social and emotional learning: A meta-analysis of school-based universal interventions. *Child Development, 82,* 405–432.

Fishbein, D., Miller, S., Herman-Stahl, M., Williams, J., Lavery, B., Markovitz, L., . . . Johnson, M. (2016). Behavioral and psychophysiological effects of a yoga intervention on high-risk adolescents: A randomized control trial. *Journal of Child and Family Studies, 25,* 518–529.

Flook, L., Goldberg, S. B., Pinger, L., & Davidson, R. J. (2015). Promoting prosocial behavior and self-regulatory skills in preschool children through a mindfulness-based kindness curriculum. *Developmental Psychology, 51,* 44–51.

Flook, L., Smalley, S. L., Kitil, M. J., Galla, B. M., Kaiser-Greenland, S., Locke,

J., . . . Kasari, C. (2010). Effects of mindful awareness practices on executive functions in elementary school children. *Journal of Applied School Psychology, 26*, 70–95.

Galla, B. M., Baelen, R. N., Duckworth, A. L., & Baime, M. J. (2016a). Mindfulness meet self-regulation: Boosting out-of-class meditation practice with brief action plans. *Motivation Science, 2*, 220–237.

Galla, B. M., Kaiser-Greenland, S., & Black, D. S. (2016b). Mindfulness training to promote self-regulation in youth: Effects of the Inner Kids program. In A. K. Schonert-Reichl & R. W. Roeser (Eds.), *Handbook of mindfulness in education: Integrating theory and research into practice* (pp. 295–311). New York: Springer.

Galla, B. M., Plummer, B. D., White, R. E., Meketon, D., D'Mello, S. K., & Duckworth, A. L. (2014). The Academic Diligence Task (ADT): Assessing individual differences in effort on tedious but important schoolwork. *Contemporary Educational Psychology, 39*, 314–325.

Goyal, M., Singh, S., Sibinga, E. M. S., Gould, N. F., Rowland-Seymour, A., Sharma, R., . . . Haythornthwaite, J. A. (2014). Meditation programs for psychological stress and well-being. *JAMA Internal Medicine, 174*, 357–368.

Gregoski, M. J., Barnes, V. A., Tingen, M. S., Harshfield, G. A., & Treiber, F. A. (2011). Breathing awareness meditation and LifeSkills Training programs influence upon ambulatory blood pressure and sodium excretion among African American adolescents. *Journal of Adolescent Health, 48*, 59–64.

Gross, J. J. (1998). The emerging field of emotion regulation: An integrative review. *Review of General Psychology, 2*, 271–299.

Hofmann, S. G., Sawyer, A. T., Witt, A. A., & Oh, D. (2010). The effect of mindfulness-based therapy on anxiety and depression: A meta-analytic review. *Journal of Consulting and Clinical Psychology, 78*, 169–183.

Holistic Life Foundation. (2016). Stress reduction and mindfulness curriculum. Retrieved from *https://htfinc.org/programs-services/stress-reduction-mindfulness-curriculum.*

Huppert, F. A., & Johnson, D. M. (2010). A controlled trial of mindfulness training in schools: The importance of practice for an impact on well-being. *Journal of Positive Psychology, 5*, 264–274.

Johnson, C., Burke, C., Brinkman, S., & Wade, T. (2016). Effectiveness of a school-based mindfulness program for transdiagnostic prevention in young adolescents. *Behaviour Research and Therapy, 81*, 1–11.

Johnson, C., Burke, C., Brinkman, S., & Wade, T. (2017). A randomized controlled evaluation of a secondary school mindfulness program for early adolescents: Do we have the recipe right yet? *Behaviour Research and Therapy, 99*, 37–46.

Kabat-Zinn, J. (1990). *Full catastrophe living: Using the wisdom of your body and mind to face stress, pain, and illness.* New York: Dell.

Kaiser-Greenland, S. (2010). *The mindful child.* New York: Free Press.

Kuyken, W., Weare, K., Ukoumunne, O. C., Vicary, R., Motton, N., Burnett, R., . . . Huppert, F. (2013). Effectiveness of the Mindfulness in Schools Project: Non-randomised controlled feasibility study. *British Journal of Psychiatry, 203*, 126–131.

Maloney, J. E., Lawlor, M. S., Schonert-Reichl, K. A., & Whitehead, J. (2016). A mindfulness-based social and emotional learning curriculum for school-aged children: The MindUP program. In K. A. Schonert-Reichl & R. W. Roeser

(Eds.), *Handbook of mindfulness in education* (pp. 313–334). New York: Springer.

McClelland, M. M., Acock, A., Piccinin, A., Rhea, S. A., & Stallings, M. C. (2012). Relations between preschool attention span-persistence and age 25 educational outcomes. *Early Childhood Research Quarterly, 28,* 314–324.

McClelland, M. M., & Cameron, C. E. (2012). Self-regulation in early childhood: Improving conceptual clarity and developing ecologically valid measures. *Child Development Perspectives, 6,* 136–142.

Mendelson, T., Greenberg, M. T., Dariotis, J. K., Gould, L. F., Rhoades, B. L., & Leaf, P. J. (2010). Feasibility and preliminary outcomes of a school-based mindfulness intervention for urban youth. *Journal of Abnormal Child Psychology, 38,* 985–994.

Metz, S. M., Frank, J. L., Reibel, D., Cantrell, T., Sanders, R., & Broderick, P. C. (2013). The effectiveness of the Learning to Breathe program on adolescent emotion regulation. *Research in Human Development, 10,* 252–272.

Moffitt, T. E., Arseneault, L., Belsky, D., Dickson, N., Hancox, R. J., Harrington, H., . . . Caspi, A. (2011). A gradient of childhood self-control predicts health, wealth, and public safety. *Proceedings of the National Academy of Sciences of the USA, 108,* 2693–2698.

Napoli, M., Krech, P. R., & Holley, L. C. (2005). Mindfulness training for elementary school students: The attention academy. *Journal of Applied School Psychology, 21,* 99–125.

Noggle, J. J., Steiner, N. J., Minami, T., & Khalsa, S. B. S. (2012). Benefits of yoga for psychosocial well-being in a US high school curriculum: A preliminary randomized controlled trial. *Journal of Developmental & Behavioral Pediatrics, 33,* 193–201.

Parker, A. E., Kupersmidt, J. B., Mathis, E. T., Scull, T. M., & Sims, C. (2014). The impact of mindfulness education on elementary school students: Evaluation of the Master Mind program. *Advances in School Mental Health Promotion, 7,* 184–204.

Poropat, A. E. (2009). A meta-analysis of the five-factor model of personality and academic performance. *Psychological Bulletin, 135,* 322–338.

Powell, L., Gilchrist, M., & Stapley, J. (2008). A journey of self-discovery: An intervention involving massage, yoga and relaxation for children with emotional and behavioural difficulties attending primary schools. *European Journal of Special Needs Education, 23,* 403–412.

Quach, D., Mano, K. E. J., & Alexander, K. (2016). A randomized controlled trial examining the effect of mindfulness meditation on working memory capacity in adolescents. *Journal of Adolescent Health, 58,* 489–496.

Raes, F., Griffith, J. W., Van der Gucht, K., & Williams, J. M. G. (2014). School-based prevention and reduction of depression in adolescents: A cluster-randomized controlled trial of a mindfulness group program. *Mindfulness, 5,* 477–486.

Ramadoss, R., & Bose, B. (2010). Transformative life skills: Pilot study of a yoga model for reduced stress and improving self-control in vulnerable youth. *International Journal of Yoga Therapy, 20,* 73–78.

Raveepatarakul, J., Suttiwan, P., Iamsupasit, S., & Mikulas, W. L. (2014). A mindfulness enhancement program for 8 to 11 year-old Thai children: Effects on mindfulness and depression. *Journal of Health Research, 28,* 335–341.

Schonert-Reichl, K. A., & Lawlor, M. S. (2010). The effects of a mindfulness-based education program on pre- and early adolescents' well-being and social and emotional competence. *Mindfulness, 1,* 137–151.

Schonert-Reichl, K. A., Oberle, E., Lawlor, M. S., Abbott, D., Thomson, K., Oberlander, T. F., & Diamond, A. (2015). Enhancing cognitive and social–emotional development through a simple-to-administer mindfulness-based school program for elementary school children: A randomized controlled trial. *Developmental Psychology, 51,* 52–66.

Sibinga, E. M., Perry-Parrish, C., Chung, S. E., Johnson, S. B., Smith, M., & Ellen, J. M. (2013). School-based mindfulness instruction for urban male youth: A small randomized controlled trial. *Preventive Medicine, 57,* 799–801.

Sibinga, E. M., Webb, L., Ghazarian, S. R., & Ellen, J. M. (2016). School-based mindfulness instruction: An RCT. *Pediatrics, 137,* 1–8.

Taylor, R. D., Oberle, E., Durlak, J. A., & Weissberg, R. P. (2017). Promoting positive youth development through school-based social and emotional learning interventions: A meta-analysis of follow-up effects. *Child Development, 88,* 1156–1171.

Taylor, T. (2016). 22% of companies now offering mindfulness training. Retrieved from *www.hrdive.com/news/22-of-companies-now-offering-mindfulness-training/424530.*

Thierry, K. L., Bryant, H. L., Nobles, S. S., & Norris, K. S. (2016). Two-year impact of a mindfulness-based program on preschoolers' self-regulation and academic performance. *Early Education and Development, 27,* 805–821.

Thierry, K. L., Vincent, R. L., Bryant, H. L., Kinder, M. B., & Wise, C. L. (2018). A self-oriented mindfulness-based curriculum improves prekindergarten students' executive functions. *Mindfulness, 9,* 1443–1456.

van de Weijer-Bergsma, E., Langenberg, G., Brandsma, R., Oort, F. J., & Bögels, S. M. (2014). The effectiveness of a school-based mindfulness training as a program to prevent stress in elementary school children. *Mindfulness, 5,* 238–248.

Viafora, D. P., Mathiesen, S. G., & Unsworth, S. J. (2015). Teaching mindfulness to middle school students and homeless youth in school classrooms. *Journal of Child and Family Studies, 24,* 1179–1191.

Vickery, C. E., & Dorjee, D. (2016). Mindfulness training in primary schools decreases negative affect and increases meta-cognition in children. *Frontiers in Psychology, 6,* 2025–2038.

Viglas, M., & Perlman, M. (2017). Effects of a mindfulness-based program on young children's self-regulation, prosocial behavior and hyperactivity. *Journal of Child and Family Studies, 27,* 1150–1161.

Weare, K., & Nind, M. (2011). Mental health promotion and problem prevention in schools: What does the evidence say? *Health Promotion International, 26,* 29–69.

Wieczner, J. (2016, March 12). Meditation has become a billion-dollar business. Retrieved from *http://fortune.com/2016/03/12/meditation-mindfulness-apps.*

Wright, L. B., Gregoski, M. J., Tingen, M. S., Barnes, V. A., & Treiber, F. A. (2011). Impact of stress reduction interventions on hostility and ambulatory systolic blood pressure in African American adolescents. *Journal of Black Psychology, 37,* 210–233.

PART II

EXAMINING ROLES AND RESPONSIBILITIES FOR SCHOOL TRANSFORMATION

CHAPTER 3

Turn and Listen

Strengthening Compassion and Leadership in the Adult Community in Schools

PAMELA SEIGLE
CHIP WOOD
LISA SANKOWSKI

May This Be a House of Joy

May this be a House of Joy.
May we be open here to dreams,
and to each other.

May all who enter in these magic halls
feel love and feel respect
for learning and each other.
May we always be friends to life.
May we walk in that friendship.
May learning live in this house.
May it never leave.

—CLIFTON (1993, n.p.)

The poet Lucille Clifton wrote this invocation for the Hollywood Elementary School in Hollywood, Maryland, at its inaugural dedication in 1993, when our friend and colleague Kathleen Glaser was the principal. Over the years, this poem has become something of a mission statement for us and for our work in schools. We have dedicated our careers to the belief that every school should be a place of learning and of genuine friendship with love, and respect for all children and adults who are members of the community.

We've also learned from long experience that hoping for this joyful alchemy does not alone make it so. Developing community among colleagues in PreK–12 education that models and teaches what we aspire to for our students requires an intentional and unending commitment to the daily challenges inherent in the work. Building a trustworthy community where learning thrives requires fostering the capacity of adults to be self-aware, mindful, and compassionate with themselves, their colleagues, and their students and families. When mindfulness and compassion are understood and practiced in the adult community, these attitudes are passed on by example and instruction to students.

Qualities of self-awareness, mindfulness, and compassion provide a foundation for educators who take seriously the charge that schools be the cradle of our democracy. Schools share a responsibility to ensure that every voice is heard, that different perspectives and cultural realities are shared and respected, and that the practice of civility is upheld. Teachers, administrators, and staff, however, may have difficulty teaching and modeling these qualities and ideals. More (and more regimented) academic curriculum to cover and assessments to conduct increase educator stress, and students often bring to the classroom their own anxiety stoked by conditions in their lives outside of school and by the emotional and academic demands within schools.

Increasingly, educators are responding by introducing mindfulness and SEL programs into schools with promising results (Newman, Flynn, Suttie, & Smith, 2017). Typically, these programs teach personal mindfulness practices for educators or introduce relaxation, attention, and self-regulation techniques to children. Over the last several years, we've witnessed in the schools we work with a resurgence of social–emotional learning (SEL) alongside academics, both in elementary school curriculums and in advisory programs at the middle and high school level.

In this chapter we describe our efforts to take the next step—from personal mindfulness practices to engaging in practices of mindfulness and reflection in the community, particularly in the adult community, in PreK–12 schools. Our own journey to prioritizing this focus on the adult community is an extension of our work as founders and co-founders of national SEL programs for children and of our ongoing collaborations with many dedicated colleagues. After years of bringing SEL programs to classrooms, we became aware that a common obstacle to effective implementation was a misalignment between what we were teaching students and the culture and behavior of adults in the school community. Teachers want their students to know and care about each other, to treat each other with respect, and to seek out and value each other's contributions. But we regularly encountered school communities where educators knew little about each other aside from day-to-day work and felt isolated from other colleagues and where the same voices predominated in meetings while others fell silent. And we noticed a correlation between a lack of trust and connection among adults and a school's struggle to be consistent and effective in implementing our SEL curricula in classrooms. We began to understand that training and coaching teachers in SEL curricula was not enough. In fact we became convinced that the *most* crucial factor in how successful our SEL programs were in schools depended on how strong and respectful relationships were between adults in the school community.

A major turning point in our thinking about the adult community of schools came when we were introduced to Parker J. Palmer (1997) and his groundbreaking book, *The Courage to Teach: Exploring the Inner Landscape of a Teacher's Life*. Palmer named a truth often hidden in plain sight: "We teach who we are." Our gifts and our limitations and our culture and life experiences are all part of what we bring to the enterprise of teaching and leading. The extent to which we do this with self-awareness determines how we share our (best) selves in our interactions with students, colleagues, and the community. Palmer writes:

> The question we most commonly ask is the "what" question—what subjects shall we teach? When the conversation goes a bit deeper, we ask the "how" question—what methods and techniques are required to teach well? Occasionally, when it goes deeper still, we ask the "why" question—for what purposes and to what ends do we teach? But seldom, if ever, do we ask the "who" question—who is the self that teaches? How does the quality of my selfhood form—or deform—the way I relate to my students, my subject, my colleagues, my world? How can educational institutions sustain and deepen the selfhood from which good teaching comes? (1997, p. 4)

In the late 1990s, we became facilitators for the Center for Courage & Renewal retreat series and other programs that put Palmer's ideas into action, first for teachers and principals, and eventually for professionals in other fields, such as nonprofit leadership and health care. The Courage to Teach and Courage to Lead programs we facilitated in education created a space that allowed individuals to reflect on their life and work and to listen more deeply to themselves and others. These programs focused on the inner life of the teacher and how this focus might fuel professional growth and renewal.

We learned from participants' feedback that the retreats were often transformative in renewing their commitment to their work as educators, and that participants developed deep bonds of trust with one another. While the retreats were designed to be invitational and developed for groups of individual educators from different schools and districts, we wondered how this work might also be integrated into entire schools.

Research Lights the Way

At first, our intuition that adult relationships were crucially important to SEL program success was just that—intuition. Our introduction to the extensive research in relational trust, first described in the 2002 book *Trust in Schools: A Core Resource for Improvement,* provided us with empirical evidence that we were on the right track. Anthony S. Bryk and Barbara Schneider, along with their colleagues, studied 12 elementary schools in Chicago undergoing school reform initiatives. They identified relational trust in the adult community of schools as a key variable that drove success.

> Good schools are intrinsically social enterprises that depend heavily on cooperative endeavors among the varied participants who comprise the school community. Relational trust constitutes the connective tissue that binds these individuals together around advancing the education and welfare of children. Improving schools requires us to think harder about how best to organize the work of adults and students so that this connective tissue remains healthy and strong. (Bryk & Schneider, 2002, p. 144)

Bryk and Schneider, with Julie Kochanek, identified the key aspects of this trust among adults working in schools as respect, competence, personal regard for others, and integrity (2002, pp. 23–26).[1]

We sought to understand how this research could be operationalized and how reflective and mindfulness practices could best be implemented intentionally in the adult community of additional schools. We hypothesized that a commitment to nurturing adult community and trust through reflective and mindfulness practices could provide a strong foundation for achieving other school goals, while strengthening the capacity for effective collaboration. In essence, if we want teachers to care for, listen to, and raise up the voice of every student, we need to create adult learning communities where colleagues afford each other the same dignity and respect.

To this end, in 2012 we launched a pilot of a new leadership program of the Center for Courage & Renewal called Leading Together: Strengthening Relational Trust in Schools. Leading Together rests on the premise that clear and effective school leadership plays a critical role in school success and that social interactions among adults in the school community impact the quality of instruction in the classroom. Although many professional development programs are designed to improve the quality of principals or improve teaching, we emphasized improving leadership capacity for both

---

[1] Over the years, others have furthered this exploration of the key aspects of relational trust as originally defined. See Bryk, Sebring, Allensworth, Luppescu, and Easton (2010) and Tschannen-Moran (2014).

principals and teacher leaders, including classroom teachers, school counselors, and other school staff, so that adults can work together to build trust among themselves and create a supportive learning environment for their students. This pilot was grounded in a logic model developed in collaboration with Dr. Sara Rimm-Kaufman and her team at the Social Development Laboratory at the Curry School of Education of the University of Virginia, which also conducted a comprehensive evaluation (Rimm-Kaufman, Leis, & Paxton, 2014).

We began this pilot with a 4-day summer institute that brought together leadership teams, including principals and teacher leaders, from 10 urban and suburban schools in eastern Massachusetts and Connecticut. This was followed by 2 day-long retreats over 2 years, and by two on-site coaching visits at each school annually by program facilitators. Central to the program is a guidebook (Seigle, Sankowski, Wood, & Center for Courage & Renewal, 2016) containing protocols and practices for use with entire school staffs and with students' parents and guardians. These training days gave the school teams a lived experience of many protocols in the guidebook, opportunities to learn from peers on other school teams, and time to plan as a team how they would introduce guidebook activities and protocols to their entire adult community.

The training and guidebook were grounded in the following principles of the Center for Courage & Renewal:

- Everyone has an inner teacher.
- Inner work requires solitude and community.
- Inner work must be invitational.
- Our lives move in cycles like the seasons.
- Appreciating paradox enriches our lives and helps us hold greater complexity.
- We live with greater integrity when we see ourselves whole.
- A hidden wholeness underlies our lives.
  (Center for Courage & Renewal, n.d.-b)

We also drew extensively on resources from the fields of SEL, mindfulness, other contemplative and reflective practices and protocols, as well as from the arts.

Early outcomes have been promising in schools that fully implemented the approach: an improved capacity to share leadership, enhanced relational trust, and increased professional capacity (educators' confidence in their collective ability to reach and motivate their students) (Rimm-Kaufman et al., 2014). Nora Bond, then a graduate student at Tufts University, undertook a qualitative evaluation of a subsequent introductory pilot. She observed:

This is the essence of the work—the nearly imperceptible personal changes that inevitably shift an entire community. Choosing to wonder why a colleague is acting this way, instead of assuming, judging, and lashing out. Seeing a co-worker as a person with inherent worth and unique perspectives. This work is not necessarily calling for staffs to all become close friends; it is not trying to redefine professional behavior. It is offering a perspective that subsumes and transcends that spectrum. It is calling for people to respect each other, to see each other as unique and worthy of regard as an individual with dignity. It wants to build communities that respect the complex work educators do. (2016, pp. 11–12)

While the focus of this research was on relationships between teachers and between teachers and principals, all members of the adult community were drawn into the program. In addition to classroom teachers, the Leading Together team often included assistant principals, special educators, school counselors, or specialty teachers. After the first year of training, schools expanded their teams to include any interested staff member. The teams introduced protocols and practices to the entire school staff through staff meetings and other small-group meetings. Parents were introduced to the concept of relational trust, and listening became an important focus of parent meetings and conferences. As we continue to develop Leading Together, we are considering adding parents, students, paraprofessionals, and school committee members as part of the Leading Together team that receives the initial training, and expanding participation to encourage *all* adults in the school community to commit to their own personal development and contribute to a welcoming, respectful learning community based on trust.

Case Example: A Principal's Journey

Ellen, a committed and passionate principal of a middle school west of Boston for 14 years, was both skeptical and intrigued when a colleague invited her to join a series of dinner meetings called "Courage to Lead." Her experience with professional development had never engaged her in work that focused on herself. Once given the opportunity to reflect on her own life and work, she gained new insights into how "who she is" affected her work and how she was perceived in her school. She learned that while she was well respected, her intensity sometimes made staff members feel that she was not accessible, and they were reluctant to approach her. This was confirmed in the results of a survey on school climate.

Over the course of her involvement in the Courage to Lead program, Ellen noticed some shifts in her thinking and behavior. Her staff noticed it too. She describes it this way.

"I found myself slowing down internally—being aware of how I listened and responded, and consciously working to slow down my thinking and how I responded to people. I tried to really listen, without coming up with solutions on the spot. I was more attentive and calmer. I walked more slowly, made more eye contact with students and adults, and really tried to smile a lot. I worked on my breathing, sometimes closing the door to my office when things got really stressful. Then I took a minute or two to focus on my breath."

Because of the personal growth Ellen experienced, she eagerly accepted an invitation to bring a team from her school to the pilot of Leading Together. At the next all-staff meeting at her school following the first Leading Together training, Ellen framed the program to her staff as a "gift." Her personal experience and commitment to developing the capacities of the adult community, starting with herself, allowed her to present a strong rationale. Over the previous 2 years, they had focused on the curriculum and then on relationships with students. Now it was time to intentionally focus on the adult community. Ellen's presentation of the research linking relational trust to student achievement, and clear definitions of Bryk and Schneider's key aspects of relational trust posed as questions (developed by David Gordon, 2002) to ask as a community, resulted in positive buy-in from most of the faculty.

- *Respect.* Do we acknowledge one another's dignity and ideas? Do we interact in a courteous way? Do we genuinely talk and listen to each other?
- *Competence.* Do we believe in each other's ability and willingness to fulfill our responsibilities effectively?
- *Personal regard.* Do we care about each other both professionally and personally?
- *Integrity.* Can we trust each other to put the interests of the students first, especially when tough decisions have to be made?

As Ellen invited her staff into reflective and mindfulness practices, she remembered her own initial discomfort in trying new things and made participation voluntary, which undercut resistance. She realized that her own initial bias about this work was related to a sense that data and tangible results are more valued in education than feelings and personal connections, but she says, "I always knew that education really is all about forming relationships, and that has to evolve over time."

Ellen and her team worked on bringing new relational activities, protocols, and practices into the life of the school. They started to introduce them on a regular basis within meeting structures that already existed, for example, in monthly after-school faculty meetings, weekly leadership team meetings, and curriculum leader morning meetings. Some of the activities were brief and introductory energizers or short getting-to-know-you exercises, while others went deeper. Ellen found that a 5- to 10-minute activity was a great way to jump-start everyone. Sometimes they used mindfulness meditation or listening exercises, but the staff especially enjoyed using poetry. One such activity centered on a poem by Judy Brown.

Fire

What makes a fire burn
is space between the logs,
a breathing space.
Too much of a good thing,
too many logs
packed in too tight
can douse the flames
almost as surely
as a pail of water would.
So building fires
requires attention
to the spaces in between,
as much as to the wood.
When we are able to build
open spaces
in the same way
we have learned
to pile on the logs,
then we can come to see how
it is fuel, and absence of the fuel
together, that make fire possible.
We only need to lay a log
lightly from time to time.
A fire
grows
simply because the space is there,
with openings
in which the flame
that knows just how it wants to burn
can find its way.

(Brown, 2012, p. 147)

After reading this poem together twice, everyone took some time to journal on these questions, followed by taking time to share reflections in small groups.

- What are the logs you lay on your fire? Can you name them?
- What logs do others lay on?
- When do you pile on too many logs?

- How and where do you practice building open spaces?
- What ways have you found to tend your fire, your passions?

In the discussion following the small groups, the staff talked about self-compassion and self-care and how they contribute to their capacity to be fully present for their students and colleagues.

These practices strengthened relationships among the team, resulting in more productive work on curricular and other issues. The benefits extended to relationships across the school community and helped people to slow down and listen to each other better, to know each other better, and to know themselves better.

All these changes were evident in the way Ellen's leadership team planned its first professional development day the following year. The school jazz band welcomed everyone with music. Parents set up tables with flowers and provided snacks. In small groups and then in the whole group, everyone shared their hopes and aspirations for the school year. Then they asked what guidelines were needed for their work together as an adult community in order to make all their hopes and aspirations possible. In small groups, they generated adult community guidelines that would best support everyone's work. Each small group shared its ideas, and the leadership team later synthesized them for ratification by the entire staff. Over the year, the staff continually revisited these simple guidelines to reflect on whether they were working and what might need to be modified.

- Consider positive intent when interacting with others.
- Listen carefully and be as present as possible with colleagues and students.
- Remind yourself to be flexible and realistic.

Teachers also began to adapt many examples of the new reflective and mindfulness practices they were experiencing for the classroom, including the following:

- Seventh-grade students learned Tai Chi practices. Later they asked their teachers if they could use Tai Chi to help them prepare before taking an upcoming state assessment.
- Sixth graders joined a new mindfulness group, and guided by their teacher, focused on their breath as they sat at their desks and noticed where they felt tension in their bodies.
- The whole school engaged in a discussion of civility in the school community, inspired by P. M. Forni's book (2003) *Choosing Civility: The Twenty-Five Rules of Considerate Conduct*. Using Todd Nelson's (2008) metaphor of a footprint, they reflected on the skills and behaviors that enable us to leave a "civility footprint."

When Ellen retired, her staff planned a series of presentations at her retirement party as a surprise. They devoted a segment of the party to Leading Together and offered their perspectives on the positive impact it had on them and on the school. It was enormously gratifying to Ellen to hear them talk proudly about the contemplative work and about the culture at the middle school. Because the staff was so committed and enthusiastic, the trusting adult culture that Ellen worked so hard to create has been sustained in the school under new leadership.

The Four "R's"

As we worked with Ellen's school and the other schools in that first pilot, and experimented with colleagues at the Center for Courage & Renewal to find new ways of sharing Leading Together more broadly, we focused on four transformational considerations for building a trustworthy adult community where individuals thrive and bring their best selves to their students and colleagues.

1. Relationships
2. Reflection
3. Resilience
4. Renewal

Relationships

Relationships, both intrapersonal (evidenced by our own internal dialogue with ourselves) and interpersonal (connecting with others), are foundational to learning for adults and students. Palmer frames his focus on self-knowledge as serving the students we teach and the communities we relate to, and our capacity to work together and collaborate effectively is dependent on our relational capacities (1997, p. 3). When we bring mindful awareness to our interactions with colleagues, we begin to understand and appreciate who they are and the gifts and experiences they bring to their work. Yet taking time to develop adult relationships is not generally seen as important in school. We've found that even taking the time to do a team-building exercise or a reflective activity in small groups helps us not only get to know each other better, but also to learn to pay better attention to each other and to work more productively together.

We have particularly tried to focus on the relationships between school principals and teacher leaders. By inviting schools to send to training a group comprising the principal and three or four teacher leaders, we give them the space and opportunities to deepen relationships and foster leadership capacity as a team. And by bringing teams together from different schools to learn from one another, it is often easier for participants to develop empathy and compassion for the respective roles principals and teachers play. Teams return to their schools ready to introduce and practice with their entire staff and broader adult community the team-building activities, reflective and mindfulness practices, listening exercises, and approaches to structured conversation that they experienced in training sessions. To deeply consider and arrive at a shared understanding of relationships in the adult community of schools today, it is important to cultivate a shared belief in the primacy of relationships in human endeavors in general. From the moment we are born, we learn from significant others. Learning is a social activity. Noted anthropologist Barbara Rogoff explains, "For example, children's ways of learning vary across communities, such as in formal schooling, apprenticeships, or helping on the farm. At the same time, however, all children learn from observation and participation in *some* kind of community activities" (2003, p. 64).

The importance of relationships between teachers and students has always been obvious to those working in schools. This intuitive understanding is now corroborated by a growing body of research demonstrating social and emotional learning's connection to academic and behavioral skills (Collaborative for Academic, Social, and Emotional Learning, n.d.). Equally important, the relationships between teachers, staff, administrators, and families in the adult community of schools create an overall school culture supportive of each adult that increases the collaboration and concentration necessary to achieve the development of each student. We need to provide avenues for listening, dialogue, shared understanding, and realistic ideas about scheduling adequate time for nurturing trusting relationships in the adult community of schools.

Reflection

Reflection is the process of taking time to thoughtfully consider our experiences and actions in a way that allows us to continually learn from them. Carol Rodgers, a John Dewey scholar, provides four compelling criteria that define reflection.

1. Reflection is a meaning-making process that moves a learner from one experience into the next with deeper understanding of its relationships with and connections to other experiences and ideas. It is the thread that makes continuity of learning possible, and ensures the progress of the individual and, ultimately, society. It is a means to essentially moral ends.
2. Reflection is a systematic, rigorous, disciplined way of thinking, with its roots in scientific inquiry.
3. Reflection needs to happen in community, in interaction with others.
4. Reflection requires attitudes that value personal and intellectual growth of oneself and of others. (2002, p. 845)

Reflective exercises in small groups contribute to our capacity to know each other and to work productively together, but in schools we rarely give ourselves the time to be reflective. Whether it's about a difficult interaction with a student or colleague, or a lesson that didn't go well, too often we react out of habitual thoughts and feelings that we haven't taken time to process or understand. In his book *Leadership Without Easy Answers,* Ron Heifetz (1998) talks about the importance of taking time to "get on the balcony." Our view is often limited when we're in the action of our classroom, or our grade level, or our busy mind. Being able to develop habits of reflection allows us to respond to ourselves and others with more care and compassion. When we give educators opportunities to experience reflection in faculty meetings, grade-level, or department meetings, in one-on-one supervisory conferences, and even in parent meetings, these experiences influence the pace of the day and the culture of the entire school in positive and important ways.

Daniel J. Siegel, author of *The Mindful Brain* and director of the UCLA Mindful Awareness Research Center, contends, "The basic ingredients of well-being and compassionate social living are, in fact, teachable. Reflection is the common pathway by which our brains support such abilities, our relationships come to thrive in them, and our minds can achieve a state of internal attunement and sense of harmony" (2007, p. 259). In reference to teaching and learning, he writes, "Reflection is the skill that embeds self-knowing and empathy in the curriculum" (p. 261).

Reflection helps place learning into memory. This is true for both students and adults. How we use and manage time in school is especially important in this regard. By resisting the temptation to teach content right up to the bell and instead allowing a good 5 to 10 minutes for students to reflect with us, we reinforce for them what it is we hope they will remember. This is one example of how we can improve our instruction by better utilizing reflective practices. Faculty meetings, like many classes, are often crammed with agendas that are too ambitious for the time we have to devote to them. Reserving 5 to 10 minutes for partner reflections and hearing out how people experienced the meeting can help to create a more trustworthy adult culture.

Resilience

Practices that develop relationships and encourage reflection also build the muscle for resilience in the service of deepening relational trust in the adult community. Resilience is experienced as the social–emotional and intellectual strength to deal with stress in productive ways. Louis Cozolino (2013), author of *The Social Neuroscience of Education: Optimizing Attachment and Learning in the Classroom,* notes that developing resilience is not easy, particularly in the context of the workplace, where our performance (as students, teachers, parents, or principals) is assessed. Stress produces cortisol, which can compromise neural growth and the immune system. "Because chronic stress inhibits neural plasticity," Cozolino writes, "success in school depends upon a student's ability to somehow decrease their stress." This applies equally to teachers and supervisors. He goes on, "From specific stress-reduction techniques to the soothing effects of a supportive student-teacher relationship, stress modulation and academic success go hand in hand" (pp. 235–236). Resilience is nurtured by positive relationships, but also by one's own capacity to hold positive and optimistic attitudes in the face of stress (Konnikova, 2016).

Renewal

There are many factors that affect our ability to be fully engaged in our work in schools. Renewal is a core value of the Center for Courage & Renewal. "When we take time to slow down, quiet ourselves, reflect, renew ourselves, and recall our commitments, important changes can happen within us and around us. As we are renewed, we in turn can contribute to the renewal of our professions, workplaces, and communities" (Center for Courage & Renewal, n.d.-a). One of the ways we support ourselves in the midst of demanding and challenging work is to incorporate into our lives, in an ongoing way, the sources of renewal that sustain us. Perhaps our renewing practices take the form of a meditation, or spending time with a good friend, or reading, or being part of a choir, or allowing ourselves to fully experience joy in an aspect of our work that is the most rewarding.

But where do we find the time for renewal? In educational settings we typically rely on vacations or so-called personal days to experience relaxation or a sense of renewal so that we are able to return "recharged" to our demanding jobs. We encourage people to identify their personal sources of renewal so that they can work it into their day, and encourage schools to make time for activities that reduce stress for both adults and students, providing ideas for using time to breathe and collaborate in enjoyable and meaningful ways in the workplace. Such experiences help us and our students learn and consolidate new skills as well as express our understanding of what we are learning in diverse ways.

The Indispensable Foundational Skill: Listening

If you're looking for a way to begin this work in your school, start by teaching and practicing listening. As we help school communities nurture the four R's, we are increasingly aware of the central power that listening plays in deepening adults' capacities for shared leadership, learning from colleagues, appreciating different perspectives, and renewing their commitment to those we teach. This critical skill is central to Bryk and Schneider's definition of the first key element in relational trust: *respect*. "In the concept of schooling," they note, "respect involves recognition of the important role each person plays in a child's education and the mutual dependencies that exist among various parties involved in this activity. *Key in this regard is how conversation takes place within a school community. A genuine sense of listening to what each person has to say marks the basis for meaningful social interaction*" (Bryk & Schneider, 2002, p. 23, emphasis added).

In recent years, teachers at all levels in PreK–12 education have become familiar with a teaching strategy called "turn and talk," in which students are given a question to discuss about something they are reading or learning. Initiate an Internet search of this strategy, and you will find a plethora of descriptions for how to use it to enhance students' oral fluency and consolidate knowledge and skills. Students are assigned or choose a partner to talk to and are told how long they have to talk. A timer is set, and partners begin discussing the topic. When the timer goes off, the teacher may ask students to share something from their conversation about the topic or invite them to ask follow-up questions. In almost all the Internet searches on turn and talk, the heavy emphasis is on *talking*.

We flipped the concept of "turn and talk" to "turn and *listen*," both in the classroom and in the adult community. When we talk with principals and school leaders about shifting to a turn and listen approach, they immediately understand and recognize how hard it is to listen with mindful awareness. Though we think we know how to listen, the pace and demands of the school day make it challenging to listen attentively, whether to a student or to a colleague.

In Leading Together, we teach how to hold space for listening by practicing a number of structured activities. First, we give partners the experience of having a few minutes to listen to each other (about 2 minutes for each partner) about a particular topic without interrupting or conversing, and then give them few minutes to talk with each other about what the activity was like for them. Practicing listening with another person, even for a short period, is for many a first experience of interpersonal mindfulness.

This simple, but surprisingly revealing, activity opens the door to understanding the meaning of respect as a leading indicator of relational trust. Reflecting on what it was like to listen or to be listened to in this way, adults often comment on how the listening slowed the pace, how it felt great just to be heard, how it gave them time to hear themselves, and how just listening helped them better understand their partner's perspective.

For some, 2 minutes of listening and 2 minutes of talking seemed like short periods of time, and for others, too long. Some found not being able to respond in a conversational way awkward or uncomfortable, which, of course for many, it is. In the busy and stressful world of education, turn and listen is a lesson about our need as educators to give someone our full attention, to see ideas from someone else's point of view, and to have the time to pause and reflect on what someone is telling us.

Additional structured listening exercises include inviting both the listener and speaker to practice taking time to internally pause in conversation. The speaker becomes aware of when she is not connected to what she is saying and takes a moment to pause before continuing. The listener notices when she is not paying attention to the speaker and gently brings her attention back to listening.

Another activity that can be used after reflecting or journaling about a poem or text involves inviting each person to speak, and having listeners represent their response in a sketch or drawing of what they heard from the speaker. A key practice of the Center for Courage & Renewal is that of asking open, honest questions to help the speaker become clearer about an issue or dilemma being considered. Learning to ask these kinds of questions requires attentive listening and an awareness of when a question is sparked by the listeners' agenda or curiosity rather than that of the speaker. After an issue is briefly presented by the speaker, listeners respond only with open, honest questions.

These are all demanding practices that build the muscle to listen this way in the course of daily life and in ongoing relationships.

Council is another structured protocol for circles of 8 to 10, in which each person takes a turn speaking for 2 minutes without interruption on a topic of common interest, while others in the circle listen attentively without comment or judgment and without rehearsing in their own minds what they plan to say when it's their turn. Everyone speaks before any connections are made. The purpose of this protocol is not to problem-solve, but to share insights and observations before problem solving. In Courage & Renewal, we call this "the work before the work."

Still another activity is an adaptation and abridgement of a consultancy protocol that participants have found useful at grade-level and at student-support meetings. A teacher describes an issue or concern to her colleagues. They respond by asking honest, open questions about her concern, which she answers briefly. The teacher then moves outside the circle and listens to her colleagues discuss her concern while she takes notes. She may choose to ask them to talk more about her issue or ask for one or more suggestions, but she is entirely in charge of the amount of input she wants—another form of respectful interaction with colleagues.

Most important, we stress that good listening is a *practice,* something we need to intentionally engage in over and over. And so in praise of the repetition of practice, we'll end this section as we began. If you're looking for a way to begin this work in your school, start by teaching and practicing listening.

Case Example:
The Gratitude Project at Harriet Street School

Some of the schools that participated in our initial pilot project quickly moved from close adherence to the guidebook to developing their own innovative communitywide projects. At Harriet Street School, Jed, the principal, described the impact of the turn and listen strategy in deepening relationships, increasing everyone's capacity to work together creatively and productively, and helping them simply enjoy each other. With this work as a foundation, a focus on gratitude seemed to be a natural extension of their work.

Aspects of the practice of gratitude touch all of the four R's. We deepen our relationships when we acknowledge our interdependence and provide opportunities to tell those we value exactly why we appreciate them. Practicing gratitude demands regular reflection on our experiences and our interpersonal interactions. Actively looking for things we are grateful for each day fuels a positive mindset that is central to resilience. And in the context of schools, engaging in a collective practice of gratitude is an opportunity to "take a deep breath together" that contributes to renewal.

Harriet Street School's gratitude project began with their leadership team and other interested staff keeping gratitude journals—in which they recorded each day the things they were thankful for—and inviting students to do the same. The team shared research on gratitude with the entire staff and the school committee, and a focus on gratitude became part of their school improvement plan and the schoolwide theme for the year.

Faculty meetings began with a gratitude circle—a practice of taking 5 minutes at the beginning of a meeting to allow staff members to respond aloud to prompts such as, "I appreciate . . . ," "I was delighted by . . . ," "I want to thank . . . " The first time this practice was done at a meeting, a staff member came in late, just after the gratitude circle ended and as the staff transitioned to business. She sat down and exclaimed, "What happened? Did we get good news? There is so much excitement in this room." The gratitude practice had so shifted the energy in the meeting and the collective mindset of the faculty that she found it clearly obvious.

The entire school community engaged in approaches not only to recognize moments of gratitude, but to actively nourish it with a practice of changing one's perspective from negative to positive when encountering a challenging situation. For example, in meetings, staff members learned to include gratitude in how they framed challenges. They were more likely to express gratitude for the openness or respectful tone of a conversation, even if was difficult and did not lead to an agreement. This change increased their capacity to disagree respectfully, to see the benefit that can come from difficult conversations, and to continue to nurture relational trust.

For students, this practice helped them to see that they have a choice in how they view situations. For one school project, students created eyeglasses that symbolically enabled them to change or enlarge their perspective using a different lens. They would first look at a situation without gratitude glasses—for example, "I got too many problems wrong on the math assessment." With their gratitude glasses on, they were able to see it differently: "I know what I need to learn next, and my teacher can help me."

By teaching everyone about perspective taking, the school began to see the seeds of gratitude take root. A gratitude bulletin board invited the staff to post thank-you notes for each other. Each student's family received a gratitude journal with suggestions for how to grow gratitude in their family lives. Students decorated the covers of their family journals with pictures of things they were grateful for. Parents brought up gratitude in parent–teacher conferences and gave their children thank-you notes to show their appreciation after student-led conferences.

Gratitude practices were shared with adults in the neighborhood and beyond as well. Teachers and students in each class thought of someone who had changed their classroom for the better and painted gratitude rocks to honor that person. They sent or presented these rocks and gratitude letters to the people they wanted to thank. Some of the recipients of rocks included children's favorite authors and local police and firefighters. These expressions of gratitude made adults and students aware of how many individuals from the local community and the larger world contributed to their lives.

Jed talked about the contagious feeling of being able to spread gratitude throughout the school and his own sense of gratitude for being at Harriet Street School for 20 years. The practice of gratitude became tangible throughout the school and community and has continued to affect everyone, underlining the fundamental importance of relationships to creating a school culture in which everyone can thrive.

This project, which was developed as part of a collaboration with the Greater Good Science Center's Expanding the Science and Practice of Gratitude initiative, resulted in the creation of a supplement to the Leading Together guidebook that focused on gratitude practices as a powerful approach to building trust in the adult community.

Conclusion: Raising and Respecting Every Voice

As we have experimented with ways to intentionally and persistently nurture relational trust in the adult community in schools, we always come back (in the spirit of practice) to listening, which is an act of love and respect for another's voice. Every voice in school today deserves to be heard. Every student voice and teacher voice, every parent and caretaker's voice, every principal and secretary's voice, every custodian and cafeteria worker's voice, every paraprofessional's voice deserves to be respected and heard. Each voice has something important to say every day, no matter the role or status in the school or broader community. We must come to a true understanding that we are all in this work together by bringing more mindful awareness, empathy, and compassion to all the work we do.

Starting a staff meeting with check-ins or turn and listen activities provides a sense of welcome to every person, often at the end of a busy school day. Making sure that a few minutes of every adult meeting ends with reflections about how people are feeling about the meeting, or what was accomplished, or what comes next, gives each person in the meeting an opportunity to be heard. Sadly, some voices, such as those of many paraprofessionals, other school staff, or parents, are not even present for these meetings, because contracts do not provide even 1 extra hour a week at minimum wage for their attendance, or, in the case of parents, is limited by the number of times for meaningful face-to-face contacts with teachers.

The most important voices needing to be heard and listened to are, of course, those of our students. This democracy will be theirs long after it is ours. It is our hope that our ideas and the many other wonderful ideas in this book will become commonplace and help schools function as safe and caring places of learning where students not only come to know, but to be known by others. We have to continue to cultivate a shared belief in the importance of relationships. The basic ingredients of well-being and compassionate social living are, in fact, teachable. We need to provide avenues for listening, dialoguing, shared understanding, and realistic ideas about scheduling adequate time for building trusting relationship in the adult community of schools.

We need to listen to each other with mindful attention in order to learn from each other. And we need to learn from each other so we can lead together in our schools. To do this, each of our voices must become as significant a learning standard as every other, demonstrated by our commitment to turn and listen to each other without judgment, interruption, or disruption. Only by turning and listening, and then acting together with courage and compassion, will we be able to call our schools of learning houses of joy.

Acknowledgments

We wish to thank the Center for Courage and Renewal, the Angell Foundation, the 1440 Foundation, the Einhorn Family Charitable Trust, and the Greater Good Science Center as part of their Expanding the Science and Practice of Gratitude project funded by the John Templeton Foundation, for supporting the development of Leading Together.

References

Bond, N. (2016). *Final report: Leading together program evaluation*. Unpublished manuscript.
Brown, J. S. (2012). *The art and spirit of leadership*. Bloomington, IN: Trafford.

Bryk, A. S., & Schneider, B. (2002). *Trust in schools: A core resource for improvement.* New York: Russell Sage Foundation.

Bryk, A. S., Sebring, P. B., Allensworth, E., Luppescu, S., & Easton, J. Q. (2010). *Organizing schools for improvement: Lessons from Chicago.* Chicago: University of Chicago Press.

Center for Courage & Renewal. (n.d.-a). The circle of trust approach. Retrieved November 27, 2017, from *www.couragerenewal.org/approach.*

Center for Courage & Renewal. (n.d.-b). Our mission and values. Retrieved November 27, 2017, from *www.couragerenewal.org/about/mission.*

Clifton, L. (1993). *May this be a house of joy.* Unpublished manuscript.

Collaborative for Academic, Social, and Emotional Learning .(n.d.). SEL research. Retrieved November 27, 2017, from *www.casel.org/research.*

Cozolino, L. (2013). *The social neuroscience of education: Optimizing attachment and learning in the classroom.* New York: Norton.

Forni, P. M. (2003). *Choosing civility: The twenty-five rules of considerate conduct.* New York: St. Martin's Griffin.

Gordon, D. T. (2002). Fuel for reform: The importance of trust in changing schools. *Harvard Education Letter, 18*(4), 1–4.

Heifetz, R. A. (1998). *Leadership without easy answers.* Cambridge, MA: Harvard University Press.

Konnikova, M. (2016, February 11). How people learn to become resilient. Retrieved November 27, 2017, from *www.newyorker.com/science/maria-konnikova/the-secret-formula-for-resilience.*

Nelson, T. (2008). Our civility footprint or—walk this way. Retrieved November 27, 2017, from *www.teachers.net/gazette/MAR08/nelson.*

Newman, K., Flynn, M., Suttie, J., & Smith, J. A. (2017, December 27). The top 10 insights from the "Science of a meaningful life" in 2017. Retrieved March 8, 2018, from *www.greatergood.berkeley.edu/article/item/the_top_10_insights_from_the_science_of_a_meaningful_life_in_2017.*

Palmer, P. J. (1997). *The courage to teach: Exploring the inner landscape of a teacher's life.* San Francisco: Jossey-Bass.

Rimm-Kaufman, S. E., Leis, M., & Paxton, C. (2014). Innovating together to improve the adult community in schools: Results from a two-year study of the initial implementation of leading together. Retrieved November 27, 2017, from *www.couragerenewal.org/PDFs/UVA_LeadingTogether_July_11_2014_Final_Full_Report.pdf.*

Rodgers, C. (2002). Defining reflection: Another look at John Dewey and reflective thinking. *Teachers College Record, 104*(4), 842–866.

Rogoff, B. (2003). *The cultural nature of human development.* New York: Oxford University Press.

Seigle, P., Sankowski, L., Wood, C., & Center for Courage & Renewal. (2016). *Leading together: Building adult community in schools* (2nd ed.). Seattle: Center for Courage & Renewal.

Siegel, D. J. (2007). *The mindful brain: Reflection and attunement in the cultivation of well-being.* New York: Norton.

Tschannen-Moran, M. (2014). *Trust matters: Leadership for successful schools.* San Francisco: Jossey-Bass.

CHAPTER 4

Modeling Mindfulness

Principal Leadership and Development for Personal and Organizational Growth

ELEANOR DRAGO-SEVERSON
JESSICA BLUM-DESTEFANO

No matter how hard or how long I work, there's always something that demands my attention—right away. Being a principal is like being a mom, a teacher, a boss, a firefighter, a judge, a mediator, and a marathon runner—*all at the same time* [emphasis hers]. I've worked really hard to try to balance this.
—VETERAN ELEMENTARY SCHOOL PRINCIPAL

If I could just catch my breath, I think I'd be able to do a better job—to be less stressed and more present for everyone. But [pause] I'm always multi-tasking. At any given moment, if you could look into my mind, you'd see that I'm triple- if not quadruple- or quintuple-tasking.[1]
—FIRST-YEAR HIGH SCHOOL PRINCIPAL

School principals, at all stages of their careers and regardless of school context or level, often share with us that they are—above all else—*busy*. This situation, we have learned, is a global phenomenon. Like the two principals

---

[1]These quotes are representative, composite examples drawn from our research and teaching.

whose words are featured in the chapter's opening, school leaders are tasked with the Herculean feat of supporting essentially everyone and everything in schools, while also managing the intense—and mounting—accountability, policy-related, and ethical pressures from above, outside, and within themselves. Perhaps it's no surprise, then, that roughly 50% of principals leave their jobs within 3 years (School Leaders Network, 2014). How could someone possibly keep up this pace—particularly on one's own, as is so often the case in traditional school leadership models?

While the stresses and pressures of the principalship may be particularly intense and hard to sustain (Drago-Severson, 2009a, 2012, 2016; Drago-Severson & Blum-DeStefano, 2018; Drago-Severson, Maslin-Ostrowski, & Blum-DeStefano, 2017, 2018; Riley, 2015), they also parallel the "excessive driving and striving" that characterize leadership across professions today (Sinclair, 2015, p. 7). In fact, it is this habitual, internalized pressure to always *go, go, go*—coupled with the standardization and routinization that accompany accountability mandates (like those in the education and business fields)—that make mindfulness such a promising path for school leaders, and for school principals in particular. Yet, how might principals' internal capacities influence their experiences with and openness to mindfulness practice—and their ability to set a mindful tone in their schools? Addressing this question is at the heart of our inquiry.

More specifically, in this chapter, we posit that an awareness of adult developmental theory offers a new and promising lens for better understanding the different ways that school leaders (and all adults) may orient to mindfulness. As such, it can serve as a road map for understanding *how* to differentiate the developmental supports and challenges (i.e., psychological stretching) that educators need in order to grow in their mindfulness practice. As we discuss, many of the goals and tenets of mindfulness—such as the ability to take a bigger perspective on the self and others, to recognize interconnection, and to think systemically—accord with complex internal capacities that can be developed over time with effort and intentionality. In other words, these abilities are not things people just automatically *possess*—but they are ways of being, seeing, and knowing that can be developed over time with the appropriate supports and challenges. Despite these connections, the parallels between mindfulness and adult development—from a constructive–developmental perspective—have not been explicitly explored in relation to school contexts, so this chapter offers something new for school leaders who hope to develop their own and others' capacities. Importantly, it also offers guidance for all of us who strive to support and be present to school leaders in our care.

To begin, we review what we see as some of the key possibilities and benefits of mindfulness for principals, as outlined in the literature, and then introduce four qualitatively different ways of knowing—or developmental meaning-making systems—that research suggests comprise the trajectory of growth in adulthood (Drago-Severson, 2004a, 2009a, 2012, 2016; Kegan, 1982, 1994, 2000). In our combined decades of research and teaching we have found that understanding these unfolding, cumulative patterns of development can help principals—and school leaders at all levels—more effectively support individual and organizational growth across domains, as well as their own growth. More important, just as a developmental lens sheds new light on the qualitatively different orientations adults bring to teaching, learning, and leading, so too does it illuminate mindfulness as a complementary, synergistic approach to leadership and life. In fact, we see adult developmental theory as key to understanding our own and others' progress as mindful practitioners. Even though a number of scholars increasingly recognize mindfulness as a developmental journey (e.g., Levenson, Jennings, Aldwin, & Shiraishi, 2005; Roeser & Eccles, 2015; Wilbur, 2000), this chapter is the first, to our knowledge, to explicitly bring a constructive–developmental perspective to mindfulness practice in school leadership.

To extend this discussion, we then describe the great power of modeling a mindful, developmental stance as a school principal, and provide a series of developmental strategies and questions that principals can employ to thoughtfully encourage mindfulness in adults with different ways of knowing. By looking inward first—and meeting others where they are with care and compassion—principals can even more effectively tap into the deep stores of possibility in themselves, others, and their school communities to lead meaningful growth and change.

Mindfulness: The Promise of the Present Moment for Principals

Our life is what our thoughts make it.
—MARCUS AURELIUS

Attention is the rarest and purest form of generosity.
—SIMONE WEIL

For millennia, people have looked to mindfulness as a path toward richer experience, greater fulfillment, and more impactful, generative engagement with the present moment (Nagy & Baer, 2017; Sinclair, 2015). Although the practices and tenets of mindfulness—which have roots in ancient Eastern culture and religion—have been blossoming in educational, corporate, and clinical settings for decades (Hornich-Lisciandro, 2013; Langer, 1993; Sinclair, 2015), it is important to note that scholars and practitioners today are increasingly looking to mindfulness as an integral dimension of leadership, leadership development, and leadership preparation (Boyatzis & McKee, 2005; Hougaard & Carter, 2017; Nadler, 2011; Richards, 2009; Sinclair, 2015).

Specifically, it is becoming clear that leaders—like all people—can benefit from more purposeful, intentional *pausing*. Given the hurried and "nonstop" pace of school leadership (as principals describe it), taking a few moments to pause—to breathe and slow down with conscious intention—is vital to renewal and sustainability. According to leading mindfulness scholar Jon Kabat-Zinn (1994), "Our actions are all too frequently driven rather than undertaken in awareness" (p. 9). In other words, what we do, say, think, and feel are—more often than not—byproducts of "automaticity and unconsciousness" (Kabat-Zinn, 1994, p. 3). Psychologist Relly Nadler (2011) similarly reports that—nearly half of the time—we are operating on a kind of autopilot. On the contrary, mindfulness—which Kabat-Zinn (1994) defines as "the art of conscious living" (p. 6)—can help us pause to catch our breath *and* pay careful and thoughtful attention to our bodies, actions, and reactions. For example, when we stop to notice how we're acting and reacting in a given moment, we can actually move forward in more optimal, thoughtful, and productive ways—rather than be "run" by our heat-of-the-moment impulses. As Kabat-Zinn (1994) put it, "the stopping actually makes the going more vivid, richer, more textured" (p. 12). It also protects us from the reactionary, *fight-or-flight* responses that can cloud our better judgment while we're in the thick of things—an ever-present danger for principals working on the front line of education.

Importantly, the purposeful pausing and increased self-awareness that can come from practicing mindfulness can also help principals (a) foster greater renewal and sustainability and (b) reframe time in more humane, manageable ways. These are pressing concerns for principals—and for others who devote themselves to the care of children and adults in schools and elsewhere. We discuss both of these intrinsic benefits in greater detail next.

Renewal and Sustainability

The greatest weapon against stress is our ability to choose one thought over another.

—WILLIAM JAMES

Given the hectic pace and urgent pressures of the principalship described earlier, the fact that mindfulness has been linked to *reduced* stress and worry and *increased* feelings of well-being and renewal (Hornich-Lisciandro, 2013; Nagy & Baer, 2017; Ricard & Singer, 2017; Roeser, Skinner, Beers, & Jennings, 2012) may be of particular interest to leaders striving for personal growth and sustainability. As renowned peace activist and Buddhist monk Thich Nhat Hanh (1975) explained, after practicing mindful meditation, "You will be refreshed and gain a broader, clearer view of things, and deepen and strengthen the love in yourself" (p. 42). In addition, mindfulness has been shown to help leaders across sectors find greater pleasure and satisfaction in their work and to feel less worn down by day-to-day urgencies (Sinclair, 2015). While it can be challenging and even counterintuitive for many principals, the kind of self-care associated with mindfulness can actually have demonstrable and positive effects not only on their individual well-being, but also on the health and flourishing of entire school communities (Dadaczynski & Paulus, 2014; Drago-Severson, 2012; Drago-Severson & Blum-DeStefano, 2018; Richards, 2009).

Reframing Time

In tandem with infusing each moment with greater possibility for renewal and sustainability, mindfulness can also help leaders reframe—and recapture—time. When we ask principals in the United States and other countries about their most pressing challenges, *time* emerges, again and again, as one of the most frequently named (Drago-Severson & Maslin-Ostrowski, 2017; Drago-Severson, Maslin-Ostrowski, & Blum-DeStefano, 2018). To help drive this point home, we offer the example of Adler, an elementary school principal in our research who recently and representatively offered the following observation: "I was working 80, 90 hours a week easy after school, and then I'd be home, you know, after my kids went to bed. I'd be up working on the computer sending emails, preparing stuff. There was basically only work and no life" (Drago-Severson et al., 2018). Likewise reflecting on how hard it was *to fit everything in,* Matt, a seasoned elementary school director, described his detailed use of a daily planner to organize himself and his time.

> So I have these lists where it's broken up into To Do Right Away, To Do Soon, To Do Later, My Personal Life, things that I've done but I need to make sure they've gotten done, and then all the different meetings that I have. . . . I get better at prioritizing what goes in the To Do Right Away box or [the] To Do Soon box, but sometimes it is thirty things (laughs) and then I've got to do these right away. (in Drago-Severson, Blum-DeStefano, & Asghar, 2013, pp. 206–207)

For other principals, like Kristina, who led a charter elementary/middle school, the time pressures of the job meant that she had *no* personal time, that she'd altruistically sacrificed her own interests and renewal in service to others. "I found oftentimes I was putting off the things that meant something to me because work was more important, doing for the kids. Everyone else became more important" (Drago-Severson et al., 2018).

Whether these school leaders were giving away their time or dividing it methodically in order to stay afloat, it seems clear that—for them and so many other dedicated principals like them—time was very rarely their own. Yet, we recognize how a mindfulness lens could help reframe this orientation with an emphasis on *conscious awareness* of the present moment. Capturing the power of this simple but profound shift in his foundational work *The Miracle of Mindfulness,* Hanh (1975) presented the story of Allen, a busy husband and family man. We share it here because we have found it resonates powerfully with the leaders in our care. Like school principals, Allen often felt his attention pulled in many directions at once—including by his children, Joey and Ana, and his wife, Sue. Reflecting on this situation, Allen offered the following thoughts (which we quote at length given their inspiring applicability).

> I've discovered a way to have a lot more time. In the past, I used to look at my time as if it were divided into several parts. One part I reserved for Joey, another part was for Sue, another part was to help with Ana, another part for household work. The time left over I considered my own. I could read, write, do research, go for walks. . . . But now I try not to divide time into parts anymore. I consider my time with Joey and Sue as my own time. When I help Joey with his homework, I try to find ways of seeing his time as my own time. I go through his lessons with him, sharing his presence and finding ways to be interested in what *we* [emphasis ours] do during that time. The time for him becomes my own time. The same with Sue. The remarkable thing is that now I have unlimited time for myself! (in Hanh, 1975, p. 2)

While Hanh (1975) acknowledged how easy it is to slip out of the mindset of unlimited time described by Allen, he also stressed the power of practicing sustained, conscious mindfulness throughout the day and over time. In other words, mindfulness isn't just for meditation retreats or mitigating routine tasks, but rather an aspiration for recapturing every moment of every day. When we think of infusing this idea of unlimited time into the principalship (even sometimes), the possibilities seem limitless and liberating! In fact, it reminds us of Arnold Toynbee's aphorism, "The supreme accomplishment is to blur the line between work and play."

Yet, what might it take for principals to embrace mindfulness as a goal *and* a process? While we recognize that there is no single answer to this question, we turn our attention next to the different ways of knowing in adulthood as one promising lens for better understanding and supporting mindfulness in school leaders and schools.

First, though, in the spirit of purposeful pausing, we invite you to take a moment to consider the reflective questions in Figure 4.1.

Patterns of Mind: Ways of Knowing as a Lens for Enhancing Mindfulness

We don't see things as they are, we see them as we are.
— ANAÏS NIN

In recent years, scientists have begun to trace the physical manifestations of mindfulness in the brain—to explore the rewiring of neurons and the rerouting of mental pathways that accompany mindful meditation (Langer,

1. What thoughts, feelings, or ideas bubbled up for you as you read the chapter so far?

2. What does mindfulness mean to you? What kinds of images come to mind when you think about what mindfulness looks like?

3. How, if at all, do you practice mindfulness in your work life?

4. What are some activities or moments that you might want to reframe—more mindfully—as part of your own *unlimited time*? How might this make a difference for you? For others?

FIGURE 4.1. A purposeful pause.

2014; Ricard & Singer, 2017; Sinclair, 2015). Although mounting evidence suggests that mindfulness has multiple benefits and effects, the practice itself is arguably *larger* than the brain, as it includes phenomenological experience more broadly (Kabat-Zinn, 1994). As Kabat-Zinn (1994) explained, it's "really about human development" (p. 81).

We agree. In fact, as teachers and researchers of adult development, we recognize mindfulness as a powerful support to internal capacity building and transformation. Moreover, as mentioned earlier, we see adult developmental theory as a promising lens for better understanding the evolving shifts of knowing that mindful practice can promote. Just as many believe in the benefits of coupling neuroscience and the mindful arts, we see developmental psychology—and particularly constructive–developmental theory, as pioneered by Harvard psychologist Robert Kegan and extended by Drago-Severson (Drago-Severson, 2009a, 2012, 2016; Kegan, 1982, 1994, 2000)—as a complementary and parallel field of study and vision.

For example, constructive–developmental theory outlines four distinct *ways of knowing* that, collectively, reflect the developmental meaning making of most adults. Even though ways of knowing are not correlated directly with age, they do emerge in a particular order (albeit at different paces), with each one serving as a prerequisite of sorts for the next. More specifically, when one grows to make meaning with a new and more complex way of knowing, it marks the emergence of new and more complex internal capacities (i.e., along four lines of development: cognitive, affective, interpersonal, and intrapersonal). Growing from one way of knowing to the next, more complex way of knowing enables a person to gain a greater perspective on aspects of one's self, others, and one's relationships with others. Taking a greater perspective means that a person is able to see more deeply into the self, into others, and the relationship between the two. Development of this kind is—in essence—about perspective taking. As a person develops greater internal capacities along the developmental lines just mentioned, he/she/they is able to gain a better perspective on aspects of oneself, of others, and of the relationship between the two that previously they were not able to see, to take responsibility for, or to control. This type of growth is associated with acquiring a greater awareness of the formerly unconscious aspects of one's self. Like mindfulness, then, development—seen through a constructive–developmental lens—is about increasing the *internal* capacities to be able to take a greater perspective on one's self, others, the world, and the interrelationship among all three. Also like mindfulness, development can continue throughout the life span when people are fortunate enough to benefit from supports and challenges that meet them where they are (we will say more about this soon). Furthermore, moving from one developmental stage to the next does not involve *losing* capacities. Rather, it's like adding a new ring to a tree or a layer to an onion—whereby new capacities become part of a larger, more encompassing self-system (i.e., a meaning-making system or *way of knowing*). For ease of reference, a visualization and summation of the four ways of knowing can be found in Figure 4. 2.

Next, we present a brief description of the four qualitatively different

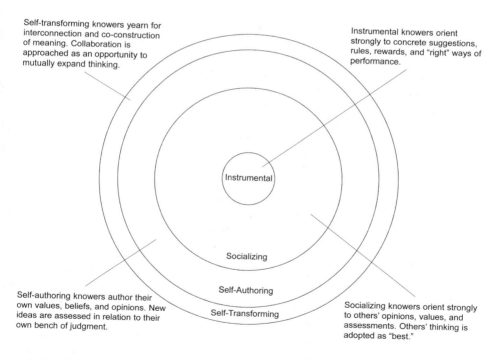

FIGURE 4.2. Four developmental ways of knowing in adulthood. From Drago-Severson and Blum-DeStefano (2018, p. 25). Reprinted with permission from ASCD.

ways of knowing in adulthood. It is important to emphasize that they are *structures* of mind (i.e., how a person orients to the world) rather than personality traits (e.g., introvert or extrovert). For more detailed discussions of ways of knowing, see Drago-Severson (2004b, 2009, 2012, 2016), Drago-Severson et al. (2013), and Drago-Severson and Blum-DeStefano (2016, 2017, 2018). For a detailed discussion of the administration and scoring of the developmental assessment employed to assess a person's way of knowing (i.e., the Subject–Object Interview, a 90-minute qualitative interview), see Lahey et al. (1988) and Lahey, Souvaine, Kegan, Goodman, and Felix (2011).

As depicted and summarized in Figure 4.2, the first way of knowing in adulthood outlined by constructive–developmental theory—the *instrumental*—is marked by a concrete, right–wrong orientation to the world and the way things are "supposed" to be. Instrumental knowers can be as kind and caring as other people; however, their kindness and caring are expressed in a concrete manner, and they tend to measure progress and value in relation to tangible outcomes. While adults who make meaning in this way can control their own impulses and desires (e.g., if an instrumental knower feels like saying or doing something to another person, he/she/they can decide not to do it), they have not yet developed the internal capacity to see things clearly from another's perspective. In other words, they cannot take on another person's point of view—or stand in another person's shoes (metaphorically speaking). Instead, they tend to be guided by their own needs—as well as the external beliefs about the world they have internalized as true or universal (e.g., right or wrong ways to teach and lead).

Over time and under the right conditions of support and developmental challenge (i.e., what we refer to as psychological stretching), instrumental knowers may gradually develop capacities that are the hallmark of a new and more complex way of knowing—what we call the *socializing* way of knowing. When this happens, adults are able to take a broader perspective on their previously unquestioned worldviews and develop the capacity to more fully adopt other people's perspectives. The challenge—or growing edge—for socializing knowers becomes disentangling their sense of self from the judgments, opinions, and assessments of valued others, as reality for socializing knowers is co-constructed. In other words, socializing knowers adopt valued others and authorities' expectations and judgments of them as *their own*.

In fact, the ability to take a larger perspective on one's relationships—to not be run by or so identified with them that a person cannot see them objectively—is a hallmark of the next way of knowing in adulthood: *self-authoring*. Adults who have grown into a self-authoring way of knowing have developed the capacity to author—or generate—their own beliefs, values, and opinions, and to strongly defend them. While they may still deeply value relationships, self-authoring knowers feel more equipped to engage in conflict and difficult conversations, as they have come to see them as integral parts of collaboration and progress. Yet, self-authoring knowers remain tied to their own ideologies, and can have a hard time taking in or considering ideas that they feel are diametrically opposed to their own. While self-authoring capacities accord with many traditional notions of and expectations for leaders and leadership—for example, having the capacity to stand up for one's beliefs, to engage in difficult conversations, and to promote a strong vision—it is arguably valuable to look beyond one's own bench of judgment when leading change in today's complex schools and world.

In fact, it is the fourth way of knowing described by constructive-developmental theory—the *self-transforming* way—that most closely mirrors some of the highest goals and principles of mindfulness. Adults who have grown to make meaning with a self-transforming way of knowing have developed the internal capacities to take a wider perspective on their values and beliefs, and to understand them as manifestations of larger systems and constellations that coexist within themselves. For instance, self-transforming knowers recognize that there are many parts to themselves (i.e., different self-systems) and that some parts are better developed than others. Not only do these adults have the capacity to recognize this, but they are also constantly seeking to develop the parts of themselves that are less well developed. As such, they orient toward deep and intimate—in the psychological sense—interconnection with others as essential to growth. This is different from the way in which adults with a socializing way of knowing orient to valued others (i.e., loved ones, important friends, authorities, and supervisors in their lives). For socializing knowers, reality is co-constructed, and valued others are needed in order for them to feel like and *be* a complete, whole person. For self-transforming knowers, on the other hand, intimate relationships help them to feel *more* complete—more fully human. They recognize that no one person could possibly see or understand everything needed as a single individual and, as such, seek to explore how their consciousness, ideas, and identities can inform and be informed by others. In these ways, self-transforming knowers seem to be able to even more fully experience several aspects of Kabat-Zinn's (1994) description of mindfulness, including "seeing more deeply into the cause and effect and the interconnectedness of things" (p. xv)—or, rather, becoming "conscious of a connectedness which has been here all the time" (p. 215).

Just as important, a developmental lens helps us recognize that—just like Stephen Covey's (2005, 2013) habits of effectiveness—mindfulness and developing greater internal capacities are not things people can simply *do* because they want to. Although understanding the patterns and trajectory of development can certainly bring conscious awareness to new aspects of ourselves and our experiences, relationships and contexts that support our development are still needed, as well as time to grow. Inspiringly, research suggests that more people are beginning to develop higher-order capacities, perhaps given the complexity of life today. Estimates from just a few decades ago placed the number of adults with some degree of self-transforming capacity at only 3–5% (Kegan, 1994); current estimates—based on meta-analyses—now place the number at 8–11% (at least within the United States) (Kegan, 2013). This change, we think, is remarkable.

It also aligns—loosely but compellingly—with the recent findings reported by organizational psychologist Tasha Eurich (2018), who esti-mated that 10–15% of leaders (based on a study of nearly 5,000 partici-pants) demonstrate high levels of both internal and external self-awareness (i.e., an intuitive coupling and valuing of both self and other that aligns with a self-transforming orientation). Equally interesting, Eurich (2018)—who studies self-awareness—reports four different archetypes of this crit-ical element of mindfulness, with each representing an advance in lead-ership effectiveness and capacity: *seekers* (who have not developed clear understandings of self or how others see them), *pleasers* (who prioritize others' feelings and fulfillment over their own), *introspectors* (who have a clear sense of self but not their own blind spots), and people who are *aware* (i.e., the aforementioned people who have a clearer sense of self but also look outward to other's diverse ideas, feedback, and opinions). In the spirit of mindful interconnection, it seems clear that these archetypes correspond closely with ways of knowing. A developmental lens also helps underscore the fact that we can *move through* these levels of self-awareness with time and practice. And that is a wonderful thing.

In addition to Figure 4.2—and all that we've offered in order to paint a picture of the *most* important characteristics of these different ways of knowing in adulthood—we encourage readers to review another introduc-tion to ways of knowing and its practical application in workplace and classroom settings by viewing our *Yes! Magazine* chart (Drago-Severson, 2009b). This chart presents brief synopses of adults' qualitatively different ways of knowing, as well as guiding questions that can be employed to help explore the kinds of developmental supports and challenges that can be employed for internal capacity building.

Making More Connections between Ways of Knowing and Mindfulness

Often, when we teach principals and aspiring and practicing educators across all levels of schools and other systems about ways of knowing, we describe each way of knowing as a unique pair of semipermanent glasses that we wear all the time—even when we're sleeping. What we mean by this is that our way of knowing—which, while we're *in* it, tends to feel more like who we are rather than something we have (Drago-Severson, 2009a, 2012, 2016)—influences how we see and make sense of every aspect of our world and ourselves. Recognizing that our perceptions of reality are actually *constructions*—and that they can change and *develop* over time—is most often a liberating and hopeful experience for people, as it opens up new possibilities for growth and transformation.

For example, after learning about constructive–developmental theory in one of our graduate classes, Carter, an aspiring principal, shared a powerful insight about something his father used to tell him: "There's no 'out there.'" What this illuminates is the ultimate power of our constructions. In other words, everything is a construction—something we *create*—as we make sense of events and experiences in our minds. As Carter explained:

"Whenever I was nervous as a kid, my father would remind me that "there's no 'out there'" to help me remember that my feelings were really coming from inside me, and that I had the power to change them if I wanted to. I'm not sure I fully understood what he meant at the time, but learning about ways of knowing has really given this concept new meaning. I get it—and it's true!"

Like developing our ways of knowing, mindfulness is also about breaking through the veil of our habitual assumptions and sense making. It is about recognizing, as Hanh (1975) explained, that we are "seeing reality through imagination" at every moment of our lives, and working to observe ourselves in ever-clearer ways through purposeful attention and contemplation (p. 56). As Kabat-Zinn (1994) similarly argued, "Sometimes our thoughts act like dream glasses. . . . Without knowing it, we are coloring everything, putting our spin on it all" (p. 26). Both mindfulness and developmental theory, then, can help us become even more intimately familiar with our own and others' patterns of thinking, and to embrace our experiences with compassion and "greater non-judgmental receptivity and acceptance" (Kabat-Zinn, 1994, p. 57). After all, no matter our ways of knowing, they've gotten us as far as we've already come, so it's important to honor the great value in that. Every part of our experience matters and is integral to what comes next. Moreover, wisdom from both paradigms reminds us that caring for and staying present in each moment can help us engage more consciously and intentionally in ways that will support development and positively benefit the future.

Beyond the Self-Transforming Way of Knowing

Before turning next to a few essential mindfulness strategies that principals can employ to promote growth in themselves and in their schools, we want to briefly acknowledge how the practice of mindfulness also accords with development *beyond* the self-transforming way of knowing. For example, like advanced mindfulness practitioners, a number of psychologists have mapped out the terrain of an ego-transcendent phase of development currently experienced by less than 2% of the population (Cook-Greuter, 2013; Wilber, 2000). People who make meaning in this way have begun to recognize the impermanence of their own selves as mental constructs. In other words, they have come to take a perspective on what theorist Susan Cook-Greuter (2013) described as the fundamental non-separateness of who they are in relation to everything surrounding them. In keeping with more Eastern, Buddhist understandings of self, people who make meaning in this way have come to recognize the experience of self as itself a subjective construct. Although research suggests that the trajectory of growth described by constructive–developmental theory is relevant regardless of culture, gender, race, or other demographics (Bridwell, 2013; Drago-Severson, 2004a; Kegan et al., 2001), the theory does derive from a Western psychological paradigm. As such, we think this overlap with the more Eastern understandings of mindfulness and identity helps bring new unity to the theory and its applicability in diverse schools and contexts.

Modeling Mindfulness for Individual and Organizational Growth: Developmental Strategies for the Mindful Principal

> To create a sense of belonging takes dedicated time and space to listen and to care for each other. . . .
> —ILSE CRAWFORD

So far, we have explored the potential benefits of mindfulness—as well as the developmental dimensions of mindfulness practice— for school principals. This is a very important point that we'd like to underscore, especially in relation to how adults' internal capacities will influence how they engage in mindfulness practice. For instance, a teacher or principal with an instrumental way of knowing will need explicit guidelines—and steps to follow—when practicing mindfulness. As discussed earlier, understanding that instrumental knowers do not yet have the internal capacity to think abstractly or to make generalizations from one context to another—and that they will want to do it "the right way"—is important to consider when encouraging an instrumental knower to engage in mindfulness practices as depicted by the literature. In the same way, it is essential to offer developmental supports and stretching to help educators with all ways of knowing grow as mindful practitioners and principals.

Given that principals and school leaders have different ways of knowing as adults, what—ideally—can principals *do* to promote greater mindfulness in themselves and others in their schools? In general, the consensus holds that leading mindfulness is primarily about *modeling* it—about practicing it rather than preaching about its promise (Kabat-Zinn, 1994; Sinclair, 2015). Accordingly, while the literature is rife with powerful breathing exercises and meditation techniques that principals can employ (and encourage others to employ, too), we focus here on the *internal* work of mindful leadership—and the ways it can radiate outward to touch others' lives and experiences. In keeping with a developmental lens, we present four strategies for modeling mindful leadership that align, loosely, with the growing edges of each of the four ways of knowing in adulthood. While leaders with any way of knowing can work on and toward each or all of these goals, we tease them apart here to shine further light on the promising connections between internal capacity building and mindful leadership.

1. Looking beyond certainty and measurable outcomes.
2. Valuing mistakes and discomfort as opportunities for growth.
3. Letting go of the "intoxicating shield of image and aura" (Kabat-Zinn, 1994, p. 65).
4. Sharing yourself and your presence.

We offer these four strategies as *goals to work toward*—and as grounding concepts to hold in mind and heart—rather than as items to add to your "do now" list. Since they are synthesized and integrated from both the mindfulness literature and our work supporting developmental leadership within schools and across the educational system, we hope you find them helpful in your own noble practice—and modeling.

Looking Beyond Certainty and Measurable Outcomes

As both mindfulness and a developmental perspective make clear, investing time into undoing the certainty and automaticity of our convictions is a transformative act in and of itself. As Kabat-Zinn (1994) wrote, "we usually fall, quite unaware, into assuming that what we are thinking—the ideas and opinions that we harbor at any given time—are 'the truth' about what is 'out there' in the world and 'in here' in our minds. Most of the time, it just isn't so" (p. xiv). Nadler (2011) acknowledged this psychological deception by dubbing our thoughts a "facts fallacy." While this can be true for all of us to some degree, for instrumental knowers, the lure of certainty—of rigid right and wrong thinking, of being *sure*—can even more frequently close off avenues of inquiry, connection, and possibility that seem essential to progress in today's schools and world. After all, many of the most pressing challenges in education—including closing the opportunity gap and achieving more equitable, just outcomes and experiences for a diverse student body—are *adaptive* in nature (Heifetz, 1994; Heifetz,

Grashow, & Linsky, 2009), and thus not reducible to technical solutions or approaches. When facing adaptive challenges, pre-made solutions do not exist, there are no experts who can solve these problems for us, they often require changes in cultural norms, and they demand the internal capacity to handle enormous amounts of complexity and ambiguity. Yet, making room for uncertainty and not knowing—and opening ourselves to the possibility that things could always be otherwise—may be one of the most important ways that we can begin to address adaptive challenges and the many -isms that underlie them (Drago-Severson & Blum-DeStefano, 2017; Magee, 2015).

Of course, and especially for instrumental knowers, embracing the invisible benefits of mindfulness and internal capacity building can be a developmental challenge. This is especially true in light of what Kabat-Zinn (1994) described as the "effort but non-doing" and the "energy but no tangible product" generally associated with mindful practice (p. 75). In other words, it can be a developmental challenge for instrumental knowers (and many other adults) to invest the time and energy into mindfulness when the results aren't immediately measurable, and when it's harder to pinpoint just what's different or better because of the effort in the short term. For example, when invited to participate in new initiatives or reforms (such as mindfulness), teachers and principals with an instrumental way of knowing sometimes ask, "Does this count? Am I being evaluated on this?" Yet, in the case of mindfulness, this outcomes-based focus may crowd out the intention of the practice itself. That is why we list this strategy *first*—as it seems a foundational element of mindful principal leadership. We further discuss strategies for effectively introducing mindfulness to instrumental knowers later in this chapter.

Valuing Mistakes and Discomfort as Opportunities for Growth

One of our most powerful takeaways from the mindfulness literature involves avoiding the tendency of going along just to get along or of doing (once again) what we've always done before. Especially in the fast-paced world of schools, it can be all too easy to stay within the lines of our most comfortable routines and relationships. This may feel especially true for principals, who inhabit a *very* public role at the intersection of many competing demands (Ackerman & Maslin-Ostrowski, 2002). Avoiding risk and difficult conversations can thus feel akin to survival. Yet, we know that acknowledging and even valuing mistakes are critical for growth—both personally and organizationally (Drago-Severson & Blum-DeStefano, 2016; Eurich, 2018; Hoy, Gage, & Tarter, 2006; Kegan & Lahey, 2016; Nadler, 2011). After all, taking stock of limitations, seeking out critical feedback, and owning the discomfort this may cause can help us better understand and address pressing challenges, rather than sweep them under the rug (or invest great stores of energy trying to hide them from ourselves and others).

While, again, mindfully facing personal and organizational shortcomings is something that all principals can practice and employ, it is a strategy that may sit at the growing edge for socializing knowers, especially, who orient to external approval, and will likely be hesitant to disrupt the flow of a school's *culture of nice* (MacDonald, 2011). From both a mindful and a developmental perspective, however, understanding the roots and branches of our orientations to critical reflection can be a liberating experience, and something we can cultivate with sustained commitment, support, and practice. Again, we share more about gently supporting mindfulness in socializing knowers at a later point.

Letting Go of the "Intoxicating Shield of Image and Aura"

Many people, research suggests, overestimate their strengths and effectiveness (Nadler, 2011). For leaders, in particular, past successes, extensive experience, little access to feedback, and the internalized expectations of others can fuel feelings of having—or needing to have—all the answers (Eurich, 2018; Heifetz, 1994; Sinclar, 2015). In our research, many principals we have had the honor of learning with and from likewise lament the pressure they feel to be the expert leader, "to know the answers," and to hold things up largely on their own (Drago-Severson, 2009a, 2012; Drago-Severson & Blum-DeStefano, 2016, 2018; Drago-Severson et al., 2013, 2017, 2018). Will they be perceived as weak, they worry, if they let down their guard? If they admit they don't know something? If they ask for help?

From both mindful and developmental perspectives, it seems clear that the answer, nearly always, is *no*. On the contrary, letting go of what Kabat-Zinn (1994) described as the "intoxicating shield of image and aura" (p. 65) is vital to deepening leadership, learning, living, and mindfulness. And, embracing vulnerability—even in small ways—can help deepen relationships and trust in all domains of our lives (Brown, 2012; Drago-Severson, 2012, 2016; Drago-Severson & Blum-DeStefano, 2016, 2018; Drago-Severson, Roy, & von Frank, 2015). It can also help us to open up more authentically to the needs and experiences of others in our care, and to lead more by listening and collaborating than by doing and deciding (Drago-Severson, 2009a, 2012, 2016; Drago-Severson & Blum-DeStefano, 2016, 2018; Nierenberg, 2009). This, Sinclair (2015) aptly explained, will help people "feel more heard and more held" (p. 6).

Of course, vulnerability as leadership can be hard for anyone to continually embody and model—which is where mindful attention comes in—but we recognize, too, that this approach may be especially pertinent (developmentally speaking) for self-authoring knowers, as they identify so firmly with their personal competencies and visions. Similar to Kabat-Zinn's (1944) image of ego as a shield, we often describe self-authoring capacities as a suit of armor self-authoring knowers can wear to advocate for important ideas and engage in conflict for a greater good (Drago-Severson, 2012; Drago-Severson & Blum-DeStefano, 2017, 2018). Yet, just as a suit of armor can protect us from harm, it can also block out new ideas—even those that may help us. Accordingly, we argue that lifting up the visor of one's self-authoring suit of armor is key to leadership development and internal capacity building, as one person's range of vision is, by definition, limited. After all, we can only know what we know at any moment in time, and principals, like all people, need others to grow and effect change. Additional strategies for supporting mindfulness in self-authoring knowers will be shared toward the end of this chapter; stay tuned.

Sharing Yourself and Your Presence

Our fourth suggested mindfulness strategy for principals—*sharing yourself and your presence*—speaks to the transformative power of being genuinely and generously present with and for others in your leadership. According to Kabat-Zinn (1994), mindfulness flourishes when "you practice sharing the fullness of your being, your best self, your enthusiasm, your vitality, your spirit, your trust, your openness, [and] above all, your presence" (p. 62). This idea makes perfect sense, as the biggest gifts we can give to others stem from both ourselves and our attention. In our experience, people know and feel when you are *with them* (psychologically, not just technically or physically), and this caring attention can make a tremendous difference. It also serves as a foundation for all kinds of generative leading, teaching, coaching, and therapeutic contexts (e.g., Duckworth, 2001; Hougaard & Carter, 2017; Kegan, 2014; Rogers, 1961). As educator and theorist Eleanor Duckworth (2001) has found—in her decades of research—simply paying *real* attention can be a tremendous support to another's growth and development.

For principals, it can also help them tap back into the joy of their work and professional relationships—which, as noted earlier, can sometimes become dulled when jumping, hour after hour and day after day, from one important meeting (and urgent demand) to the next. Like reframing shared time as (also) one's own, having a purposeful and authentic presence can be mutually generative and can radiate outward in ways that make a significant difference with and for others in an organization (Hougaard & Carter, 2017; Reb, Narayanan, & Chaturvedi, 2014). Describing the expanding influence of personal growth, Hanh (1975) again offered a foundational idea, which we think applies equally to school leadership.

In a family, if there is one person who practices mindfulness, the entire family will be more mindful. Because of the presence of one member who lives in mindfulness, the entire family is reminded to live in mindfulness. If in one class, one student lives in mindfulness, the entire class is influenced. (p. 64)

Indeed, we contend that a similar truth holds for adult development, as "the growth that happens within each of us matters immensely for the growth of our students, schools, systems, democracies, and world communities" (Drago-Severson & Blum-DeStefano, 2018, p. 137).

Yet, just as with the other strategies we've offered, sharing oneself and one's presence can be a developmental challenge for some principals—depending on one's way of knowing—and on other internal preferences. Perhaps ironically, given their preference for mutuality and interconnection, self-transforming principals may feel a tug at their growing edges when enacting this strategy. More specifically, self-transforming principals may sometimes need help in *pulling back* their attention from others and from seeking harmony, especially when needing to delegate responsibilities or make quick decisions. In other words, they may need support when working to balance their urge to connect with the urgencies of the principal role (and its inherent imperatives toward decisive action). Like all of the strategies we've offered then—including looking beyond certainty and measurable outcomes, valuing mistakes and discomfort as opportunities for growth, and letting go of the "intoxicating shield of image and aura" (Kabat-Zinn, 1994, p. 65)—sharing yourself and your presence will require *different* supports and challenges for leaders with different ways of knowing.

In the next section, we offer developmental strategies for supporting the mindful practice of educators in this and other ways.

Differentiating Mindfulness Supports and Challenges for Others: A Developmental View

While, in general, modeling remains a highly effective path for principals toward promoting a culture of mindfulness in schools, there may also be times when more direct invitations, supports, and challenges for colleagues seem appropriate. Just as sharing developmental ideas can help create a common language for thinking and talking about growth in a school community (Drago-Severson, 2004b, 2009a, 2012, 2016), sharing the promise of mindfulness and its connection to development can similarly broaden collective understandings and foster robust and meaningful conversations. As we have learned about and worked to design professional learning opportunities of all kinds, however, it is essential to remember that adults will orient *differently* to mindfulness conversations and activities depending on their ways of knowing (and other factors of personality and identity) (Drago-Severson, 2004b, 2009a, 2012, 2016; Drago-Severson et al., 2015; Richards, 2009). Accordingly, thinking strategically about how to *differentiate* the supports and challenges you offer to colleagues in support of mindfulness is another powerful dimension of mindful and developmental leadership.

While by no means an exhaustive list or how-to guide, in Table 4.1 we offer (1) developmental suggestions for introducing and framing mindfulness in ways that align with the four different ways of knowing and (2) reflective questions you could employ to gently expand and encourage colleagues' engagement with mindfulness *just along their growing edges*. This is important because, as we often teach in our developmental leadership classes, growth happens at the intersection of support *and* challenge.

Also, in terms of how to address your own or others' ways of knowing, there's no quick quiz or assessment you can use to "diagnose" your own or others' ways of knowing.[2] Please do not be disheartened, though. You can use the ideas we've discussed here to help with gauging your own and others' ways of knowing. Actually, what we suggest to be of help is sharing this and other work on ways of knowing in order to develop (1) a common language for understanding and talking about adult development and mindfulness (and their connection); (2) a developmentally oriented curriculum (e.g., an infrastructure of collaborative practices and professional learning opportunities) that supports mindfulness and internal capacity building; and (3) a culture wherein adults work to support *each other's* growth and mindfulness practices.

Table 4.1 can assist you in your important growth-enhancing and mindfulness work. We offer this chart not to box you or any of your colleagues in to a particular way of making meaning—but rather to honor and anticipate the developmental diversity that will likely be present in nearly any of your groups or teams (Drago-Severson, 2009a, 2016; Drago-Severson & Blum-DeStefano, 2016, 2018).

In other words, we share these strategies not as tools for recruiting people into "team mindfulness," but to help you even more intentionally *adapt* your leadership practices to meet people where they are. As always, we hope they are helpful to you and those in your care.

---

[2]As mentioned briefly earlier, there *is* an assessment called the Subject–Object Interview (Lahey et al., 2011), which is a valid, reliable, developmental measure (tested and employed since 1982) that can assess reliably a person's way of knowing. However, this formal interview takes 90–120 minutes to complete and should be administered and scored by a trained developmental interviewer.

TABLE 4.1. Developmental Framing and Reflective Questions for Mindful Practice

Way of knowing	Strategies for framing and introducing mindfulness	Reflective questions to encourage mindfulness and perspective taking
Instrumental (concrete)	Share evidence about the positive effects of mindfulness on the brain and for leadership outcomes (e.g., how the practice and processes help with sustaining leadership and renewing oneself and helping others to sustain and renew themselves over time). Share this as a rationale for *considering* mindfulness (i.e., not the end goal). Share examples/models and step-by-step guides to effective mindfulness practices.	"How would you describe your feelings right now?" "What's most important to you about _____?" "What's the worst thing that would happen if _____ didn't happen?" "What would be the best thing if _____ were to happen to you and for you?" "How do you think _____ would feel about _____?"
Socializing (other-focused)	Share stories and examples of how mindfulness has helped you grow and learn as a leader and how it has helped you in your practice of work–life balance, in sustaining and caring for yourself, and in developing ongoing practices for self-renewal. Offer to support mindfulness as an expression of care (i.e., not as a critique or a need for improvement). Provide a menu of options for and examples of mindfulness practices that may work for the individual.	"What are the parts of your work that bring you joy?" "What did it feel like for you when _____?" "What would you do if you didn't have to worry about _____?" "What would be the best thing about that—if _____ were to happen to you and for you?" "What would make _____ better or easier for you?"
Self-Authoring (reflective)	Ask about personal experiences with, feelings about, and understandings of best practices for mindfulness. Ask about how the person thinks and feels about trying out mindfulness practices or enhancing those that the person already employs. Emphasize the flexibility and autonomy inherent in mindfulness given a self-authoring knower's orientation toward demonstrating personal competence.	"What parts of your work do you feel most confident about?" "What does it feel like for you when things are going well?" "What are some parts of your life that you wish you could better prioritize and/or that you wish were different?" "What would be the best thing about that—if _____ were to happen to you and for you?" "What aspects of _____ might you not be able to see on your own, given your positionality?" "What could you do to learn more about _____?"

(continued)

TABLE 4.1. (*continued*)

Way of knowing	Strategies for framing and introducing mindfulness	Reflective questions to encourage mindfulness and perspective taking
Self-Transforming (interconnecting)	Make time for self and others in the school community to offer and experience mutual, reciprocal supports for growing as mindful practitioners. Provide time and space to think together about experiences with mindfulness and progress made. Create ongoing spaces to discuss the complexities, inconsistencies, and paradoxes associated with carving out time to engage in mindfulness practices. Gently encourage moving from thinking about issues, dilemmas, situations, and inconsistencies and toward acting when needed.	"What's working well in your mindfulness practice?" "What does _____ feel like for you?" "What's something you'd like to grow?" "What would be the best thing about that—if you were able to grow yourself in that way?" "What would you do if you had to decide *right now*, given what you've already learned?"

Conclusion

All truths are easy to understand once they are discovered.
—GALILEO GALILEI

For nearly three decades, one of us (Eleanor Drago-Severson) has worked to bring the promise of an adult developmental perspective to educators and schools. For the past decade, both of us have had honor of learning and working together to advance this knowledge and mission in the field. While we feel deep gratitude when educators across the country and around the world find value in developmental ideas and practices, teaching about adult development in schools is not always free from pushback. Sometimes, people initially wonder, "Aren't schools—and learning—supposed to be for *kids*?" Busy educators sometimes ask, "How can we make time for adults when there's so much *else* we need to do—like, right now?" Still others confide, when first introduced to the concept of adult development, that they think, "But I'm already an adult—what more do I have to learn?"

Most often, learning about and experiencing developmental leadership can be a transformational experience for aspiring and practicing leaders—and one that seems to make a difference in real-life leadership long after classes and workshops are over (Drago-Severson et al., 2013). While this may simply be the case because supporting adult development *works* (i.e., it's been directly linked to improved student outcomes; see Donaldson,

2008; Guskey, 1999)—we like to think that there is also something nour-
ishing, restorative, and contagious (in a good way) about putting people
and their growth *first*. In fact, the more we learn about leading change,
building collaborative cultures, and communicating effectively up and
down the system, the more we see internal capacity building—for self and
others—as *the center of gravity* of the contemporary principalship. In the
same way, mindfulness is not just some add-on or new-agey fad for principals to experiment with on the margins. Supporting mindfulness, like supporting adult development and internal capacity building, is about building
and growing our world and ourselves. It is *life giving*. And, from our viewpoint, it is a natural outgrowth and extension of the developmental work
of leading and an orientation to leadership that can help drive personal
and organizational development. In other words, coupling mindfulness and
development is a win-win. For these reasons and more, we are *so* excited to
bring these two powerful lenses together—and to even more purposefully
infuse each moment of our leadership and daily lives with developmental
intentionality *and* mindfulness. As we think more about the possibilities of
bringing these two promising leadership lenses together, we end this chapter just as we began it—with hope.

APPENDIX 4.1. Case Study: Spreading Mindfulness

LINDA ROSENBURY
former middle school principal;
doctoral candidate, Harvard Graduate School of Education

In this vignette, Linda Rosenbury describes her own journey through mindfulness practices as a middle school principal in New York City. At age 28
she was appointed principal of Middle School 22 in the Bronx, a 700-student
school that was previously named one of the city's 12 most violent schools.
After serving as the principal for 5 years, she worked with a group of local
parents to found the Brooklyn Urban Garden Charter School (BUGS), an
independent, community-based school serving 300 students. She is now
receiving her Doctorate in Education Leadership at Harvard's Graduate
School of Education.

My mindfulness journey began when I started practicing yoga. I remember
being confused the first time the teacher announced things like, "Wherever you
are in the pose is fine." "If you can not go as far today as you did yesterday,

that is fine." There was no end goal for everyone. It was the first time in life that I understood that there may not be one "right" way, that development is not always linear, that pushing oneself may not be as effective as listening to and accepting one's self. The yoga studio was also the first place where I began to meditate. Sitting still for long periods of time was challenging, but I approached it from an instrumental knower perspective. I wanted to be "good" at staying still. If the Dalai Lama doesn't flinch when a fly is circling his face, neither will I. As my mindfulness practice developed over the coming years, my perspective evolved to include more self-authoring and self-transforming ways of knowing.

My school's support organization invited me and educators from other schools to the CARE (Cultivating Awareness and Resilience in Educators) for Teachers retreat at the Garrison Institute. At the time, I was a new principal feeling very overwhelmed by the day-to-day challenges of running a school. Each day, I was bombarded with school-based problems and stories of personal tragedy and left the building not knowing how to process the many things that had happened and the pain I had witnessed. At CARE, I learned helpful practices that supported me in meeting these challenges, such as active listening, setting an intention, mindful walking, and compassion meditation. Unlike other work retreats that felt very goal oriented and focused on student outcomes, this retreat was really about caring for oneself. At first, I felt a bit guilty or self-indulgent. But being with other educators in a sponsored cohort gave me the permission to acknowledge my own emotions as a central component of who I am while at work and to learn to regulate them. If the higher-ups were investing in this practice, I would follow along.

It has been almost a decade since I began integrating the practices I first learned about at CARE into my work and personal life, and the impact has been transformational for my relationships, my efficacy, and my level of resilience in the face of day-to-day challenges. Active listening is a key practice that has transformed my principalship. Before intentionally integrating this practice, I would often enter a conversation thinking about how to bring the other participants to the outcome I envisioned. As they spoke, I was often having judgmental "scripts" in my head about what they were saying or thinking about what I was going to say in response. When I began to listen with an open mind, I was better able to pick up on the nuances of their thinking and to incorporate their ideas to make our working together stronger. Instead of feeling like the staff members were people separate from me that needed convincing, I started to conceive of us as one group that could reason together about ways to work more effectively.

Mindful walking was one way that I modeled intentionality and connectedness as a leader. While I didn't always find time to sit down and meditate during the school day, I could be mindful about how I transitioned from activity to activity throughout the school building. Before learning about this practice, I often would read and send email as I walked from one meeting or event to another. I would hardly look up, typing away until I needed to do the next thing, which led to ever-more-distracted and bogged-down beginnings and disconnection with those I need to have the strongest connections with. When I started to instead keep my phone in my pocket and feel my feet on the ground and my body in space, I would tune in to the stress that I was carrying from one event to the next and process it before letting it bleed over into the next conversation. I was looking up at my school environment and becoming more in tune with what was going on, which led to more informed decision making.

Compassion meditation improved my relationship with one staff member who directly reported to me. Before learning about it, I would often approach our interactions with dread and become frustrated by his comments, leading to ineffective communication. We couldn't work together to help children if we couldn't even hear each other. When I learned how to cultivate feelings of warmth toward him, I began to enter our conversations ready to listen and able to use his ideas to reach a compromise that advanced our goals. I stopped seeing him as a problem and started feeling empowered to positively influence his thinking and learn from him.

I immediately embedded two of the practices from the retreat into my staff meeting protocols. My hope was that just as I felt permission to engage in self-care by my school support organization, I could act, as principal, to give my staff permission to dedicate time to mindfulness. We would begin the meeting by closing our eyes, breathing, and thinking about how we were feeling in each part of our bodies (body scan). This practice "reset" everyone before we dug into the meeting content, resulting in more effective interpersonal communication. People then carried this practice into other meetings (like stressful ones with parents or entering a difficult class!) allowing them to be more in tune with their emotions and respond more strategically.

In addition to the body scan, I started leading my staff in setting an intention for the day or week—not what we were to accomplish but how we were going to *be* as we move about the school. We started to be more conscious of how our facial expressions, our tone, and our body language created a powerful atmosphere in the school. We prioritized the demonstration of compassion for ourselves and others as a tool that gave us the energy and stamina to achieve our goals, instead of prioritizing "getting things done" in spite of our needs and the needs of others. The result of this reprioritization meant that instead of reacting to student situations, we felt empowered to proactively create a climate in the school wherein students felt heard and cared for.

After incorporating these two practices into the culture of our school, we started giving each other feedback throughout the day. When I heard a staff member yelling at a student, I felt comfortable walking over, touching him softly on the shoulder, and gently saying, "Are you okay?" This reminded him of his intention. He reset and began to approach the student in a more productive way. Staff members also felt comfortable giving me feedback. When they saw me worked up, they reminded me to stop and breathe for a minute. This brief pause allowed me to reenter the task at hand more aware of my emotions and able to regulate them. Creating the space for the staff to give me feedback increased my awareness and allowed me to grow in my emotional regulation at a much faster rate than if I maintained a more hierarchical approach.

In my new school, I went even further in supporting mindfulness by embedding twice-daily meditation into our school schedule for all students and staff members, thereby incorporating mindfulness practices even more fully into our school community. When we started the Brooklyn Urban Garden Charter School, we partnered with the David Lynch Foundation to pilot the Quiet Time program in New York City. Schools in California that had used this program had seen increases in attendance and decreases in discipline incidents, and it aligned with our values of community and awareness. The entire school, including the main office, is silent for 15 minutes each morning and afternoon. The security officer at the door stops visitors to notify them that the school is meditating, and they need to wait to enter. Staff members double up in each classroom, taking turns modeling meditation for the students or monitoring the students.

After multiple years in the principalship and daily applications of these practices, I began to realize that the people in charge didn't necessarily have all the answers. If I continued to dutifully follow preset rules or trust the decisions of the current leaders, I would not necessarily meet my goal of better serving children. I realized that I must be part of transforming the system. I started looking at system leaders through a critical lens and developed my ability to give them feedback. Instead of looking to others to determine if I was doing things the "right" way, I began to self-author. This process was painful, because I lost a sense of certainty and security. Over time, however, I became more confident in my instincts and felt comfortable being driven by my personal values.

Incorporating mindfulness practices into my life made me a better principal and person. By being more aware and in control of my own emotions, I am able to better understand other people. I can determine each person's strengths and limitations and provide the individualized supports and challenges needed to grow. In one-on-one meetings, I know when people just need me to practice active listening and when I can challenge them to adapt their behavior and perspectives on themselves and their work. Sometimes these difficult conversations can be painful and uncomfortable but with the mindfulness practices, I am now equipped to navigate the associated emotions. Engaging all staff members in these reflective practices is necessary for their personal and professional growth and my responsibility as their leader.

Acknowledgment

We thank Michael Marino for his help during an early stage of our literature review.

References

Ackerman, R., & Maslin-Ostrowski, P. (2002). *The wounded leader: How real leadership emerges in times of crisis.* San Francisco: Jossey-Bass.

Boyatzis, R., & McKee, A. (2005). *Resonant leadership: Renewing yourself and connecting with others through mindfulness, hope and compassion.* Boston: Harvard Business School Press.

Bridwell, S. D. (2013). A constructive–developmental perspective on the transformative learning of adults marginalized by race, class, and gender. *Adult Education Quarterly, 63*(2), 127–146.

Brown, B. (2012). *Daring greatly: How the courage to be vulnerable transforms the way we live, love, parent, and lead.* New York: Avery.

Cook-Greuter, S. R. (2013). Nine levels of increasing embrace in ego development: A full-spectrum theory of vertical growth and meaning making. Retrieved from *www.cook-greuter.com/Cook-Greuter%209%20levels%20paper%20 new%201.1'14%2097p%5B1%5D.pdf.*

Covey, S. R. (2005). *The 8th habit: From effectiveness to greatness.* New York: Free Press.

Covey, S. R. (2013). *The 7 habits of highly effective people: Powerful lessons in personal change* (25th anniversary ed.). New York: Simon & Schuster.

Dadaczynski, K., & Paulus, P. (2014). Healthy principals—healthy schools?: A neglected perspective to school health promotion. In V. Simovska, & P. Mannix McNamara (Eds.), *Schools for health and sustainability* (pp. 253–273). Dordrecht, the Netherlands: Springer.

Donaldson, G. A. (2008). *How leaders learn: Cultivating capacities for school improvement.* New York: Teachers College Press.

Drago-Severson, E. (2004a). *Becoming adult learners: Principles and practices for effective development.* New York: Teachers College Press.

Drago-Severson, E. (2004b). *Helping teachers learn: Principal leadership for adult growth and development.* Thousand Oaks, CA: Corwin.

Drago-Severson, E. (2009a). *Leading adult learning: Supporting adult development in our schools.* Thousand Oaks, CA: Corwin.

Drago-Severson, E. (2009b). How do you know? Retrieved from *www.yesmagazine.org/issues/learn-as-you-go/four-ways-of-knowing.*

Drago-Severson, E. (2012). *Helping educators grow: Strategies and practices for leadership development.* Cambridge, MA: Harvard Education Press.

Drago-Severson, E. (2016). Teaching, learning, and leading in today's complex world: Reaching new heights with a developmental approach. *International Journal of Leadership in Education, 19*(1), 56–86.

Drago-Severson, E., & Blum-DeStefano, J. (2016). *Tell me so I can hear you: A developmental approach to feedback for educators.* Cambridge, MA: Harvard Education Press.

Drago-Severson, E., & Blum-DeStefano, J. (2017). The self in social justice: A developmental lens on race, identity, and transformation. *Harvard Educational Review, 87*(4), 457–481.

Drago-Severson, E., & Blum-DeStefano, J. (2018). *Leading change together: Developing educator capacity within schools and systems.* Alexandria, VA: ASCD.

Drago-Severson, E., Blum-DeStefano, J., & Asghar, A. (2013). *Learning for leadership: Developmental strategies for building capacity in our schools.* Thousand Oaks, CA: Corwin.

Drago-Severson, E., Maslin-Ostrowski, P. (2017). In translation: School leaders learning in and from leadership practice while confronting pressing policy challenges. *Teachers College Record, 120*(1), 1–44.

Drago-Severson, E., Maslin-Ostrowski, P., & Blum-DeStefano, J. (2017). *Inside out: How principals' internal experiences influence their leadership and advocacy through pressing challenges.* Paper presented at the annual conference of the University Council of Educational Administration, Denver, CO.

Drago-Severson, E., Maslin-Ostrowski, P., & Blum-DeStefano, J. (2018). Looking behind the curtain: Principals' internal experiences of managing pressing challenges. *Journal of School Leadership, 28*(3), 315–343.

Drago-Severson, E., Roy, P., & von Frank, V. (2015). *Reach the highest standard in professional learning: Learning designs.* Thousand Oaks, CA: Corwin.

Duckworth, E. (2001). *"Tell me more": Listening to learners explain.* New York: Teachers College Press.

Eurich, T. (2018, January 4). What self-awareness really is (and how to cultivate it). Retrieved from *https://hbr.org/2018/01/what-self-awareness-really-is-and-how-to-cultivate-it.*

Guskey, T. R. (1999). *New perspectives on evaluating professional development.* Paper presented at the annual meeting of the American Educational Research Association, Montreal, Quebec, Canada.

Hanh, T. N. (1975). *The miracle of mindfulness: An introduction to the practice of mindfulness.* Boston: Beacon Press.

Heifetz, R. (1994). *Leadership without easy answers.* Cambridge, MA: Harvard University Press.

Heifetz, R., Grashow, A., & Linsky, M. (2009). *The practice of adaptive leadership: Tools and tactics for changing your organization and the world.* Boston: Harvard Business Press.

Hornich-Lisciandro, T. (2013). Mindfulness in education. *Education Digest, 79*(2), 66–68.

Hougaard, R., & Carter, J. (2017, December 13). If you aspire to be a great leader, be present. Retrieved from *https://hbr.org/2017/12/if-you-aspire-to-be-a-great-leader-be-present.*

Hoy, W. K., Gage, C. Q., III, & Tarter, C. J. (2006). School mindfulness and faculty trust: Necessary conditions for each other? *Educational Administration Quarterly, 42*(2), 236–255.

Kabat-Zinn, J. (1994). *Wherever you go, there you are: Mindfulness meditation in everyday life.* New York: Hyperion.

Kegan, R. (1982). *The evolving self: Problems and process in human development.* Cambridge, MA: Harvard University Press.

Kegan, R. (1994). *In over our heads: The mental demands of modern life.* Cambridge, MA: Harvard University Press.

Kegan, R. (2000). What "form" transforms?: A constructive–developmental approach to transformative learning. In J. Mezirow & Associates (Eds.), *Learning as transformation* (pp. 35–70). San Francisco: Jossey-Bass.

Kegan, R. (2013, January). *Adult development in the 21st century.* Keynote address presented at the 22nd annual Conflict Resolution Symposium, Ottawa, Ontario, Canada.

Kegan, R. (2014, October 15). *Empathic listening. Lecture notes.* Cambridge, MA: Minds at Work Coach Certification Program.

Kegan, R., Broderick, M., Drago-Severson, E., Helsing, D., Popp, N., & Portnow, K. (Eds.). (2001). *Toward a "new pluralism" in the ABE/ESOL classroom: Teaching to multiple "cultures of mind"* (Research Monograph of the National Center for the Study of Adult Learning and Literacy, No. 19). Boston: World Education.

Kegan, R., & Lahey, L. L. (2016). *An everyone culture: Becoming a deliberately developmental organization.* Boston: Harvard Business Review Press.

Lahey, L., Souvaine, E., Kegan, R., Goodman, R., & Felix, S. (2011). *A guide to the Subject-Object Interview: Its administration and interpretation.* Cambridge, MA: Minds at Work.

Langer, E. J. (1993). A mindful education. *Educational Psychologist, 28*(1), 43–50.

Langer, E. J. (2014). *Mindfulness* (25th anniversary ed.). Philadelphia: DaCapo Press.

Levenson, M. R., Jennings, P. A., Aldwin, C. M., & Shiraishi, R. W. (2005). Self-transcendence: Conceptualization and measurement. *International Journal of Aging and Human Development, 60*(2), 127–143.

MacDonald, E. (June 2011). When nice won't suffice: Honest discourse is key to shifting school culture. *Journal of Staff Development, 32*(3), 45–47, 51.

Magee, R. V. (2015, May 23). How mindfulness can defeat racial bias. Retrieved from *www.contemplativemind.org/archives/3621.*

Nadler, R. (2011, August 24). The illusion of self-awareness: We are more unaware than aware. Retrieved from *www.psychologytoday.com/US/blog/leading-emotional-intelligence/201108/the-illusion-self-awareness.*

Nagy, L. M., & Baer, R. A. (2017). Mindfulness: What should teachers of psychology know? *Teaching of Psychology, 44*(4), 353–359.

Nierenberg, R. (2009). *Maestro: A surprising story about leading by listening.* New York: Portfolio.

Reb, J. M., Narayanan, J., & Chaturvedi, S. (2014). Leading mindfully: Two studies on the influence of supervisor trait mindfulness on employee well-being and performance. *Mindfulness, 5*(1), 24–36.

Ricard, M., & Singer, W. (2017, December 17). Neuroscience has a lot to learn from Buddhism: A scientist and a monk compare notes on meditation, therapy, and their effects on the brain. Retrieved from *www.theatlantic.com/international/archive/2017/12/buddhism-and-neuroscience/548120.*

Richards, C. (2009). Toward a pedagogy of self. *Teachers College Record, 111*(12), 2732–2759.

Riley, P. (2015). *Australian principal occupational health and wellbeing survey report.* Melbourne: Australian Catholic University, Institute for Positive Psychology and Education.

Roeser, R. W., & Eccles, J. S. (2015). Mindfulness and compassion in human development: Introduction to the special section. *Developmental Psychology, 51*(1), 1–6.

Roeser, R. W., Skinner, E., Beers, J., & Jennings, P. A. (2012). Mindfulness training and teachers' professional development: An emerging area of research and practice. *Child Development Perspectives, 6*(2), 167–173.

Rogers, C. (1961). *On becoming a person: A therapist's view of psychotherapy.* New York: Houghton Mifflin.

School Leaders Network. (2014). Churn: The high cost of principal turnover. Retrieved from *http://connectleadsucceed.org/sites/default/files/principal_turnover_cost.pdf.*

Sinclair, A. (2015). Possibilities, purpose and pitfalls: Insights from introducing mindfulness to leaders. *Journal of Spirituality, Leadership and Management, 8*(1), 3–11.

Wilber, K. (2000). *Integral psychology: Consciousness, spirit, psychology, therapy.* Boston: Shambhala.

CHAPTER 5

Embodied Teacher Mindfulness in the Classroom

The Calm, Clear, Kind Framework

CYNTHIA TAYLOR
PATRICIA A. JENNINGS
ALEXIS HARRIS
DEBORAH L. SCHUSSLER
ROBERT W. ROESER

Teaching is a demanding profession. In order to be effective with students in the classroom and successfully meet the demands inherent in teaching, it is becoming increasingly clear that teachers need to embody certain skills and dispositions beyond those related to subject matter and pedagogical knowledge. Several factors, such as (1) teachers' understanding of what their students bring to the classroom, not just intellectually, but also developmentally, socially, and emotionally; and (2) teachers' embodiment and ability to teach students basic attention and social–emotional skills related to mindful attention, emotion regulation, and harmonious and prosocial relationships with others, are beginning to be discussed in relation to effective teaching (e.g., Hamre & Pianta, 2001; Jennings & Greenberg, 2009; Roeser, Skinner, Beers & Jennings, 2012). As such, various scholars of education are expanding their theories of what constitutes "good teaching," as well as of the constellation of skills and dispositions associated with the good or expert teacher. These theories go beyond the traditional view that good teaching involves content and pedagogical knowledge to include teachers' professional beliefs about students, teachers' empathic concern and prosocial intentions for their students, their enthusiasm and emotion expression in the classroom, and their mental flexibility and awareness (e.g., Darling-Hammond & Bransford, 2005). However, this domain of teacher expertise or knowledge is, as yet, unnamed. It is precisely these kinds of dimensions of teacher expertise that may be amenable to cultivation through mindfulness training (Mind and Life Education Research Network, 2012).

This chapter presents the Calm, Clear, Kind Conceptual Framework of the Mindful Teacher (see Rickert, 2016; Rickert, Skinner, & Roeser, 2018; Taylor, 2016) as a means of summarizing research on teacher dispositions and showing how teacher mindfulness represents an "unnamed domain" of teacher expertise. We describe the "mindful teacher" as one who is clear minded and aware (not distracted), calm bodied (and not reactive), and kindhearted (and not critical, coercive, or biased) in word and deed in interactions with students in the classroom (Taylor, 2016). In addition to presenting this conceptual framework, the goal of this chapter is to review evidence that various mindfulness training programs can teach mindfulness-related skills and dispositions (calmness, clarity, and kindness) that then may "show through" in observable behaviors of teachers in the classroom. Toward this end, we review both quantitative and qualitative research on the impacts of teacher mindfulness programs, and provide anecdotes that exemplify these attributes as they are experienced by teachers in these various programs.

The "Unnamed Domain" of Teacher Expertise

Various theorists have proposed novel aspects of teacher expertise that go beyond the traditional domains of content knowledge and pedagogical content knowledge expertise. For instance, Dottin (2009) refers to "professional dispositions" (e.g., patterns of behavior or capacities) as a key part of teacher expertise. He posits that such dispositions allow teachers to "address the gap between abilities and actions" (p. 89) and to be more effective in the classroom, thus connecting with their students in meaningful and productive ways. The concept of "habits of mind" also seems relevant here. Habits of mind are defined as the ability to behave prosocially and intelligently when confronted with the inevitable instructional and interpersonal challenges that arise in the classroom (Costa & Kallinick, 2011). Research on such professional dispositions and habits of mind in relation to teachers' classroom behavior or classroom climate is still limited at this time.

Similarly, Jennings and Greenberg (2009) have discussed the importance of teachers' social–emotional competencies (SEC) in relation to the implementation of social–emotional learning programs in particular, and to healthy climates for student learning more generally. These authors define teacher SEC in terms of the five core competencies of social–emotional learning, including self- and social awareness, self- and relationship management, and responsible decision making (CASEL, 2018). Teachers high in SEC are thought to be able to generate and use positive emotions to engage students, understand students' emotions and how their own emotions influence students, and manage behavior and emotions in positive ways even in the face of challenging classroom situations (Jennings & Greenberg, 2009). SEC is posited to be important for teachers, because it not only supports effective behavior management and student engagement in learning, but also because students' tendencies toward prosociality are supported when teachers are able to model prosocial behaviors for them. Research examining the measurement, conceptualization, and impact of teacher SEC; teachers' efficacy and belief in social–emotional learning programs; and program implementation and classroom climate is just beginning (e.g., Jennings & Frank, 2015; Ransford, Greenberg, Domitrovich, Small, & Jacobson, 2009; Reyes, Brackett, Rivers, Elbertson, & Salovey, 2012).

Finally, Rodgers and Raider-Roth (2006) proposed a quality called "teacher presence." They define teacher presence as "a state of alert awareness, receptivity and connectedness to the mental, emotional, and physical workings of both the individual and the group in the context of their learning environments and the ability to respond with a considered and compassionate next step" (p. 266). The authors stress the importance of presence in teachers' cultivation of relationships with students, stating that it supports empathy, relationship authenticity, connected teaching, and mutuality (see also Brown, Simone, & Worley, 2016).

The Calm, Clear, Kind Framework of the Mindful Teacher

Despite increasing attention to this unnamed domain of teacher expertise, consensual definitions as to its content and conceptualization do not yet exist, as attested to in the previous works. Many theorists seem to agree that these teacher qualities are important to being a "good teacher," although there is little research on these variously named qualities at this time. In this chapter, we conceptualize this "unnamed domain" in relation to teachers' mindfulness-related skills and dispositions, as well as the influence that these skills and dispositions have on teachers' embodied mindfulness in the classroom. A novel contribution of this perspective is that embodied teacher mindfulness is defined in terms of a teacher's capacity to be calm, clear, and kind in his or her speech and behavioral interactions with students in the classroom despite the uncertainty and the many challenges and demands of the classroom setting (see Colaianne, Galla, & Roeser, 2019; Rickert, 2016; Rickert et al., 2016, 2018; Taylor, 2016).

As subsequently discussed, embodied teacher mindfulness, defined in terms of calmness, mental clarity, and interpersonal kindness, is hypothesized to rely on underlying mindful skills and dispositions related to the regulation of attention and emotion and to prosocial dispositions toward others; in other words, the attentional, emotional, and social skills and dispositions that are viewed as the main outcomes of teacher mindfulness training (see Roeser, 2014, for a review). Attention regulation and emotion regulation are understood here as key self-regulatory processes associated with the capacity to consciously and intentionally bring attention and emotion to bear on relevant goal-related behavior (e.g., Carlson, Zelazo, & Faja, 2013; Rothbart, Posner, & Kieras, 2006). In addition, teachers' ability to be kind in relationships with others is hypothesized to rest on their skills of empathy, compassion, and forgiveness (also referred to as "prosocial dispositions"). Empathy is defined as perceiving and understanding the feelings and needs of others (Singer & Lamm, 2009). Compassion, which includes empathy, is defined as an awareness and feeling of concern for another person's suffering, accompanied by a subsequent desire to alleviate that suffering through action (e.g., Goetz, Keltner, & Simon-Thomas, 2010). Last, forgiveness is defined as a prosocial change in an aggrieved individual's thoughts, emotions, and/or behaviors toward a blameworthy transgressor. This change includes a reduction or elimination of resentment and motivation toward revenge and decreased behavioral avoidance of the transgressor (Enright & Fitzgibbons, 2000; McCullough, 2000; Worthington, 2010). Such attentional, emotional, and social skills are thought to be among the key outcomes of mindfulness training, and are also hypothesized to have effects on stress management, efficiency in carrying out tasks, and interpersonal harmony.

Conceptualizing Teacher Mindfulness and the Unnamed Domain

In order to articulate just what the unnamed domain of teacher expertise is in relation to mindfulness, we believe it is useful to conceptualize mindfulness at two different levels of analysis (Rickert, 2016; Taylor, 2016). First, at the level of teacher behavior, mindfulness can be conceptualized as referring to the invisible attentional, emotional, and social skills just described. For instance, mindfulness has been operationalized psychologically by Bishop and colleagues (2004) as a two-facet phenomenon consisting of the self-regulation of attention, "so that it is maintained on immediate experience, thereby allowing for increased recognition of mental events in the present moment" (p. 232), and present-moment orientation toward one's experiences "that is characterized by curiosity, openness, and acceptance" (p. 232). This definition operationalizes Jon Kabat-Zinn's (1990) classic definition of mindfulness as "paying attention, on purpose, to the present moment, and non-judgmentally." Cullen (2011), following Kabat-Zinn, has also described a general orientation of heartfulness as central to the definition of mindfulness. Heartfulness can be described as a general kindness toward the inner, outer, and other realms of experience. Increasingly, research with adults generally, and teachers in particular, supports the claim that mindfulness training can cultivate the skills of attention regulation (present-centered focus), emotion regulation (nonreactivity and nonjudgment), and kindness toward others (see Hölzel et al., 2011; Roeser, 2014; and Vago & Silbersweig, 2012, for reviews). How might these skills and dispositions, cultivated in the context of mindfulness training, show through in teachers' visible verbal and nonverbal behaviors in the classrooms?

We propose that mindfulness training for teachers, as a unique form of professional development, may result in changes not only in teachers' mindfulness-related skills and dispositions, but also in their visible embodied behaviors in the classroom being calmer in their demeanor and clearer and kinder in their words and interactions with students. Thus, at the level of teachers' classroom behavior, we propose that mindfulness can be conceptualized in relation to certain visible, related behaviors, such as emotional calm, verbal clarity, and kindness. To summarize, we propose that the skills teachers learn through participation in mindfulness training may gradually become embodied and transferred to the classroom context in such a way that they "show through" in teachers' classroom behavior and interactions with students. Why are these factors important, and thus, why might they constitute the "unnamed domain" of teacher expertise?

Emotional Calm in the Classroom

The capacity to be calm in mind and body is essential to effective teaching (Hargreaves, 1998; Jennings & Greenberg, 2009; Roeser et al., 2012). For instance, it is crucial for the creation and maintenance of positive teacher–student relationships, which have been shown to be foundational for student success, teachers' enjoyment of their profession, and overall positive classroom climate (Jennings & Greenberg, 2009). Indeed, some of the most stressful job demands that teachers face are related to their interactions with students (e.g., pupils who lack readiness and motivation and maintaining discipline; Kyriacou, 2001). Therefore, teachers with an ability to be calm when faced with classroom challenges should have more success in cultivating good relationships with their students and in setting a positive tone in the classroom than do those who do not.

Further, teaching is emotionally intensive, in that when it is going well it can be highly emotionally rewarding. However, the reverse is also true: emotionally intensive labor can be a drain on resources when teachers have poor working conditions or are expected to suppress or mask emotions to suit others' needs or purposes (Grandey, 2000; Hargreaves, 2000; Jennings & Greenberg, 2009). From an emotional labor standpoint, to the extent that teachers can manage emotions, such that reactivity and negativity are down-regulated and joy and enthusiasm are up-regulated, strong relationships with students and positive classroom climate should be visible.

Jennings and Greenberg (2009) proposed that teachers who are better able to regulate their emotions (e.g., SEC) cultivate warm and supportive relationships with their students by helping them deal effectively with conflict and behave cooperatively and also by being good role models for the kinds of respectful and prosocial behaviors they want their students to learn and exhibit. They are also better able to generate the joy and enthusiasm that create a positive classroom climate and motivate student learning. The authors further propose that these types of teacher actions lead to an "optimal social and emotional climate" that is characterized by observable behaviors, which include low levels of conflict, misbehavior, and off-task behavior; expressions of positive emotions and respectful communications among all members of the classroom; and teachers' ability to quickly respond to and effectively support students' social–emotional and academic needs. Finally, being calm is also thought to underpin another key skill set that can support teachers—the capacity to attend to others with kindness, or prosociality (Eisenberg, Fabes, & Spinrad, 2006), which is discussed following the next section.

Mental Clarity in the Classroom

Classrooms are inherently challenging contexts in which to function, as they can be dynamic, multifaceted, and ambiguous environments. For example, teachers must be consistently and simultaneously attuned not only to the content they are delivering, but also to the needs and behavior of 25–30 unique students. It is posited here that mental clarity is integral to effective classroom management and that changes in teachers' capacity to be clear as a function of mindfulness training might be observable in terms of how teachers carry out this aspect of teaching. Although there are many conceptualizations of what it means to manage a classroom, most have in common establishing and maintaining order (e.g., clear routines, monitoring, and minimizing off-task behavior) and keeping students engaged in the process of learning (Emmer & Stough, 2001).

Keeping in mind the dynamic and fast-paced nature of the classroom, teachers who effectively manage student behavior are clear in their think-ing and perceptions as they consistently monitor the classroom as a whole and recognize student behavior that needs redirection amid all the stimuli present in a classroom at any given time (e.g., alerting, orienting), particu-larly that which might not be the most salient (e.g., off-task, nondisruptive behavior vs. off-task, disruptive behavior). Teachers who are more aware of the ongoing state of the classroom and less prone to distraction may be better able to be proactive rather than reactive in managing student behavior, by addressing misbehavior before it escalates. Teachers who are consistently proactive and clear about their expectations for student behav-ior and who can quickly redirect behavior that violates those expectations with firmness and warmth should be more effective in managing behavior overall (Marzano, Marzano, & Pickering, 2003). Clear expectations and effective redirection also mean that the likelihood of using strategies, such as consequences or punishments for misbehavior, will be less frequent.

Finally, a large part of what teachers do in the classroom on a daily basis is to support students in their engagement with learning, which, as with behavior management, necessitates an awareness of specific students within the larger classroom context who are having difficulty. Often, they need one-on-one attention, during which time the teacher cannot lose sight of what is unfolding in the classroom as a whole. Additionally, supporting these needs sometimes requires teachers to adapt what they know about students, curriculum, and learning "on the fly," which necessitates a clear understanding of the student's issue and accessing and manipulating the information necessary to help solve it.

Interpersonal Kindness in the Classroom

The capacity for kindness influences the ways in which teachers interact with students and one another in the process of building relationships, such that those interactions are characterized by kindness, or attunement to others' needs, as opposed to coercion, or attunement to one's own needs (Skinner & Belmont, 1993). Establishing relationships characterized by kindness and an other-directed focus in the classroom can be challeng-ing for teachers. Students often come to school with emotional states and experiences (e.g., learning difficulties, behavior problems, and trauma) that are difficult for a teacher to see beyond to a student's underlying need state, thereby making it more likely that the teacher's response will be more self-focused and coercive (i.e., "Stop that or else!"), as opposed to other focused and kind (i.e., "Would you tell me what is going on?") (Jennings, 2018). Therefore, empathy and compassion are instrumental for teachers' awareness of students' expressed and unexpressed academic and social–emotional needs, which often involve the need for safety, car-ing, reassurance, or limit setting (Pianta, Mashburn, Downer, Hamre,

& Justice, 2008). Learning how to modulate empathetic reactions and respond to others' distress with compassion should be evident in teachers' behavior and enhanced relationships with students. These relationships should arise as a function of teachers' awareness of students' academic and/or social–emotional needs and effectiveness in addressing those needs in an other-focused way, whether they require academic support or help in managing behavior.

Further, common humanity is posited to foster not only compassion for oneself, but for others as well. If understanding that one's own suffering is part of a common experience of what it means to be human can help one to be more self-compassionate, then, by definition, that compassion can extend to others as well. Additionally, Neff, Kirkpatrick, and Rude (2006) found that self-compassion was related to reduced feelings of anxiety and improved overall psychological well-being for individuals when confronted with threats to self-esteem. Self-compassion therefore can help teachers in their efforts to be more compassionate in their interactions with students, while also promoting resilience. Self-compassion can help teachers to better cope with inevitable failures and setbacks, allowing them to "bounce back" rather than get caught in a negative cycle of rumination and other threats to well-being. Being resilient in this way can be expected to manifest itself in teachers' ability to generate positive affect and enthusiasm in the classroom.

In summary, we believe that teacher mindfulness, conceptualized as both invisible skills and dispositions and their visible manifestation in emotional calm, mental clarity, and social kindness in the classroom, offers one fruitful way to conceptualize the "unnamed domain" of teacher expertise. Furthermore, as we discuss in the next section, there is mounting evidence that such skills, dispositions, and embodied behaviors can be cultivated through teacher mindfulness programs.

Programs and Previous Research

In this section, we describe three teacher mindfulness programs that have shown some promise in cultivating teachers' mindfulness at both the mental and embodied behavioral levels of analysis. We briefly describe each program as well as key research findings that emerge from their evaluation.

Mindfulness–Based Emotional Balance

Mindfulness-Based Emotional Balance (MBEB) is a fully manualized program designed specifically for teachers (Cullen & Pons, 2015). The MBEB program, based on Jon Kabat-Zinn's widespread Mindfulness-Based Stress Reduction (MBSR) program, uses approximately 50% of the same mindfulness meditation and movement practices. About 30% of the program is devoted to emotion theory and mindful emotion regulation. The remaining 20% of the program focuses on the theory and practice of compassion and forgiveness.

MBEB includes explicit instruction on emotions and stress, and on how to use mindfulness to regulate them more effectively (Bishop et al., 2004; Chambers, Gullone, & Allen, 2009) through the teaching of body awareness, focused attention meditation, and open monitoring meditation. The program aims to cultivate more mindful and efficacious emotion regulation through components such as (1) a lecture on emotion, emotion regulation, and how mindfulness can help regulate emotion and reduce stress, rumination, and fatigue; (2) extensive, guided mindfulness practices, including focused attention, open monitoring, and loving-kindness meditations; (3) exercises and homework designed to help teachers explore the "inner geography" of challenging emotions, such as fear and anger in the classroom; and (4) weekly discussions about how such practices are operating in the personal and professional lives of participants.

MBEB also includes a session on forgiveness during which participants are guided through a mindful exploration of forgiveness and lack of forgiveness (called "unforgiveness"). Participants also engage in loving-kindness practice, in which benevolent feelings are silently extended to oneself, to others, and perhaps, to those by whom one feels aggrieved. MBEB concentrates a great deal on cultivating teachers' attitudes of compassion through practices (e.g., compassionate meditation) and through question-and-answer sessions, in which the instructor teaches about and models compassion for oneself and others. Furthermore, the habit of equanimity, which is the ability to be present to positive/neutral/negatively valanced events, is reinforced in each moment of mindfulness practice by instructing participants to relate to their minds, bodies, and social experiences with kind acceptance and curiosity rather than with aversion toward, fixation on, and criticism of oneself or others.

In randomized controlled trials of MBEB, results showed that compared with teachers in the wait-list control condition, teachers who participated in the program showed improvements in mindfulness (e.g., attentional awareness and nonreactivity) and emotion regulation and reductions in occupational stress, burnout, anxiety, and depression at post-program and follow-up (Akiva, Arel, Benn, Eccles, & Roeser, 2011; Roeser et al., 2013). Roeser et al. (2013) also found improvements in sustained attention and working memory among teachers following mindfulness training. In addition, these studies have shown that mindfulness training has an effect on the specific skills and mindsets we discussed, including focused attention, mindful awareness, self-compassion, forgiveness, and reduced work rumination while at home (Crain, Schonert-Reichl, & Roeser, 2017; Roeser et al., 2013, Taylor et al., 2015).

Cultivating Awareness and Resilience in Education

Cultivating Awareness and Resilience in Education (CARE) is a comprehensive professional learning model designed to reduce teachers' stress and to promote and support teachers' social and emotional competences over the course of one full school year. Adhering to best practices in adult learning, CARE introduces material sequentially by utilizing a blend of didactic, experiential, and interactive learning processes. The program presents a structured set of mindful awareness and compassion practices, as well as didactic and experiential practices to promote emotion awareness and emotion regulation. CARE is typically delivered in 30 hours over 5 in-person training days (of 6 hours each) over the course of several weeks. The breaks in between sessions give teachers an opportunity for practice, reflection, and application of the material to their teaching. Teachers typically receive coaching via phone between sessions to support this process.

The efficacy of the program was assessed using a cluster randomized trial design involving 36 urban elementary schools and 224 teachers (Jennings et al., 2017). Teachers were randomized within schools to receive CARE or to be assigned to a wait-list control group. At pre- and postintervention, teachers completed self-report measures and assessments of their participating students. Teachers' classrooms were observed and coded using the Classroom Assessment Scoring System (CLASS; Pianta, La Paro, & Hamre, 2008). CARE had statistically significant direct positive impacts on adaptive emotion regulation, mindfulness, psychological distress, and time urgency, or stress associated with time pressure. CARE also had a statistically significant positive impact on the emotional support domain of the CLASS, which included positive impacts on teacher sensitivity and positive emotional climate. The program also had a positive impact on classroom productivity, or efficient use of classroom time, and had a direct positive impact on student engagement. Among students with low social skills at baseline, students of CARE teachers had higher reading competence at the end of the year than students in the control condition. Among students with teachers low in mindfulness at baseline, students of CARE teachers had higher end-of-year motivation and higher end-of-year reading competence than students of low mindfulness teachers in the control condition, lending support to the notion that teachers' mindfulness played a role in supporting the student outcomes (Brown et al., 2017).

Community Approach to Learning Mindfully

The Community Approach to Learning Mindfully (CALM for Educators) program was developed to provide educators a school-based opportunity to develop and practice mindfulness-based skills for resilience and well-being. The program is offered as an invitational space and time for self-care at the start of the school day, and all teachers and staff are encouraged to attend as often as they like. The CALM program is implemented by trained yoga instructors and not only includes many mindful awareness practices found in other mindfulness-based interventions for educators, but also daily gentle yoga and intentional breathing practices. Because CALM program sessions last only 15–20 minutes, they emphasize accessibility, and they follow a structured and scripted format. Each session opens with a couple of minutes of getting grounded in the present moment through mindful awareness of body and mind, three breaths together, and setting an intention for the practice. This exercise is followed by a breathing practice, which may include breath awareness or an intentional breathing exercise. Then participants engage in gentle yoga movement and revisit the breathing practice. The session closes with a few minutes devoted to a final mindful awareness practice that rotates between relaxation, caring and compassion, and gratitude. The practice ends with setting an intention for the teaching day. Participants are given personal practice cards containing a specific, brief practice to try in the classroom or at home and a reflection on the week's theme.

The CALM program explores 16 weekly conceptual themes that guide the content and are integrated into the intention-setting, breathing, movement, and reflection practices. These themes include concepts like balance, slowing down (nonreactivity), acceptance, gratitude, and joy. For example, in the unit on balance, participants might set an intention for the practice to bring awareness to the muscles that work to balance their bodies while sitting, standing, and moving. They then practice an "even-in–even-out" balanced breathing exercise, focusing on matching the length of their inhalations and exhalations, and explore yoga poses that challenge their balance. A final meditation might include cultivating and/or extending care to someone who brings a balancing energy of joy and laughter to the stress and effort of the school day. The take-home practice for the week includes a reflection on the ways that we can find balance in different aspects of our lives, such as in work or leisure or in stillness or movement.

The CALM program has been evaluated in one trial with 64 participants, in which one middle school served as an implementation group and another middle school served as a wait-list control group (Harris, Jennings, Katz, Abenavoli, & Greenberg, 2016). Teachers and staff in the school who participated in the CALM program developed mindfulness (observing internal and external experience) and distress tolerance (a meta-emotion-regulation skill), and had decreased burnout and physical symptom scores compared to the control school. Compared to the control group, they also improved in their efficacy for classroom management. Benefits of the program were also seen in physiological measures related to stress and well-being, including blood pressure and cortisol functioning. Focus groups emphasized not only the development of more positive methods of dealing with stress, but also a strong sense of relational benefits, such as camaraderie and positive regard, within the community of teachers.

Core Program Practices and Qualitative Illustrations

Each of the programs that have been described introduces core practices that promote calm, clear, and kind teacher behaviors. In the following section, we describe examples of specific practices that promote such embodied teacher attributes, followed by qualitative, anecdotal examples from teachers about how the practices have helped them in the classroom. It is important to note that these teacher mindfulness programs contain similar activities, and we highlight examples from each program, some of which may or may not be unique. The intention is to provide an overview of the types of activities each program offers that may not only cultivate the skills of mindfulness, but also demonstrate how these skills are instantiated in calm, clear, and kind teacher behaviors in the classroom.

Mindfulness-Based Emotional Balance

Calm

The mindfulness meditation practice called the "body scan" is one way that emotion regulation skills and a sense of calm in the body and mind are taught in the MBEB program. The body scan involves drawing attention to awareness through the body from the head to the foot, scanning for how the body is feeling, for sensations that are present, or for any other noticings. This practice can result in attentional focus and calming of the mind and an increase of somatic awareness—a key "front-end" process in emotion regulation, insofar as emotion often arises in the body, and thus somatic awareness can provide early signals that activating emotion regulation strategies (e.g., stopping, pausing). Thus, knowing the body can both be calming and supportive of the awareness needed to regulate emotions mindfully.

Teachers who participated in MBEB were interviewed post-program and asked to describe professional benefits derived from the intervention. With regard to a sense of calm, teachers reported being better able to regulate emotions and practice nonreactivity, to experience the benefits of pausing, and to manage stress more effectively as a result of program participation (Taylor et al., 2017). Nonreactivity and being better able to manage stress were especially salient for several of the early-career teachers in the study:

"I think that I am definitely less prone to get angry quickly. I've noticed myself thinking 'Oh I'm getting angry right now, what do I want to do about that?' Which is really helpful, because I don't just react as much. And I feel like I got a lot of other tools in the class that helped me reflect on that [being reactive] and notice the times that I'm reacting and help me to not be as quick to react."

Often, being calm and clear were described together, particularly in the case of behavior and classroom management, as illustrated in this quote from a teacher of 17 years. The teacher found that learning to pause and manage stress and emotions provided better insight into what was happening in the classroom:

"I think it's helped me to remember to breathe and just remembering to take that moment to pause and not getting so bound up and stressed out in the moment. And to kind of reflect on what am I reacting to and what is really making me angry about things? Certain kids or certain situations. I think it's helped me be able to reflect better on that. Before it [classroom/student behavior] would get out of control, and I would get really stressed and I'd leave the day crying. Now I don't see that it gets to me quite as much—when the kids are unruly, I just take a breath and go okay—I'm able to think it through better and therefore I don't get frustrated with them [students] and feel like I'm yelling at them. And they don't get frustrated with me because I'm always grouchy."

Clear

In the MBEB program, developing mental clarity is accomplished, in part, through an attentional training practice called open monitoring (OM) meditation. In OM meditation attention is directed toward any sensations, feelings, images, and thoughts that arise while maintaining awareness of the phenomenal field of awareness as a nonattached observer (see Lutz, Dunne, & Davidson, 2007). For example, after a period of focus on the breath, teachers are instructed to notice when a thought arises and then label it (e.g., thinking, worrying, planning) and observe what happens to the thought without being carried away by it (Cullen & Pons, 2015). This monitoring cultivates meta-awareness, a kind of reperceiving, de-fusion, or noting, in which one is aware of what is occurring cognitively, emotionally, and somatically, and may even initially react to what is happening, but is not "fused" with such mental contents and processes in ways that lead to automatic and reactive behaviors. Rather, one remains aware and open to new information prior to response. Eventually, through training, the active noting of mental contents moment to moment (e.g., thinking, feelings, visualizing, and perceiving) can cease, and the process of mental noting (e.g., clarity) becomes effortless. At this point, practice has led to an efficient, decreased allotment of attentional resources to any particular feeling, image, or thought, and a concomitant increase in meta-awareness. In this way, perception is clarified, emotional and cognitive reactivity are reduced, and freedom to respond flexibly is increased.

In their interviews, teachers' statements about being clear included experiencing mental clarity with regard to their own experiences with stress, emotions, and choices, but also with regard to having new clarity about their students' needs. This clarity is illustrated in the following quote from a teacher of many challenging students whose behavior affected their learning. Following the training, this teacher was better able to recognize when students needed extra time and space to process issues that were interfering with learning:

> "I feel like I've been less focused or less strict about the priority of academic instruction and learning because sometimes it's like, 'well they're not going to do any math today.' We just need to go take a walk or talk or let them sort of lead the conversation, because sometimes it's just as important to sort of spend that time up front than to always be looking to get through the material. So, I feel like that's been a change."

This second-year teacher discussed program benefits in terms of how they influenced an understanding of, and relationship to stress.

> "This isn't a program that is going to eliminate stress—teaching is stressful and life is stressful and so this is just a way of acknowledging what those triggers are and what those things are that stress you out. It's about knowing that there are going to be stressors and that's okay—that's a normal thing. Just the thought of 'okay well I'm stressing because this is a stressful situation and that's okay. And then I can decide how best to go about dealing with those things in a positive way, rather than having them affect me negatively.' "

Kind

In the MBEB program, the capacity for kindness is cultivated through loving-kindness, forgiveness, and compassion practices. Loving-kindness involves explicit instructions for visualization (imagining others), emotion cultivation (love and forgiveness), and extension of that feeling to the imagined others (Varela, 1999). The cultivation of loving-kindness is based on the idea that all beings wish to be happy (Ricard, 2006; Salzberg, 1999).

This practice is characterized by progressively cultivating loving-kindness toward oneself, a good friend, an acquaintance, a difficult person, all four persons equally, and then gradually toward the entire universe. One visualizes each of these people in turn, and extends good wishes for happiness and freedom from suffering to them. The practice may be experienced more visually, cognitively, or emotionally, and all such states are thought to lead to a greater awareness of others, and perhaps a heartfelt intention for their well-being. Teachers engage with practices in which they extend compassion to themselves and to others in the program (Cullen & Pons, 2015).

The capacity for being kind in the classroom was discussed in several ways by the teachers in the study. Some talked about being better able to understand their students' needs and perspectives and be more accepting of their young adolescent students, and of what it means to be that age. As one teacher commented:

"The kids are awesome. They're kids, even if they're acting like knuckleheads—they're seventh graders, that's perfect."

For this same teacher, these benefits also translated into greater overall happiness and the capacity to be kind in the classroom:

"I have better patience with the kids—the way I talk to them and with them is more compassionate. I feel like I'm just truly happier to see them. Not that I wasn't before, but now the kids will walk in and I'll say 'Hey! How are you! Good to see you, how was your weekend!' I really genuinely want to know. I think that's a huge positive in my book, and it makes me happy to feel happy if that makes sense. So it puts me in an even better mood because it's like 'this is so great, I'm in a great mood.'"

There were also references to how specific compassion and forgiveness practices had impacted how teachers dealt with difficult situations and students, as is seen in this statement from another early career teacher:

"Oh, the loving-kindness thing that we did, that was so helpful. Actually, that student that I was talking about who's challenging—I've consistently done my loving-kindness meditation about that student, and it has helped me so much to be able to have this different relationship with him. We did that long retreat, and we did this loving-kindness meditation and I focused on him. Part of me felt like well, I'm in this different space because I've let go of all the stuff that happened with him and rather than holding it I've just thought 'I'm just going to let it be a new day and just be trying uh to be excited about seeing him and engaging him.' And seeing it as a gift rather than as this negative thing. And I think that has really helped with him."

Cultivating Awareness and Resilience in Education

Calm

A practice that teachers report is very helpful for calming, especially while working in the midst of the sometimes chaotic classroom, is "Three Breaths." This practice involves taking three, slow, diaphragmatic breaths, mindfully attending to the sensation of each breath. During CARE, this practice is used at the start of each session to help everyone calm themselves and to bring themselves to the present moment and be ready for the program to begin. During the program, teachers are taught to check in with how they are feeling and to make this a habit when they are teaching. If they notice that their stress level is climbing, they are encouraged to take the three slow breaths so that they can calm down. In our research, this practice has been reported by teachers to be very helpful, and they used this practice frequently during the course of the entire school year of the research (Schussler, Jennings, Sharp, & Frank, 2016; Schussler et al., 2018).

One of the most powerful ways for teachers to practice and model "calm" in the classroom is through practicing nonreactivity. Teachers who participate in the CARE program learn this skill through engaging in mindful awareness practices and through learning about emotion awareness and their own emotional triggers. By becoming more aware of what these triggers are and, more important, when these triggers are activated, they can regulate their own emotions and help establish a more positive environment for their students. For example, this teacher of almost 20 years notes how CARE helped her to be a model of calm in the classroom. She realized that though she could not change the external circumstances of what was occurring, she did have control over her own approach:

> "I think CARE just helped give me the extra support that I probably wasn't focused on, or probably didn't think about. Most of the time you just react to something. I think whatever I could've been doing I think CARE just brought in that next level to incorporate everything, so that I probably was more [able] . . . to deal with it every day. Not really expecting the child to be too much different, but I could be different."

Similarly, this teacher of less than 10 years modeled nonreactivity for her students, articulating her feelings and her need to pause before responding to a triggering event. It is also worth noting that she acknowledged that the CARE program gave her the permission to take this pause. This is something that a number of teachers expressed—that they began to realize that taking a pause and being nonreactive was both acceptable and beneficial:

> "And I also feel like the other thing that the CARE program has done for me is . . . take that time, focus on myself. . . . Like I said, the guilt, it's okay to process the things the way that you need to process them, take the time that you need to, to calm down from it, even in the moments of the classroom. Allowing that to be a central part of who I am has been a big change, as a result of the CARE program. I feel less on edge about it being important, because I feel like other people are recognizing too that, yes, it is important. So it's okay in those moments to like, take 3 breaths, or tell your students, 'You know what guys, right now I really just need a few moments, because I'm feeling this way,' and it's allowed me to make it a part of my daily life both in school and out of school, that I would not have done before."

Clear

During the CARE program, teachers learn the basic breath-awareness practice to cultivate mental clarity. During this practice, they are instructed to focus their attention on the sensations of the breath, the air going in and out of the nostrils, the air filling their windpipe and lungs, and then feeling the air as it leaves the body. They are instructed to notice when the mind has wandered into thinking or is distracted by sensations and to return the attention to the sensations of the breath in a kind and gentle way. With practice, participants notice that their minds settle, and they feel more mental clarity.

Managing many aspects of the classroom is par for the course for an elementary school teacher, especially in an urban setting where students may have a host of needs that extend beyond academic learning. In responding to a question of how they handle emotions in the classroom, many teachers in the CARE study discussed the need to balance managing the classroom for learning and managing the social–emotional dynamics of the classroom environment. This entails being flexible, as the following teacher describes:

> "Sometimes it does change my routine. Like if there's a student who's going through something I may do something different, just to lighten up the mood, or just to get them back on task or whatever. Definitely whatever is going on with them I'm aware of it and I try to make the situation better, fast."

Other teachers explicitly articulated the need for high academic expectations, coupled with an awareness of and responsiveness to student behaviors stemming from unmet emotional needs:

"Everyone has to be ready for learning, but if they have any emotional issues, if they're sad, you got to try to find out what's wrong right away and take care of it right away, so that your day can be fluid. Once a child, one child, starts something, then it's like a domino effect, the next one does it, 'I was doing it because he's doing it, or she's doing it,' so it has a great effect. The child's emotions have a great effect on how you're going to get through the day."

Teachers who experienced the CARE program were sensitized to the importance of managing both their own and their students' emotions in the classroom. They recognized the dual need to practice emotional self-regulation and to provide tools for their students to address and manage their emotions as well. This emotional self-regulation was critical for creating the space for mental clarity in the classroom.

Kind

During the CARE program, in addition to the loving-kindness or "caring" practices (as they are called in CARE) that have been described, teachers are introduced to a series of mindful listening practices. Mindful listening involves bringing one's full presence to the speaker, holding space for what the person has to say and offering kindness and care during the listening process. It also involves noticing any thoughts, feelings, or judgments that may arise during the listening process and then bringing the attention back to listening with an open heart and an open mind. During this practice, teachers are encouraged to sit side by side, rather than face-to-face, to eliminate the distractions of facial expressions that may inhibit or encourage the speaker. Typically the content of the speaking involves the description of a challenging situation, through which participants learn how powerful, kind, and caring listening can be. This observation by physician Rachel Naomi Remen exemplifies the intention of these practices in cultivating kindness and compassion:

> Perhaps the most important thing we bring to another person is the silence in us, not the sort of silence that is filled with unspoken criticism or hard withdrawal. The sort of silence that is a place of refuge, of rest, of acceptance of someone as they are. We are all hungry for this other silence. It is hard to find. In its presence we can remember something beyond the moment, a strength on which to build a life. Silence is a place of great power and healing. (2001, p. 164)

When teachers become more mindful, acting out of an awareness of their own emotional states and practicing nonreactivity to triggering stimuli, they seem more apt to practice compassion and respond to their students with empathy. Some teachers who completed the CARE program recognized that, in some ways, they had become desensitized to their students' needs, and they sought to change that. For example, one teacher noted, "You're so used to the system, and the status quo you don't realize that you're at a point where you're not connecting with the kids, even though you think you are. You're not connecting with their humanity." As a result of the CARE training, another teacher said:

> "When I did respond to the kids, it was becoming more nurturing, it was becoming more understanding, and becoming more patient. And understanding that, trying to really, really connect with the kids, rather than looking at them as little people. I look at them as a person who, like myself, wanted that attention and really yearned for it and needed it. . . . It did get so much better, so much better."

This teacher became aware of her own needs and the needs of her students. Furthermore, she made it her goal to ensure she was "connecting" and acting compassionately.

Community Approach to Learning Mindfully

Calm

Examples of components within the CALM program that encourage a calm disposition include embodied practices like gentle yoga, specific breathing exercises to facilitate relaxation, and exploration of nonreactivity in body and mind. CALM includes a daily gentle yoga practice preceded by a warm-up sequence that is repeated throughout the program. This sequence of gentle neck stretches, shoulder openers, arm movements, and spinal movements emphasizes the connection of breath and movement and facilitates the development of body awareness. It can be easily repeated in any setting as a way to reconnect with the body and release physical tension. Unit 5 of the CALM program ("Slowing Down") is thematically focused on building skills in nonreactivity by encouraging participants to slow down in body, mind, and breath, by noticing automatic reactions, and by pausing in order to respond mindfully. For example, participants learn and practice "Letting Go Breath," in which they intentionally slow or lengthen their exhalations to experience a physiological calming effect, as the heart rate momentarily slows and the parasympathetic nervous system is activated. They employ this practice again while holding yoga poses and observing their automatic mental, emotional, and physical reactions to the physical challenge, with the intention of increasing the skill of remaining calm in body and mind in moments that are less than comfortable.

Teachers in the CALM program described their experience of

developing skills that helped them exercise nonreactivity. They discussed developing awareness of their own emotions and using breathing as a means of regulating and mitigating emotional triggers:

> "I'm a very calm and patient person, so I normally don't explode when a student does something dumb, but I could say that I probably have a calmer approach to students who aren't doing their work or who are not paying attention, or at least try to be more mindful of how I handle that, the same thing, breathing if you feel yourself getting frustrated, but I don't know, I don't have a good recollection of a good blowup from before CALM, but I feel like I mindfully try to have classroom management."

In addition, for these teachers, skills related to emotion regulation frequently affected their awareness of how they were holding stress in their bodies. They then would take active measures to release this stress, thereby helping them develop calmness in their classrooms. This reaction is not very surprising given the nature of the CALM program, which integrated yoga with intention-setting practices, such as slowing down to respond mindfully rather than reacting automatically. For example, a teacher who said she took child birthing classes for her two children talked about how the breathing that was taught in those classes did not really help her, whereas the body awareness she learned about in CALM proved to be effective:

> "All that was stupid to me [breathing in child birthing class]. But this one was maybe, it worked. It just made me stop, and then I really think, I sit better, I just feel, I actually feel better. If I physically feel better, stresswise, I feel better, like 'Yeah, bring it on, keep doing that, making that poor decision and throw that thing across the room,' you know what I mean? And then I can deal with it in a calmer manner."

For a number of these teachers, breathing and body awareness were the gateway to regulating their emotions and adopting a calm demeanor in their classrooms.

Clear

Although there are many practices in the CALM program to promote mindful awareness, the brief and simple introductory practice that is repeated in each session may be the best example of how CALM promotes clarity of mind. Every CALM practice opens with a few minutes of present-centered awareness ("centering"), wherein participants are guided through transitioning their attention into the room, giving themselves permission to shift their full awareness away from worries and to-do lists and onto the present moment that they have chosen for self-care. They are encouraged to practice the simple act of noticing, without judgment, the physical sensations of the body, their sensory perceptions, and any thoughts, worries, or narratives that are pulling at their attention. They are reminded that it is normal for these distractions and mental occupations to be ever present during the school day, whether they notice them or not, and that they can always use the anchor of the breath to gently reconnect with this clear-minded present-centered awareness.

Teachers' comments about their experience revealed that this type of gentle, present-centered awareness was an essential ingredient of fostering clarity in the classroom. Teachers in the CALM program, especially those who attended more regularly, developed the habit of practicing intentional moments of awareness of their bodies, as well as awareness of their thoughts and intentions. Although the program did not specifically instruct teachers to implement particular practices in the classroom, it encouraged them to take brief moments of mindfulness for self-care and clarity throughout the day. Some teachers who were fine-tuning their sense of awareness became more aware of how they were using time and managing their classroom environment:

> "In class, I mean, every minute matters to me, so I really like, if I have something planned, I really like to get it done. I think more so this year I'm able to, like you said, just breathe, and if the kids are talking, and we really need to get something out, I can breathe and I can lose those 30 seconds. I don't have to account for every second in my class. . . . I don't think it originated with CALM, but I think it's still going because of it."

Reducing teachers' sense of feeling hurried is important for their own well-being, as it can help mitigate emotional exhaustion and burnout. It is also important for creating a classroom environment marked by spaciousness, where student and teacher social–emotional needs are met and learning can occur.

Kind

The primary method through which CALM promotes a kind orientation of the mind is through caring and gratitude practices that hold the self or members of the school community as their focal points. These are not lengthy loving-kindness practices but similarly structured brief practices of just a few minutes. For example, in one session's gratitude practice, teachers call to mind a student who has made their work week easier in some way, perhaps by causing them to laugh, by sharing kind words, or by simply listening. After they recall this experience, they notice any feelings of gratitude or appreciation that arise and shift their focus onto the experience of those feelings. They are then led through spending several breath cycles cultivating that experience of gratitude or appreciation and then imagining extending that gratitude back to the child, whose words or actions invoked it. Gratitude practices and similar caring practices are present in every unit of the CALM program. In addition there are two units of the CALM program with an overarching theme of cultivating gratitude and compassion. By practicing the association of the positive feelings of caring and gratitude with students and other members of the school community, even those with whom teachers have had challenging experiences, the hope is that neural connections begin to develop or be strengthened, whereby they may access a kind orientation more easily during daily classroom interactions.

The qualitative data reinforced the idea that the CALM program encouraged a disposition of kindness from the perspective of gratitude and care for others in the school community. Engaging in gratitude and caring practices fostered positive feelings among participating teachers that some wanted to share with others in the community. For example, one teacher who attended the program somewhat regularly, but not as much as the average participant, extended gratitude to both students and parents:

> "It definitely made me think, okay well, if this person said they were gracious toward me, that made me feel so good and it was so simple. So it made me want to do that more for my students and their parents too, in emails from students to parents and just say, you know, 'Your son or daughter is doing a really awesome job and is excelling. . . . '"

Another teacher, who attended the program regularly, adopted a new perspective as a result of feeling more gratitude, and she tried to share this outlook with one of her administrators:

> "Each morning I stand out in the hallway with the assistant principal, and we often touch base and go over the issues coming up that day, and I have talked to him about this program and about how I'm trying to find the positive in each student and in the situation, because usually when I'm dealing with a student it's over a difficult situation. So I have an opportunity to do that multiple times throughout the day."

By setting an intention to appreciate another, a number of the program participants made efforts to extend this feeling toward others, in essence demonstrating kindness by adopting a positive outlook. As one teacher succinctly said, "I think differently about students now. I'm looking for the positive."

Conclusion

In this chapter, we have proposed that teacher mindfulness, conceptualized as both mental skills and dispositions, and related embodied behaviors in the classroom in the form of emotional calmness, mental and verbal clarity, and behavioral kindness, compassion, and forgiveness, represent an "unnamed domain" of teacher expertise. Furthermore, we have described three unique programs that aim to cultivate mindful skills, dispositions, and behaviors in teachers. The results of preliminary research on these programs suggest that mindfulness is a malleable quality, and that teacher professional-development programs that focus on the cultivation of mindfulness can be helpful in supporting teachers in changing their classroom behavior and practice. Results from randomized controlled trials, as well as anecdotes from the MBEB program for teachers, the CARE program for teachers, and the CALM program for teachers all provide evidence of the malleability of teacher mindfulness and the efficacy of these different approaches to cultivating it.

This research is promising, in that it shows that a key domain of teacher expertise, one that we believe brings together other forms of expertise, namely, content knowledge, pedagogical content knowledge, and developmental knowledge of students in teachers' moment-to-moment behavior in the classroom, can be cultivated. Rather than focusing on only content-rich domains of teacher expertise that have already been named—those associated with subject matter, pedagogical content, and developmental knowledge—we believe that teacher professional-development programs should also focus on the unnamed domain of teacher expertise that refers to the kinds of procedural skills associated with mindfulness as a vehicle for transforming education.

The studies in this chapter examined teacher programs and teacher and classroom outcomes; new research might study whether or not teachers' embodiment of calmness, clarity, and kindness in the classroom is emulated by students and affects their own social–emotional and character development. Research that examines the influence of teacher mindfulness on students is just beginning (e.g., Colaianne et al., 2019).

In our view, the scholarship on teacher mindfulness programs we briefly illustrated suggests two important directions for future research and practice. First, how can mindfulness training be infused into teacher professional development programs focused on content knowledge, pedagogical practices, or understanding the developmental characteristics of students? That is, how can new hybrid programs be designed for both preservice and in-service teachers that focus on both traditional topics as well as the skills of the "unnamed domain" of teacher expertise that may allow teachers to synthesize and embody their expertise in their moment-to-moment interactions with students in the classroom?

A second future direction for this work concerns how mindfulness programs for educators can be scaled and sustained at a level beyond the individual classroom. The relevant unit of analysis in enduring forms of educational transformation, we believe, is the whole school (e.g., Sarason, 1990). Thus, we pose the question of how mindfulness programs can be offered on a wider scale in school systems and in ways that permeate not just an individual teacher's classroom, but all of the interactions in a school within and beyond the classroom that includes principals, counselors, special educators and aides, and other staff?

In summary, we believe that education is necessarily a holistic endeavor that involves educating the whole person. The concept of "good teaching" therefore entails not just imparting and scaffolding students' acquisition of subject matter knowledge, but also the embodied human qualities through which such teaching occurs. Teachers who are calm, clear, and kind as they skillfully teach subject matter may not only foster students' academic development, but also their social, emotional, and moral development. This, we believe, is the kind of education we need in the 21st century to address the global challenges of our times (e.g., Goleman & Senge, 2014).

References

Akiva, T., Arel, S., Benn, R., Eccles, J. S., & Roeser, R. W. (2011, April). *Mindfulness-based professional development for special educators: Participant observation and interview findings from a randomized control pilot study.* Paper presented at the biennial meeting of the Society for Research on Child Development, Montreal, Quebec, Canada.

Bishop, S. R., Lau, M., Shapiro, S., Carlson, L., Anderson, N., Carmody, J., . . . Devins, G. (2004). Mindfulness: A proposed operational definition. *Clinical Psychology: Science and Practice, 11,* 230–241.

Brown, J. L., Jennings, P. A., Cham, H., Rasheed, D., Frank, J. L., Doyle, S., . . . Greenberg, M. T. (2017, March). CARE for Teachers: Direct and mediated effects of a mindfulness-based professional development program for teachers on teachers' and students' social and emotional competencies. In J. Downer (Chair), *Social and emotional learning in educational settings invited symposium: Role of teacher well-being and stress in the classroom.* Paper presented at the Society for Research on Educational Effectiveness Annual Conference, Washington, DC.

Brown, R. C., Simone, G., & Worley, L. (2016). Embodied presence: Contemplative teacher education. In K. A. Schonert-Reichl & R. W. Roeser (Eds.), *Handbook of mindfulness in education* (pp. 207–219). New York: Springer.

Carlson, S. M., Zelazo, P. D., & Faja, S. (2013). Executive function. In P. D. Zelazo (Ed.), *The Oxford handbook of developmental psychology* (Vol. 1, pp. 706–742). New York: Oxford University Press.

CASEL. (2018). What is SEL? Retrieved from *https://casel.org/what-is-sel.*

Chambers, R., Gullone, E., & Allen, N. B. (2009). Mindful emotion regulation: An integrative review. *Clinical Psychology Review, 29*(6), 560–572.

Colaianne, B., Galla, B., & Roeser, R. W. (2019). *Perceptions of mindful teachers and longitudinal change in high school students' mindfulness and self-compassion.* Manuscript submitted for publication.

Costa, A. L., & Kallinick, B. (2011). Describing 16 habits of mind. Retrieved January 1, 2011, from *www.habitsofmindinstitute.org.*

Crain, T. L., Schonert-Reichl, K. A., & Roeser, R. W. (2017). Cultivating teacher mindfulness: Effects of a randomized controlled trial on work, home, and sleep outcomes. *Journal of Occupational Health Psychology, 22*(2), 138–152.

Cullen, M. (2011). Mindfulness-based interventions: An emerging phenomena. *Mindfulness, 2,* 186–193.

Cullen, M., & Pons, G. B. (2015). *The mindfulness-based emotional balance workbook: An eight-week program for improved emotion regulation and resilience.* Oakland, CA: New Harbinger.

Darling-Hammond, L., & Bransford, J. (2007). *Preparing teachers for a changing world: What teachers should learn and be able to do.* San Francisco: Jossey-Bass.

Dottin, E. S. (2009). Professional judgment and dispositions in teacher education. *Teaching and Teacher Education, 25*(1), 83–88.

Eisenberg, N., Fabes, R. A., & Spinrad, T. L. (2006). Prosocial development. In N. Eisenberg (Vol. Ed.) & W. Damon & R. M. Lerner (Series Eds.), *Handbook of child psychology: Vol. 3. Social, emotional, personality development* (6th ed., pp. 646–718). Hoboken, NJ: Wiley.

Emmer, E. T., & Stough, L. M. (2001). Classroom management: A critical part of educational psychology, with implications for teacher education. *Educational Psychologist, 36*(2), 103–112.

Enright, R. D., & Fitzgibbons, R. P. (2000). *Helping clients forgive: An empirical guide for resolving anger and restoring hope.* Washington, DC: American Psychological Association.

Goetz, J. L., Keltner, D., & Simon-Thomas, E. (2010). Compassion: An evolutionary analysis and empirical review. *Psychological Bulletin, 136*(3), 351–374.

Goleman, D., & Senge, P. (2014). *The triple focus: A new approach to education.* Florence, MA: More Than Sound.

Grandey, A. A. (2000). Emotional regulation in the workplace: A new way to conceptualize emotional labor. *Journal of Occupational Health Psychology, 5*(1), 95–110.

Hamre, B. K., & Pianta, R. C. (2001). Early teacher–child relationships and the trajectory of children's school outcomes through eighth grade. *Child Development, 72*(2), 625–638.

Hargreaves, A. (1998). The emotional practice of teaching. *Teaching and Teacher Education, 14*(8), 835–854.

Hargreaves, A. (2000). Mixed emotions: Teachers' perceptions of their interactions with students. *Teaching and Teacher Education, 16*(8), 811–826.

Harris, A. R., Jennings, P. A., Katz, D. A., Abenavoli, R. M., & Greenberg, M. T. (2016). Promoting stress management and well-being in educators: Feasibility and efficacy of the CALM intervention. *Mindfulness, 7,* 143–154.

Hofmann, S. G., Grossman, P., & Hinton, D. E. (2011). Loving-kindness and compassion meditation: Potential for psychological interventions. *Clinical Psychology Review, 31*(7), 1126–1132.

Hölzel, B. K., Lazar, S. W., Gard, T., Schuman-Olivier, Z., Vago, D. R., & Ott, U. (2011). How does mindfulness meditation work?: Proposing mechanisms of action from a conceptual and neural perspective. *Perspectives on Psychological Science, 6*(6), 537–559.

Jennings, P. A. (2018). *The trauma-sensitive classroom: Building resilience with compassionate teaching.* New York: Norton.

Jennings, P. A., Brown, J. L., Frank, J. L., Doyle, S., Oh, Y., Davis, R., A., . . . Greenberg, M. T. (2017). Impacts of the CARE for Teachers program on teachers' social and emotional competence and classroom interactions. *Journal of Educational Psychology, 109,* 1010–1028.

Jennings, P. A., & Frank, J. L. (2015). Inservice preparation for educators. In J. Durlak, C. Domitrovich, R. Weissberg, & T. Gullota (Eds.), *Handbook of social and emotional learning* (pp. 422–437). New York: Guilford Press.

Jennings, P. A., & Greenberg, M. (2009). The prosocial classroom: Teacher social and emotional competence in relation to child and classroom outcomes. *Review of Educational Research, 79,* 491–525.

Kabat-Zinn, J. (1990). *Full catastrophe living: Using the wisdom of your mind and body to face stress, pain, and illness.* New York: Delacorte Press.

Kyriacou, C. (2001). Teacher stress: Directions for future research. *Educational Review, 53*(1), 27–35.

Lutz, A., Dunne, J. D., & Davidson, R. J. (2007). Meditation and the neuroscience of consciousness. In P. Zelazo, M. Moscovitch, & E. Thompson (Eds.), *Cambridge handbook of consciousness* (pp. 499–554). New York: Cambridge University Press.

Marzano, R. J., Marzano, J. S., & Pickering, D. J. (2003). *Classroom management that works.* Alexandra, VA: ASCD.

McCullough, M. E. (2000). Forgiveness as human strength: Theory, measurement, and links to well-being. *Journal of Social and Clinical Psychology, 19*(1), 43–55.

Mind and Life Education Research Network. (2012). Contemplative practices and mental training: Prospects for American education. *Child Development Perspectives, 6,* 146–153.

Neff, K. D., Kirkpatrick, K. L., & Rude, S. S. (2007). Self-compassion and adaptive psychological functioning. *Journal of Research in Personality, 41*(1), 139–154.

Pianta, R. C., La Paro, L., & Hamre, B. K. (2008). *Classroom Assessment Scoring System (CLASS) Manual: K–3.* Baltimore: Brookes.

Pianta, R. C., Mashburn, A. J., Downer, J. T., Hamre, B. K., & Justice, L. (2008). Effects of web-mediated professional development resources on teacher–child interactions in pre-kindergarten classrooms. *Early Childhood Research Quarterly, 23*(4), 431–451.

Ransford, C. R., Greenberg, M. T., Domitrovich, C. E., Small, M., & Jacobson, L. (2009). The role of teachers' psychological experiences and perceptions of curriculum supports on the implementation of a social and emotional learning curriculum. *School Psychology Review, 38*(4), 510–532.

Remen, R. N. (2001). *My grandfather's blessings: Stories of strength, refuge, and belonging.* New York: Riverhead Books.

Reyes, M. R., Brackett, M. A., Rivers, S. E., Elbertson, N. A., & Salovey, P. (2012). The interaction effects of program training, dosage, and implementation quality on targeted student outcomes for the RULER approach to social and emotional learning. *School Psychology Review, 41*(1), 82–99.

Ricard, M. (2006). *Happiness: A guide to developing life's most important skill.* New York: Little, Brown.

Rickert, N. P. (2016). *Teacher mindfulness in the middle school classroom: Reliability and validity of a new scale* [master's thesis]. Retrieved from *https://pdxscholar.library.pdx.edu/open_access_etds/3118.*

Rickert, N. P., Choles, J. R., Saxton, E. A., Skinner, E. A., Mashburn, A. J., & Roeser, R. W. (2018, April). *Middle school student perceptions of teacher mindfulness in the classroom: Impacts on motivational outcomes.* Paper presented at the meeting of the Society for Research on Adolescence, Minneapolis, MN.

Rickert, N. P., Choles, J., Taylor, C., Harrison, J., Pinela, C., Mashburn, A. J., . . . Roeser, R.W. (2016, April). *Teacher mindfulness and student engagement in the classroom.* Poster presented at the biennial meeting of the International Symposium for Contemplative Studies, San Diego, CA.

Rickert, N. P., Skinner, E. A., & Roeser, R. W. (2018). *Development of a multidimensional, multi-informant measure of teacher mindfulness as experienced and expressed in the middle school classroom.* Manuscript submitted for publication.

Rickert, N. P., Taylor, C., Harrison, J., Pinela, C., Saxton, E., Robbeloth, J., . . . Roeser, R. W. (2016, April). *Teacher mindfulness in the classroom.* Paper presented at the biennial meeting of the Society for Research on Adolescence, Baltimore, MD.

Rodgers, C. R., & Raider-Roth, M. B. (2006). Presence in teaching. *Teachers and Teaching: Theory and Practice, 12*(3), 265–287.

Roeser, R. W. (2014). The emergence of mindfulness-based interventions in educational settings. In S. Karabenick & T. Urdan (Eds.), *Motivational interventions* (pp. 379–419). Bingley, UK: Emerald Group.

Roeser, R. W., Schonert-Reichl, K. A., Jha, A., Cullen, M., Wallace, L., Wilensky, R., . . . Harrison, J. (2013). Mindfulness training and reductions in teacher stress and burnout: Results from two randomized, waitlist-control field trials. *Journal of Educational Psychology, 105*(3), 787–804.

Roeser, R. W., Skinner, E., Beers, J., & Jennings, P. A. (2012). Mindfulness training and teachers' professional development: An emerging area of research and practice. *Child Development Perspectives, 6*, 167–173.

Rothbart, M. K., Posner, M. I., & Kieras, J. (2006). Temperament, attention, and the development of self-regulation. In K. McCartney & D. Phillips (Eds.), *Blackwell handbook of early childhood development* (pp. 338–357). Malden, MA: Blackwell.

Salzberg, S. (1999). *A heart as wide as the world: Stories on the path of lovingkindness.* Boston: Shambhala.

Sarason, S. B. (1990). *The predictable failure of educational reform: Can we change course before it's too late?* San Francisco: Jossey-Bass.

Schussler, D. L., Greenberg, M., DeWeese, A. R., Rasheed, D., DeMauro, A., Jennings, P. A., & Brown, J. L. (2018). Stress and release: Case studies of teacher resilience following a mindfulness-based intervention. *American Journal of Education, 125*(1), 1–28.

Schussler, D. L., Jennings, P. A., Sharp, J., & Frank, J. L. (2016). Improving teacher awareness and well-being through CARE: A qualitative analysis of the underlying mechanisms. *Mindfulness, 7*(1), 130–142.

Singer, T., & Lamm, C. (2009). The social neuroscience of empathy. *Annals of the New York Academy of Sciences, 1156*(1), 81–96.

Skinner, E. A., & Belmont, M. J. (1993). Motivation in the classroom: Reciprocal effects of teacher behavior and student engagement across the school year. *Journal of Educational Psychology, 85*(4), 571–581.

Taylor, C. (2016). Conceptualizing the mindful teacher: Examining evidence for mindfulness skills in teachers' classroom speech and behavior [doctoral dissertation]. Retrieved from *http://archives.pdx.edu/ds/psu/18784*.

Taylor, C., Harrison, J., Haimovitz, K., Oberle, E., Thomson, K., Schonert-Reichl, K., & Roeser, R. W. (2015). Examining ways that a mindfulness-based intervention reduces stress in public school teachers: A mixed-methods study. *Mindfulness, 7*(1), 1–15.

Taylor, C., Pinela, C., Mashburn, A. J., Skinner, E., Rickert, N. P., Choles, J. R., & Roeser, R. W. (2017, April). *Qualitative assessment of teacher and classroom impacts of a mindfulness-based intervention for middle school teachers.* Paper presented at the annual meeting of the American Educational Research Association, San Antonio, TX.

Vago, D. R., & Silbersweig, D. A. (2012). Self-awareness, self-regulation, and self-transcendence (S-ART): A framework for understanding the neurobiological mechanisms of mindfulness. *Frontiers in Human Neuroscience, 6,* 296.

Varela, F. J. (1999). *Ethical know-how: Action, wisdom, and cognition.* Stanford, CA: Stanford University Press.

Worthington, E. L. (2010). The new science of forgiveness. In D. Keltner, J. Marsh, & J. A. Smith (Eds.), *The compassionate instinct: The science of human goodness* (pp. 62–71). New York: Norton.

CHAPTER 6

Cultivating Passion for Practicing and Teaching Mindfulness

A Multiple-Case Study
of Compassionate Schools Project Teachers

POLINA P. MISCHENKO
PATRICIA A. JENNINGS

Mindfulness-based interventions (MBIs) in educational contexts have become increasingly popular, as evidenced by this volume, and existing studies of school-based MBIs generally show promising results (for reviews, see Baelen, Esposito, & Galla [Chapter 2, this volume] and Zenner, Herrnleben-Kurz, & Walach, 2014). However, the primarily quantitative outcomes-focused approach does not allow for a more situated and nuanced understanding of the processes and conditions that may affect the outcomes of these studies. To date, no study has explored classroom teachers' buy-in to the delivery of mindfulness-based curricula to schoolchildren, which is likely critical for these curricula to become widely adopted by schools and districts. This chapter presents a case study of elementary school teachers who introduced mindful awareness practices to students as part of the Compassionate Schools Project (CSP) curriculum (Compassionate Schools Project, n.d.). To examine how teachers cultivated a high level of buy-in or "passion" for practicing and teaching mindfulness, we studied three teachers who had no previous formal experience with mindfulness and varying levels of initial program buy-in, but who all presented the curriculum with high fidelity. We document their experiences and introduce a conceptual framework that outlines the necessary internal processes, such as beliefs and emotions, that helped cultivate high-fidelity teachers' passion for practicing and teaching mindfulness and the conditions that enabled these processes to arise.

Teacher Buy-In in Social–Emotional Learning Programs

Considering the lack of research on passion, enthusiasm, buy-in, or related concepts in the implementation of school-based mindfulness programs, the following literature pertains to studies involving social–emotional learning (SEL),[1] such as health and wellness and prevention programs for children and youth. SEL programs are reasonable proxies for mindfulness programs (Lawlor, 2016), because school-based mindfulness programs are essentially SEL programs that use "mindfulness" to deepen the teaching of SEL. Additionally, the SEL field is a useful arena with which to explore the role of teacher buy-in, because skepticism about the effects of SEL programing and uncertainties about the relative importance of SEL in relation to other subjects is not uncommon among school teachers (Buchanan, Gueldner, Tran, & Merrell, 2009; Elias, Bruene-Butler, Blum, & Schuyler, 2000; Reyes, Brackett, Rivers, Elbertson, & Salovey, 2012).

Greenberg, Domitrovich, Graczyk, and Zins (2005) suggest the teacher beliefs may affect the quality of implementation and the effectiveness of SEL prevention programs. To ensure successful programming, they argue that teachers (along with school administrators, support staff, and affected community members) must (1) be aware of a community need, (2) believe that change is a school–community goal, (3) perceive the problem as preventable, and (4) believe the intervention to be effective.

In 2008, Durlak and DuPre completed a review of over 500 quantitative studies on youth health interventions to assess the impact of implementation on program outcomes and of 81 program reports to identify the factors affecting the implementation process. The reviewed studies offered strong evidence that the quality of implementation matters in relation to

---

[1] Social–emotional learning (SEL) has been defined by the Collaborative on Academic and Social and Emotional Learning (CASEL) as "the process through which children and adults acquire and effectively apply the knowledge, attitudes, and skills necessary to understand and manage emotions, set and achieve positive goals, feel and show empathy for others, establish and maintain positive relationships, and make responsible decisions" (CASEL, 2018).

program outcomes. Moreover, provider[2] characteristics, such as a perceived need for the innovation, a belief that the innovation will produce the desired results, self-efficacy, and skill proficiency, have been shown to influence implementation quality. Providers with high levels of these characteristics were found to implement the programs with higher fidelity or higher levels of dosage (Durlak & DuPre, 2008).

A study involving 812 students and 28 teachers from 28 elementary schools suggested that teacher buy-in and openness to programming before implementation is essential for program effectiveness (i.e., improvements in students' social–emotional competencies) (Reyes et al., 2012). Although no main effects of implementation quality (a measure incorporating the instructional coaches' ratings of teacher buy-in and program delivery), training, or dosage were found on program outcomes, the authors reported several interactions. Among high implementation quality (i.e., high initial buy-in, high delivery rating) teachers, those who attended more training or who taught more units of the curriculum, had students who scored significantly higher on social-emotional outcomes. In other words, students who received more instruction from teachers with a consistently high rating of delivery and buy-in did better than those students who received less instruction from teachers of the same caliber. These results may suggest that teachers with high initial buy-in and high curriculum delivery may have benefitted from more training or from implementing more of the curriculum. On the other hand, when teachers with low-initial buy-in and low delivery (i.e., low quality implementors) attended more training and taught more curriculum, students outcomes were actually more negative than those teachers who did not attend the training or taught less of the curriculum. Thus, Reyes et al. (2012) recommend not including teachers with low initial buy-in in SEL training and program delivery, as doing so may result in detrimental outcomes for students.

Although the present study did not examine student outcomes in relation to teacher buy-in, it aimed to clarify our understanding of how buy-in is cultivated among teachers who were considered to be successful at implementing a mindfulness-based curriculum. We decided to study a teacher who was not represented in the research of Reyes et al. (2012)—one who was initially resistant to the program, but was considered (by instructional coaches) to deliver the curriculum with fidelity and quality. We also explored the experiences of two teachers who were passionate about teaching SEL, but did not necessarily buy in to mindfulness, considering that they knew little initially about the concept and practice. Studying teachers with low initial buy-in allowed us to develop a preliminary framework of

---

[2]Providers were nonresearch staff members of community-based organizations (e.g., staff in schools, health clinics, or community coalitions).

the conditions and mechanisms that may play a role in helping teachers to overcome their resistance to teaching mindfulness and/or to cultivate their passion for this craft.

Conceptual Framework

Teacher Passion

The National Board for Professional Teaching Standards stands by its belief in the importance of teacher passion in accomplished teaching. In a validation study of the National Board's vision for accomplished teaching, the researchers assessed whether National Board Certified Teachers (NBCTs) would score significantly higher than non-NBCTs on attributes of expert teaching, such as passion (Smith, Baker, Hattie, & Bond, 2004). Basing the analysis on student reports of their perceptions of how passionate their teacher was about teaching and learning, the researchers found that NBCTs were perceived as more passionate than non-NBCTs, and that student motivation and student self-efficacy were positively correlated with student-reported teacher passion. They concluded that accomplished teaching involves bringing passion to the subject and displaying passion during instruction.

Teachers' perceptions and beliefs regarding education initiatives that they are expected to implement have also been found to play an important role in how well teachers implement them (e.g., Polly et al., 2013; Thibaut, Knipprath, Dehaene, & Depaepe, 2018). Hunzicker (2004) refers to this phenomenon as the "beliefs–behavior connection" (p. 44). Further, a review of research showed that a large number of studies on teacher enthusiasm (e.g., passion) had unambiguously positive effects on student motivation and interest level (Keller, Woolfolk Hoy, Goetz, & Frenzel, 2016)

Passion has been defined and measured in various ways and overlaps with concepts such as "enthusiasm," "enjoyment," and "intrinsic value" in education literature (Keller et al., 2016). For example, Carbonneau, Vallerand, Fernet, and Guay (2008) conceptualized enthusiasm as a "visible sign of passion" (p. 983). Frenzel, Goetz, Lüdtke, Pekrun, and Sutton (2009) suggest that teachers' enjoyment is manifested through *enthusiastic* teaching behaviors. Moreover, valuing something or believing that it is essential or important is intertwined with the conceptualization of passion (Keller et al., 2016). Keller et al.'s (2016) definition of passion includes the importance of emotions and values: "a mixture of positive emotions and commitment toward a subjectively valuable target" (p. 749). In the realm of organizational behavior, Clawson (2011) refers to passion as the highest level of "buy-in" an individual can have. At this level, the individual is energetic and enthusiastic, and believes that the requested task is a priority and will sacrifice time beyond that which is required to accomplish it. In literature on teaching mindfulness, Brandsma (2017) defines passion as "the flame that burns in your heart, supplying you with commitment and intention" (p. 208). Building on these definitions, and in an attempt to encompass the overlapping concepts, passion is viewed here as a *high level of buy-in,* or more specifically as *a mixture of positive emotions, coupled with beliefs, that motivate intention and commitment toward a subjectively valuable target.*

Is Passion a Prerequisite for Teaching Mindfulness?

One may wonder why it is necessary to study the *highest* level of buy-in or passion with regard to teaching mindfulness; why not just study buy-in? In the book *The Mindfulness Teaching Guide: Essential Skills & Competencies for Teaching Mindfulness-Based Interventions,* Brandsma (2017) sees passion as an essential element that a teacher brings to the mindfulness teacher training program. In existing literature on teaching mindfulness or mindfulness teaching competencies, having a passion for the practice and a passion for sharing it with others is typically perceived as a given among teachers (e.g., Kabat-Zinn, 2010). In fact, mindfulness-based interventions were initially led by people who were motivated to teach mindfulness because of a desire to share with others the benefits they had experienced from the practice themselves (Kabat-Zinn, 2010). Although the assessment measure of mindfulness teacher competence does not speak directly to the concept of passion, Crane et al. (2012) refer to the importance of "the energy and motivation" that a teacher brings to mindfulness practice and "the development of perserverance and resolve" to stay with the practice throughout the teaching process (p. 20). They cite Kabat-Zinn (1990) in describing that this "energy and motivation . . . is brought to mindfulness practice as 'commitment, self discipline and intentionality'" (p. 20). The teacher who is committed to, self-disciplined, and intentional in the practice of mindfulness while teaching and who teaches from her own experience of mindfulness, is measured by the instrument and is referred to as "embodiment of mindfulness" (Crane et al., 2012, p. 3). Brandsma (2017) acknowledges the importance of "embodiment" in teaching mindfulness, describing how it is necessary to keep teachers from being blindsided by passion (more on this later), but he pays extra attention to passion as a prerequisite. Moreover, in order to have passion and embodiment one is assumed to have a personal mindfulness practice. This means that teachers are already expected to have personally experienced the effects of mindful awareness practices, be enthusiastic about sharing them, and be committed to practicing them while teaching and outside of the classroom, in other words, to have a high level of buy-in and passion for teaching *and practicing* mindfulness themselves.

This emphasis on teacher passion, embodiment, and personal practice is important to consider given recent trends in school-based MBIs that rely on classroom teachers for implementation. Although most researched school-based MBIs were initially delivered by program developers or other staff who had an extensive background in mindfulness (e.g., Kuyken et al., 2013), newer studies have employed regular classroom teachers with varying levels of background in mindfulness to deliver the programs (e.g., Schonert-Reichl et al., 2015; Broderick et al., 2018). To increase the feasibility and sustainability of these initiatives, researchers question whether teachers can learn and practice alongside students as they deliver mindfulness-based curricula (Schonert-Reichl et al., 2015) and whether more simplistic classroom-based MBIs may require less preparation in mindfulness than formal programs targeting adults (Maloney, Lawlor, Schonert-Reichl, & Whitehead, 2016). Furthermore, the subject of teacher *buy-in* for delivering school-based mindfulness-based programs remains to be empirically explored (Schonert-Reichl & Roeser, 2016).

This chapter aims to approach this gap in literature by exploring how teachers cultivate buy-in or passion for practicing and teaching mindfulness. Next we review the theoretical literature regarding (1) types of passion, (2) the mechanisms (or internal processes, such as beliefs and emotional experiences) of passion or buy-in, and (3) the conditions (external as well as internal) that have been theorized to support teacher buy-in.

Types of Passion

Brandsma (2017) cautions that although passion is a necessity for teaching mindfulness, it can also blind us if we do not also "embody" mindfulness. Vallerand and colleagues (2003) proposed a useful distinction between two types of passion that helps to clarify the type of passion we are referring to in this chapter and that speaks to Brandsma's (2017) word of caution. Vallerand et al. (2003) differentiate between "obsessive passion" and "harmonious passion." Obsessive passion comes from "intrapersonal and/or interpersonal pressure either because certain contingencies are attached to the activity, such as feelings of social acceptance or self-esteem, or because the sense of excitement derived from the activity engagement becomes uncontrollable" (p. 757). Obsessive passion can lead to inflexible persistence and loss of reason and control that results in suffering. When teaching mindfulness, obsessive passion may lead to teachers' inability to be responsive to the students, reacting out of personal bias, unsatisfied desires, or preconceptions. For example, teachers may become frustrated when the lesson does not go the way that they had originally envisioned, they may take personally the disobedience of students, and due to these reasons they may become rigid in their approach to teaching and unable to adapt their teaching to the needs of the students. On the other hand, harmonious passion occurs when "the activity occupies a significant, but not overpowering space in the person's identity and is in harmony with other aspects of the person's life" (p. 757). Harmonious passion promotes the autonomy of choice (rather than social pressure) to engage in the activity and an appreciation of new learning that occurs while engaging in the activity. When teaching mindfulness, harmonious passion can motivate teachers to persist in the teaching, while being responsive, grateful, and not attached to a particular outcome. Responsiveness, gratitude, and nonattachment are qualities that are illustrative of one who embodies mindfulness. Thus, teachers selected for this study not only had high buy-in, but were rated by their instructional coaches as embodying the qualities of mindfulness while teaching. Additionally, the teachers self-reported that curriculum content and mindfulness were in harmony with other aspects of their lives. In other words, for this study we focused on harmonious passion and included teachers who exhibited harmonious, rather than obsessive, passion.

Mechanisms in Cultivating Passion

Vallerand et al. (2003) proposed several essential elements of harmonious passion that could be considered as mechanisms that promote passion. One of these elements is valuing the activity, or finding the activity "very important" for the individual (p. 758). Harmonious passion also includes beliefs such as "The new things I discover with this activity allow me to appreciate it even more; this activity allows me to live memorable experiences; this activity is in harmony with the other activities in my life" (p. 760). In other words, individuals with a harmonious passion believe that the activity aligns with their personal commitments and has a positive, memorable, and personal impact for which they are grateful. Cultivating a belief in the value of the activity, in the alignment of the activity with other personal commitments, and in the personal impact of the activity may be essential to cultivating passion.

In education literature, teachers' motivation to deliver a program effectively seems to rest on their beliefs about the value of the activity and about their own efficacy. Valuing is associated with teachers' belief in the personal value of the activity and the value of the activity for the students (Durlak & DuPre, 2008; Greenberg et al., 2005; Turnbull, 2002). Believing in one's own understanding of and ability to effectively deliver the program (e.g., teaching efficacy) may also play a role in the motivation that teachers have for delivering the program with high quality (Durlak & DuPre, 2008; Turnbull, 2002).

Another essential element of harmonious passion is the individual's enjoyment of the activity and experience of positive emotions during and after the activity (Vallerand et al., 2003). With regard to education, enthusiasm for the subject may be essential in empassioning teachers to teach the subject (Keller et al., 2016). Teacher enthusiasm for subject has been found to be best illustrated by reporting more positively on items such as: "I find my subject exciting and try to convey my enthusiasm to the students; I engage in my subject because I enjoy it; Because engaging in my subject is fun, I wouldn't want to give it up" (Kunter, Frenzel, Nagy, Baumert, & Pekrun, 2011, p. 299).

These beliefs and emotional experiences are theorized elements of passion that are explored in this case study. We also examined the conditions that gave rise to these beliefs and emotional experiences in our informants. Next we review the literature on such conditions as they relate to SEL research.

Conditions Found to Enable Buy-In and Passion in SEL Research

The specific conditions that have been identified as factors that are controllable by program developers or school administrators include teacher participation in program selection; teacher training; support from program developers, staff members, and the school; and administrator buy-in and control over classroom implementation. All of these conditions consistently predicted teacher buy-in to a school reform program, except for teacher participation in program selection and school-level support (Turnbull, 2002). Other research has also supported the value of teacher training for motivating teachers (Greenberg et al., 2005). Training and curriculum delivery have also been found to interact with teacher quality and/or buy-in to predict desired student outcomes (Reyes et al., 2012). Another condition, teacher autonomy, has also been associated with teacher enthusiasm (see Keller et al., 2016). These conditions are directly determined and dependent on decisions made by program developers and school administrators.

Conditions that are not amenable to program developer or administrator directives and actions are also considered in the literature (Keller et al., 2016). They include the conditions of teachers' personal lives (e.g., teacher health or well-being, life and job satisfaction) and student conditions (e.g., student motivation and personal growth, well-behaved classes, and student outcomes). Although these conditions cannot be directly controlled by program developers and administrators, they can be considered in the teacher-recruitment process and indirectly supported by promoting opportunities that may allow for them to occur.

This conceptual framework, which includes our definition of passion, the different types of passion, and the mechanisms and conditions that cultivate passion, drawn from several fields of study, provides a backdrop for our case study. The study aims to refine this framework based on an examination of the mechanisms and conditions that influenced teachers' motivation to practice and teach mindful awareness practices.

Case Study Research Questions

- How do initially inexperienced (in mindfulness) elementary school teachers become passionate about practicing and teaching mindfulness?

- How might an initially resistant elementary school teacher become passionate about practicing and teaching mindfulness?

- What mechanisms, or internal processes, fueled this growth in passion and what conditions enabled the passion to arise and grow?

Methods

This case study focuses on the phenomenon of "teacher passion" in teaching mindful awareness practices to K–5 students through the CSP curriculum. Our informants were three teachers who delivered the mindfulness-based curriculum from three different schools in the same district as part of a large randomized controlled trial of CSP. We used a multiple-case-study approach to explore teachers experiences and confirm or disconfirm the interpretations drawn from individual cases to strengthen the rigor of the study (Yin, 2014).

Project Description and Setting Selection

The study took place in a large city in the southeastern region of the United States within which 23 schools in the district are implementing the CSP curriculum. This project is part of a mayoral initiative to promote compassion in the city, and there is general supportiveness for this work at the city and district levels.

The CSP curriculum is a mindfulness-based SEL program that is taught for 50 minutes per class for two times a week to every student in the school (Compassionate Schools Project, 2017). The curriculum is organized around the Collaborative for Academic, Social and Emotional Learning's (CASEL) social–emotional competencies: self-awareness, self-management, social awareness, relationship management, and responsible decision making (CASEL, 2013). In CSP, social–emotional learning activities are presented from a mindfulness perspective in which mindful awareness practices are integrated. Essential mindfulness-based elements of the lessons include Calming (taking three deep, mindful breaths) and Focusing (mindful listening to a chime) exercises at the beginning of each lesson, Mindful Movement (primarily based on yoga postures and emphasizing connection with the breath and awareness of the body), and Rest at the end of class (accompanied by a breath, body awareness, or visualization practice). Other mindful awareness practices introduced throughout the curriculum are mindful eating, mindful walking, a "Kind Mind Practice" (variations of metta/loving-kindness practice), and the body scan practice.

For each school, two teachers were assigned to deliver the curriculum during the time designated for health and physical education instruction in the school's schedule. Approximately half of these teachers were already working at the school as physical education (P.E.) teachers, and typically had no interest and/or previous experience in mindfulness, while the other half were recruited specifically to deliver this curriculum, because their interest in and/or experience with mindfulness or SEL was part of the basis for being hired. This scenario provided an unusual opportunity to explore buy-in as it related to program implementation quality.

Participant Selection

The results presented here focused on 3 passionate (high buy-in) and high-fidelity teachers out of the 46 teachers who were delivering the CSP curriculum at the time of this study.

Determining Passion (Buy-In)

These teachers were considered passionate about practicing and teaching mindfulness at the time of the interview, as evidenced by their own reported personal practice and their participation in voluntary activities to promote CSP to parents and other staff outside of their required teaching duties.[3] Their passion was also seen as harmonious based on the high rating they received on the fidelity of implementation instrument, especially as it relates to the embodiment of mindfulness in their teaching.

Operationalizing Implementation Fidelity and Quality

We selected these teachers because of their success with delivering the curriculum, as evidenced by reports from their CSP instructional coaches regarding their fidelity of implementation. Although there is a formal implementation fidelity measure, there was no formal archival data on teachers' implementation fidelity scores at the time that participants were selected for this pilot phase, owing to the timing of recruitment. Because of the exploratory nature of this study, the teachers' instructional coaches were asked to provide an overall rating of the teachers as High, Medium, and Low with respect to fidelity on the basis of their weekly classroom observations of the teachers and informal use of the measure. The three teachers in this

---

[3] This information was based on self-reports by these teachers during interviews as well as through informal conversations with instructional coaches and project administrators.

study were selected because they were rated as having High fidelity. Their high scores were later confirmed once they were formally assessed with the implementation measure.

The implementation measure assesses fidelity to curriculum and lesson components *as well as* quality of delivery and classroom management with respect to: (1) Planning, Organization, and Coverage of Curriculum; (2) Lesson Delivery; and (3) Classroom Management. Within Lesson Delivery and Classroom Management, teachers were assessed as to the extent to which they embodied mindfulness and mindfulness qualities throughout their teaching. This instrument does not capture the impacts of the program on student outcomes, and was used only as a tool to select teachers who excel at delivering the curriculum as it was envisioned by program developers. Given the criteria of this assessment tool, implementation fidelity is at times presented as a proxy for quality in this study.

Other Selection Criteria

The teachers were also chosen because of their limited initial experience with mindfulness to better understand the processes and conditions involved in developing passion. The final criteria for selection was that the teachers had different backgrounds with regard to hiring and/or initial buy-in in terms of delivering this curriculum to allow for theoretical contrast across these subgroups (e.g., an existing P.E. teacher vs. one who volunteered to apply). Ms. Jennifer was previously a P.E. teacher at the school and was unexpectedly told by her principal that she would be delivering CSP at the beginning of the year without having applied for the position. Ms. Kathy and Ms. Molly voluntarily applied to deliver CSP and had extensive experience and interest in implementing SEL curricula.

The teachers worked at three different Title I schools. The number of students with free or reduced-price lunch ranged from 74% (Dale Elementary and Ford Elementary) to 89% (Run Elementary). During the interviews, all teachers maintained that their school was ethnically diverse, with white students being a minority at all of them. To ensure confidentiality, the teachers are referred to by the pseudonym: Ms. Molly, Ms. Kathy, and Ms. Jennifer. (See Table 6.1 for participant and school descriptions.)

Professional Learning Workshops

All three teachers participated in weeklong professional learning (PL) workshops each summer before delivering the curriculum. Ms. Molly, a teacher who was part of the initial pilot study received three weeklong workshops, one per summer prior to delivering the curriculum each year. Ms. Kathy and Ms. Jennifer received two weeklong trainings (one for each year of delivery). The first 2 days of the weeklong training integrated the Cultivating

TABLE 6.1. Three Participating Teachers and Their Schools

	Ms. Molly	Ms. Jennifer	Ms. Kathy
Years teaching	> 12 years in schools	> 20 years in schools	14 years homeschooling; > 9 years in schools
Fidelity/quality	High	High	High
Previous experience with mindfulness	No	No	No
Initially interested/hired	Yes	No	Yes
Year delivering the curriculum	Third year	Second year	Second year
School	Run Elem.	Dale Elem.	Ford Elem.
Demographics	82% black; 11% white; 3% Hispanic; 4% other	15% black; 49% white; 26% Hispanic; 10% other	29% black; 28% white; 19% Hispanic; 23% other
Free/reduced lunch	89.2%	74.1%	74.2%

Awareness and Resilience in Education (CARE), a mindfulness-based PL program that included emotion-skills instruction and training in mindful awareness and compassion practices (Jennings et al., 2017) facilitated by program developer Dr. Patricia A. Jennings. The last 3 days focused on curriculum content, lesson delivery, and mindful classroom management. Each year, midyear PL included another half day of the CARE program and a half day of curriculum.

Data Collection

Approval from the University of Virginia Instructional Review Board and the school district and informed teacher consent were received before conducting the study. Participating teachers received $100 as compensation for their time. The Mind and Life Institute 1440 Grant provided funding for the study. Data collection occurred between September and October 2017.

The lead author conducted two semistructured interviews with each teacher (about 1.5–2 hours total). The first interview was conducted in person and focused on gaining insight into the teacher's meaning making of their experience with CSP; the knowledge, skills, beliefs, and values they considered important for CSP teachers to have for successful implementation; their personal areas of growth and challenges as a CSP teacher; and their perspectives on the PL and instructional support they received. The second interview was conducted by phone approximately 1 month after the initial interview for Ms. Molly and Ms. Jennifer. Ms. Kathy, preferred to do both interviews in person, within a 2-day span. The second interview concentrated more deeply on the experiences that influenced teachers' meaning making of mindfulness and their approach to delivering CSP. Interviews were audio-recorded and sent for transcription to a third-party service. Teacher- and school-identifying information were removed to maintain confidentiality.

Validity and Credibility

Although only one data collection method was used in this study, multiple cases were contrasted, and literal and theoretical replication was used to enhance the rigor of the study (Yin, 2014). The prolonged interviews allowed for in-depth understanding of the teachers' experiences. The lead author addressed possible biases in the interview process by eliminating any leading questions and continuously reflecting on ways they may be increasing the reflexive threat[4] (Yin, 2014). During the data analysis phase, the data were reviewed after the final set of codes was developed to search for confirming and disconfirming evidence. Also, the authors engaged in peer review to improve the validity of the findings. Care was taken to establish an audit trail of memos, reflexivity logs, and data analysis to ensure the dependability of the results. Additionally, participants were asked to review a draft report to ensure the accurate reflection of their experience and meaning making.

Data Analysis

We employed elements of the grounded theory approach in our analyses, and the coding system was based on partially emergent and partially *a priori* codes (Corbin & Strauss, 2015). An initial analysis suggested that CSP teachers identified the important components of teaching mindful awareness practices in the CSP curriculum to be teachers' buy-in to the curriculum and mindfulness, their enthusiasm and motivation for their work, and their effort to engage, learn, and practice mindfulness inside and outside

---

[4]The reflexive threat refers to the idea that the researchers' perspectives and behaviors can unknowingly influence the participants' responses or behaviors, which, in turn, may also unknowingly influence the researchers' responses, behaviors, analyses, and future lines of inquiry about the participants.

of the school context. Brandsma's (2017) broad conceptualization of passion as a required characteristic for the effective teaching of mindfulness motivated us to use the construct of teacher passion as the overarching core category for the case study. Data analysis involved reading and reflecting on the interview transcripts, writing memos to explore the codes, and diagramming the processes as well as the relevant conditions under which teachers' passion developed to get a better conceptualization. The lead author conducted segment-by-segment analysis of all three interviews to reduce potential researcher biases and to allow for codes to emerge from the data. This process yielded 22 codes, which were then analyzed and combined into more general analytic concepts.

The foci of this case study were on mechanisms and conditions. Mechanisms are the internal processes that were involved in the development of teachers' passion for practicing and/or teaching mindful awareness practices. Conditions are factors, usually related to the educational context or experience of the teachers, that allowed for these internal processes to occur. The final codes for mechanisms were *belief in personal need, belief in student need, feeling of personal impact, belief in student impact, and feeling of positive emotions.* The final codes for conditions were *previous experience, professional learning, curriculum delivery, curriculum flexibility, personal impact, and student impact.* These codes were created through an iterative process using the software program MAXQDA 12 and written memos.

Results

Development of Passion for Practicing and Teaching Mindfulness

In this section we present teachers' stories in separate narratives to better illustrate how they cultivated a passion for practicing and teaching mindfulness. To emphasize the final mechanisms and conditions depicted in our conceptual framework, we italicize references to these elements throughout the narratives.

Ms. Molly

Although Ms. Molly did not have *prior experience* with mindfulness or teaching mindfulness, she did have a passion for teaching SEL. Early in her career as a kindergarten teacher in a high-needs school she was inspired to teach SEL because of the need she saw for this kind of education for her students:

> "There was like cussing and fighting and just so much lacking in the field of social and emotional skills with this little group that I had, that

I realized right away—before I get into teaching math and teaching reading, we've got to start at ground zero because they didn't know how to relate to me. They didn't know how to relate to each other."

She integrated SEL activities into her classroom, without even knowing the term social–emotional learning, and became fully involved in implementing the district-adopted SEL programs.

She became interested in mindfulness and teaching mindfulness to students when a colleague told her about the CSP project:

"She gave me a little bit of a rundown of what it was and I knew right away—that's my passion. That's what I've always loved teaching—social–emotional skills. And this was just in such a new and different way that it really intrigued me."

Ms. Molly's *belief in the student need* for social–emotional learning was echoed by the CSP curriculum, and her interest was sparked by the mindfulness-based approach. Additionally, her love for teaching social–emotional skills reflects the *feeling of enjoyment* she gets from the process. Even though it meant moving from her favored "home school" to a different school selected to implement CSP, she applied, was accepted, and was invited to join the CSP teacher-preparatory PL workshops.

Ms. Molly's interest in personal mindfulness practice grew from participation in these workshops. She was impressed by the CARE part of the program's emphasis on teacher self-care and moved by the facilitator's encouragement for teachers to practice mindfulness themselves:

"With that encouragement, then it just kind of made sense. It was like I can't ask my kids to do this if I'm myself not doing this. Not only that, it's gonna help me be a better teacher because my reaction time needs help."

Ms. Molly's motivation to practice came from her *belief that it was needed for student success,* as well as from her *belief in a personal professional need* for this practice, recognizing her need to better self-regulate (e.g., "my reaction time needs help").

Once she became involved in delivering CSP and developed her own practice, she was impassioned by the impact that mindfulness had on her students and became convinced of the need students have for mindfulness. Based on her experience, Ms. Molly shared why she thought mindfulness was essential to teach to students:

"What I've seen with mindfulness is it just slows everything down for a second and allows them to stop and think about what they're doing before they're actually doing it, but it's actually putting a name to it, so that we can teach it because just telling someone to calm down and stop and think . . . wasn't really getting the response we wanted to see, but mindfulness skills, I feel like it's actually accomplishing that goal. . . . "

Ms. Molly began to see the unique way that mindfulness skills can help children to thoughtfully respond to situations and calm themselves. When reflecting on her overall experience with *delivering the curriculum*, she said that it was "fulfilling" because she "see[s] it working." Ms. Molly's *belief in the student impact* of her teaching mindfulness reinforced her belief that students need this type of education:

"It's one of the hardest courses I've ever taught . . . but it is by far the most important work I've ever done. So, I think when you weigh those two things out, especially as an educator, if you're a good teacher, then you see the importance of this and you see that this is what our kids really, really need."

This reflection shows Ms. Molly's *belief in the student's need* for CSP, *belief in student improvement* due to CSP, as well as her *belief in a personal professional need* to teach CSP given the assessed importance of the work and her intention to be "a good teacher."

The impact on the students not only motivated Ms. Molly to teach mindfulness, but it also encouraged her to practice it herself. "There's a lot of advantages to me doing this with them. And *actually* doing this with them, and not just facilitating. . . . I've seen what it can do for them, so it's helped me to know how important it is for myself." The *student impact*, she noticed, made her more committed to engage in personal practice, especially while teaching CSP.

Ms. Molly also expressed that just *delivering CSP* has made her aware of the *personal impact of mindfulness practices*, motivated her to practice, and helped her to *feel "empowered"*:

"Before this [I] never did any mindful practices. . . . So, what this has done has kind of opened up my world to the world of mindfulness, and I feel more empowered in my own ability to face [classroom] challenges, because now I do practice on my own mindfulness and I do practice those skills."

Ms. Molly felt that practicing mindfulness helped her feel empowered because she was better able to handle challenges that arise in the classroom. She shared how she believes that mindfulness improved her ability to self-regulate and "hold space" for student self-regulation, or what she called "planned ignoring"; she allowed some student dysregulation to occur, without reacting to it, in order to allow students the time and space to learn how to regulate themselves.

Another motivating personal impact of mindfulness is the role Ms. Molly believes that mindfulness plays in her personal life: "I feel like [mindfulness] allows me to be more connected to people, because it helps me kind of lower my walls that I've built up over time and notice why I've built up those walls, and ask myself why." Ms. Molly felt that her mindfulness practice had helped her to *feel more connected* with others. She also pointed out that "connectedness" is something that is important not only in her personal life, but also in her conceptualization of spirituality. This *feeling of personal impact* in aspects of Ms. Molly's life that she finds meaningful motivates her to commit to mindfulness. Besides practicing while teaching, she reported that she practices meditation and some mindful movement about 15–30 minutes for 5 days every week. She also attends yoga classes every so often and practices meditation sessions with a friend on the weekends. During the first year of the program, she also regularly attended CALM (see Taylor, Jennings, Harris, Schussler, and Roeser, 2018 (Chapter 5, this volume)), which was offered to all schools implementing CSP.

Ms. Kathy

Ms. Kathy had a history of working in the field of special education (SPED) in several elementary schools, drawing heavily on inspirations from her time teaching at a Waldorf School, which is based on an educational philosophy known for its strong emphasis on SEL. Similar to Ms. Molly, Ms. Kathy had also presented SEL programming to non-SPED students at her former school. Additionally, she noted that her experience completing the Lamaze Certified Childbirth Educator Certification Program (Lamaze International, n.d.) and working as a doula helped her "understand the connection between the mind and the body," which is emphasized in the CSP program through mindfulness. Like Ms. Molly, Ms. Kathy was encouraged to apply for the position by a colleague who noticed that her way of teaching aligned with CSP. When Ms. Kathy was asked what drew her to apply for the CSP teacher role, she shared: "This job is pretty much the synthesis of a lot of my own life skills, which really verifies the fact that these life skills are what the kids need." She *believed in the student need* for these types of skills and was thus motivated to teach CSP.

When Ms. Kathy became acquainted with the curriculum she found that CSP was highly aligned with her intentions for education and the skills she believed were essential for her students:

"I have a very different approach to education. . . . I think there should be individualized, project-based education, and the CSP curriculum helps to do that. It helps to give [students] the awareness of their bodies, of their minds, of their emotions, and help[s] them see how they fit together, and how they can be emotional–social beings. . . . There are some other programs out there that try to help, but CSP . . . goes very deep. It goes very deep into thoughts and neuroscience. . . . I appreciate the neuroscience . . . especially."

Ms. Kathy was impassioned by the alignment of the curriculum with her *beliefs regarding student needs*. She was also motivated because she enjoyed being able to be creative while teaching CSP. A unique aspect of CSP is its *flexibility and openness to adaptation* by the teacher based on the needs of the students and the strengths of the teacher. "I love that I have the freedom to change this curriculum around. . . . My biggest asset is just a God-given creativity. And that's also what makes me tick." This flexibility in the curriculum motivated Ms. Kathy to teach mindfulness.

Ms. Kathy was not previously experienced in personal mindfulness practice, but once she learned more about it, she saw the connection between her spiritual practice and mindfulness:

"I see mindfulness as prayer. And the word 'to meditate,' in the Hebrew . . . , it means to mutter, . . . and it means basically to pray. I'm an Evangelical Christian . . . Psalm 1:3 says 'Blessed is the man who meditates on the law of the Lord and he'll be like a tree planted by the rivers of living water.' And so that communion for me in meditation is a communion with my term for God. . . . So I am in the practice of doing that already. So mindfulness was not a big jump for me."

Ms. Kathy's practice includes about 30 minutes of meditation on Bible scripture and prayer each day. Her belief that mindfulness *aligns with her personal spiritual needs* motivated her buy-in to mindfulness. She also shared that mindfulness in her life has evolved beyond prayer as a product of *delivering CSP*.

"I practice mindful eating now. Since the curriculum, I've begun to be aware of eating more mindfully, and drinking, and walking more mindfully. So the curriculum, the expansion of mindfulness into the other areas of my life, has helped to do that."

Ms. Kathy also reported practicing mindful deep-breathing exercises to help her fall asleep, and regularly attending CALM, which is offered at her school. Delivering the curriculum and *seeing the impact of this in her personal life* has motivated her to embrace mindfulness as a daily practice.

Further, Ms. Kathy's beliefs about her *personal professional needs are aligned* with mindfulness. Similar to Ms. Molly, she believed that if teachers were going to teach mindfulness, they had to "embrace the mission" and practice mindfulness themselves. She also saw teaching and practicing mindfulness as the desired direction for her ongoing professional development. "We do a lot of professional development about other things, and they really don't interest me at this stage in my professional growth. Mindfulness is the way in which I want to grow." Even though Ms. Kathy felt her classroom was "kind of mediocre on the mindfulness thing," she admitted that she has improved in classroom management thanks to mindfulness:

"The mindful approach by Tish [Patricia A.] Jennings is something I'm just really working on. . . . How you can distance yourself from behavior and not be affected by it, not lose your temper, start screaming. . . . It's very difficult to describe it, but—I've learned a lot of management."

The desire and asserted *need for mindfulness in her professional life* and the *impact she has seen on her personal learning* thus far sparked Ms. Kathy's passion for personal professional growth in mindfulness.

Delivering the curriculum also made Ms. Kathy eager to continue teaching mindfulness, because of the *impact she believed it had on students* and how that positive outcome made her feel:

"The teacher paycheck is always the kid coming back and saying, 'I loved it Ms. Kathy. . . . You're the best teacher in the whole world, because you're teaching me something I love learning.' . . . Or they come back and they say, 'I taught my mom how to breathe and calm down. And when my parents were having a fight, I went in the other room and breathed.' And they say that, and they're doing it. I think that's the best reward, is that these kids are using what we teach them."

Similar to Ms. Molly, Ms. Kathy felt that the work she was doing with CSP was highly meaningful and *felt fulfilling*. She was so passionate about CSP that even though her school was not going to continue funding CSP after the 2-year trial (and she said she loved working at this school), she was ready to transfer to another school just to keep teaching CSP. "I want to try to transfer to a CSP school. . . . For me it's about teaching this curriculum, not just [at] this school." Ms. Kathy's commitment to staying with CSP demonstrate her unwavering passion and personal professional need for teaching mindfulness.

Ms. Jennifer

Ms. Jennifer was different from the other teachers in that she did not apply for the CSP teacher position. She had been a P.E. teacher at her school for 16 years and saw P.E. as her primary passion. "That's my whole heart, that's what I love," she shared. Not surprisingly, when she was told at the start of the school year that her P.E. curriculum would be replaced by CSP, she was resistant. Ms. Jennifer shared the initial shock that she experienced with colleagues placed in the same position at other schools that were part of the randomized controlled trial:

> "At first, we took offense to it, like we were not teaching the P.E. curriculum correctly. To us we thought, 'Wow, you're just gonna replace it? What we have going on is pretty great here.' Most of the teachers did not even know this until they were already at the training. . . . So then I was like, 'Wait a minute, *I* have to teach a whole different curriculum?' And so no wonder there was no buy-in. . . . "

With no previous experience or knowledge of mindfulness and feeling coerced to teach it, Ms. Jennifer was initially apprehensive about mindfulness and did not buy into the curriculum. However, when asked for three adjectives to describe her experience delivering CSP over the past year, she said it was "inspiring, enjoyable, and hopeful." She clearly had experiences that changed her orientation toward mindfulness and the curriculum.

Similar to the other two teachers, Ms. Jennifer was moved by the *CARE/CSP PL experience*. She reflected on the CARE portion of the workshop:

> "At first, I was like, 'When are we gonna get [the curriculum]?' . . . I was frustrated because we were just doing all this self-stuff and I'm like, 'I can't lay here and do this over and over again.[5] But then [by the end of the training] I was like, 'Well, it feels pretty good now.' So, by the second year, I loved it. I was so excited to see Tish[6] again. . . . "

Even though Ms. Jennifer had not bought into the practices at the outset, the actual experience of the practices changed her attitude toward them. She began to feel the difference that these practices can make and realized how they benefitted her *(feeling of personal impact and of positive emotions)*. Her experience *delivering the curriculum* further fed into her realization that these practices were valuable:

> "Then when I got into the curriculum, I'm like 'This is what I need.' So, I found that I needed it more than the kids needed it at the time. I tell them because they know me as like the P.E. guru, 'Move, exercise.'

---

[5]This is a reference to the body-scan mindfulness practice in which teachers are asked to lie down on mats on the floor (or sit in their chairs) and systematically focus their attention on the sensations in different parts of the body as way to develop body awareness.

[6]The facilitator and program developer, Dr. Patricia A. (Tish) Jennings.

So, I tell them now that this is something I really believe in because it's something I really do and it has really changed me."

Ms. Jennifer's *belief in a personal need* for these practices fueled her commitment to teach them to her students. When asked to elaborate on how the role of delivering CSP affected her personal practice and whether she would have taken up the practices with just the training, she explained:

"I don't know if I would have really had done it for myself if I [had not] continued with the curriculum. . . . The objectives, love of self, self-awareness, when you look at the main objectives of each of the units, because I'm teaching those, I'm being aware for myself. And it's just like teaching anything. You don't know something really until you teach it."

Actually *teaching the curriculum* helped her to realize a *personal need for these practices as well as the impact* of doing them on her self-awareness. One of the main turning points for Jennifer was understanding the importance of love for herself and others:

"It was [based] on just personal experience. . . . That was my big thing was self-love . . . even in the P.E. curriculum. . . . We teach kindness to others—but the kindness to self—it's always been missing. And that's most important, and I realized, wow! I feel like it's a really big need to keep going."

Self-love was something that she considered transformational for herself. *Believing in a personal need* for the curriculum content solidified her *belief of the student need* for it and her motivation to practice and teach it.

She was additionally motivated to start her own practice, because she believed that she needed to do so in order to teach the curriculum. "When I didn't, at first, I thought, 'Oh, I have got to figure this out.' So, I started doing it on my own, especially in the summer off." During the year, she downloaded mindfulness and meditation apps on her cell phone, started attending yoga classes with a friend, and even enrolled in and completed a contemplative healing course, which she thought would help her explore mindfulness more deeply. She regularly engages with mindful awareness practices at least 10 to 15 minutes per day.

The other main turning point for Ms. Jennifer was her awareness that CSP was addressing student needs. "I've seen kids using it and recognizing the need, which I didn't know anything about." Ms. Jennifer came to see a need that she was not aware of previously. She was keen to share the impression it made on her:

"Kids are actually out there using it because now I have teachers come to me and say, 'Oh, you should have seen Kayla, when we were doing map testing, she stopped and took a deep breath' so . . . I'm like, oh, this is great. They're using it."

As a result of hearing these stories, Ms. Jennifer felt that she is doing something valuable. "I mean, I find it very inspiring. I think it's necessary. At first, I was very apprehensive, but getting into the curriculum, I felt the need for it. And now, I would like—I'd like it to go further." This *feeling of inspiration* and *belief in the need* for this curriculum have motivated her intention to keep teaching mindfulness.

Ms. Jennifer also explained how she reconciled her love of P.E. with teaching CSP. She explained that she was able to make it work. "At first, I was very apprehensive because I had a good P.E. program. . . . But now that I've done it, I know that I can do both. I can put a lot of movement in it." Ms. Jennifer *felt motivated* because she could integrate her passion and love for movement into the lessons. This does not mean that she had completely bought into all the mindful awareness practices she was supposed to teach. For example, she was hesitant about the "mindful movement" portion of the curriculum, which included yoga-based postures. "That part, I'm not completely bought-on," she admitted. She said that it was likely due to the fact that it was difficult for her to "be still" and so she usually put a lot of "long planks" and quick movements into the sequences.

Partially though, she appreciated this portion of the curriculum because she *believed it met the needs of kids* who were not typically interested in P.E.:

"The kids that typically didn't like P.E. really love this program. So, therefore, I saw, wow. And ones I didn't even have a whole lot of relationship with, because I couldn't get them to do hardly anything in my P.E. class have just embraced this curriculum. . . . There's one girl in particular that just tells me that she uses all of these things at home. So, then if I just reached that one kid, then that meant that it was enough . . . that it's needed."

This statement shows that Ms. Jennifer was able to overcome some of the dissonance she felt with teaching CSP instead of P.E., because she saw an *impact on students* and *a need* from those students who were not engaged in the traditional gym class.

Additionally, the above statement aligns with a concept that frequently arose in the interviews with Ms. Jennifer: her personal and professional desire to *feel connected* to the students. She was able to satisfy this desire partially because she became more compassionate through the curriculum:

"I've gotten better at allowing kids to express themselves without judgment. . . . I have a lot more sense of empathy and compassion than I did before teaching this curriculum." Additionally, she found the curriculum conducive to developing deep connections. "You can create really great relationships with kids in this curriculum," she shared during one interview. Moreover, she found this process enjoyable:

"I was shocked actually at how much I enjoy [teaching CSP] because now I get to put myself in it, where before, you know, I taught skills, and we taught games, but now I get to show them how these calming breaths and all those things . . . helped my life. So, I get to—and I really—I just find that enjoyable, the kids, to be able to get closer connections with the kids. I find that very enjoyable."

Besides sharing her *feelings of enjoyment* for this work, here she describes how her *feeling of personal impact* helped her *fulfill her personal need* of connecting with her students at a deeper level.

Ms. Jennifer's emphasis on the importance of connection and the benefits of mindfulness for connection was also evident in her spiritual aims. Although raised as a devout Catholic, she sees herself as "more like a spiritual-based person" rather than a religious person, and believes that mindfulness helps her "battle" the "guilt and shame" that is promoted in Catholicism by offering a sense of connection and community with all beings. "I think mindfulness, just being able to stop and meditate, that does allow me to see that there is some sort of energy force around us that kind of connects us as human beings." This alignment between her personal intention of connection with others and mindfulness motivated a positive orientation toward mindfulness.

This was not all that Ms. Jennifer felt she was personally gaining from practicing mindfulness. She also *felt an impact on her personal life,* finding that mindfulness helped her to become more self-aware and helped her get out of "toxic relationships." "I was not as self-aware as I am now but I was ready for that journey too in my life, so it fell to me at the right time." She also said that it was a practice that she used with her own children in helping them resolve conflicts and that they now used mindful awareness practices to help them fall asleep.

It is important to mention that Ms. Jennifer's buy-in to CSP may also be attributable to her *previous experience* as a classroom teacher. As she observed, "I've noticed that those who have been classroom teachers have been able to accept this curriculum and really be enriched from it more so than just the strictly P.E. teachers that were trying to do P.E." She had taught a self-contained special education class for 11 years and spent 1 year teaching a regular fourth-grade class before being invited to be a P.E. teacher because of her passion for health and fitness.

Discussion

The primary goal of the present study was to explore how teachers with no previous experience with mindfulness cultivated their passion (or a high level of buy-in) to practice and teach mindful awareness practices with high fidelity through the CSP curriculum. As SEL interventions often encounter lack of teacher buy-in (e.g., Reyes et al., 2012), this study included one teacher who was initially resistant to delivering the curriculum in order to better understand how one overcomes resistance and becomes impassioned to practice and teach mindfulness. A primarily inductive process brought to the forefront five mechanisms (internal processes) and seven conditions that seemed to be essential to their development of passion (see Figure 6.1).

The internal processes related to the development of passion were *belief in personal need, belief in student need, belief in student impact, belief in personal impact*, and *feeling positive emotions*. Valuing an activity is an essential element of passion, and thus aligns with the teachers' valuing of mindful awareness practices for themselves and for their students as represented by their beliefs (Vallerand et al., 2003). Teachers' belief in the need for personal practice and belief in its impact motivated them to practice and share the practice with their students. Furthermore, the teachers' beliefs about their own mindfulness practice reflects harmonious passion—in that the practice is harmonious with other areas of their life (i.e., personal, professional, and spiritual) and invites appreciation and memorable experiences (Vallerand et al., 2003).

Believing in the student need for and in the student impact of their work was also essential to teacher passion. Becoming a believer in the students' need for mindfulness education was found to be one internal process that motivated these teachers to practice and teach the curriculum with high fidelity (as suggested by Durlak & DuPre, 2008; Greenberg et al., 2005). Seeing and hearing of the positive impact that the practices had on students also fueled their passion. Teachers reported that the experience left them feeling "fulfilled," "inspired," and "rewarded."

The feeling of positive emotions while engaging in the activity aligns with the other essential element of passion, as presented by Vallerand et al. (2003) of liking and enjoying the activity. These high-fidelity teachers experienced the type of enjoyment that motivated them to teach mindfulness and share their enthusiasm with their students (Kunter et al., 2011). They reported enjoying the teaching process and/or how much they love to teach this content. Through their personal practice, teachers also experienced a positive feeling of connectedness either with their students, with other living beings, or with God. The harmonious alignment of mindfulness with their personal and/or spiritual needs manifested through a feeling of connectedness, inspiring the teachers' passion for personal practice.

The results showed that the mechanisms associated with teacher

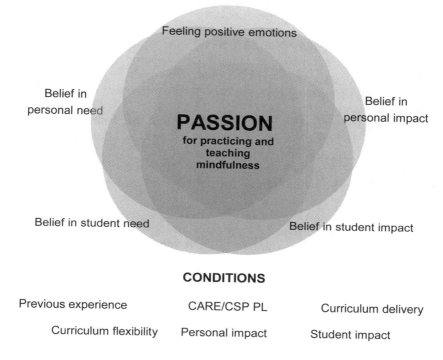

Feeling positive emotions

Belief in
personal need

PASSION
for practicing and
teaching
mindfulness

Belief in
personal impact

Belief in student need

Belief in student impact

CONDITIONS

Previous experience   CARE/CSP PL   Curriculum delivery

Curriculum flexibility   Personal impact   Student impact

FIGURE 6.1. A conceptual framework: Cultivating teacher passion for practicing and teaching mindfulness.

passion for practicing mindfulness and those that cultivate a passion for teaching mindfulness are not mutually exclusive. The mechanisms feed into each other and are reciprocally related. For example, one of the initially bought-in teachers realized a personal need for practice because of the impact she saw that it had on students. However, the belief in student impact also helped her recognize the need students had for mindfulness. To give another example, the teacher who had not initially bought into the program became motivated to teach students and saw the student need only once she believed in the personal need and impact of mindful awareness practices. Further, for all teachers, feelings of positive emotions were derived from their belief in the student impact of their teaching and from the impact they observed the practices having on the students.

A primary finding is that the five mechanisms described in this study played an essential role in the development of these teachers' passion for practicing and teaching mindfulness. This is not to say that there may not have been additional beliefs or different emotions that motivated teachers' commitment to practice and teach. For example, the belief in self-efficacy has been used in studies that measure buy-in (e.g., Turnbull, 2002) and predict implementation quality (e.g., Durlak & DuPre, 2008). However, there was insufficient evidence from the interviews to support that these teachers' belief in their ability to teach mindfulness was one of the roots of their passion. Extending the research to more teachers could help to broaden our understanding of what cultivates teachers' passion and the prevalence of these mechanisms.

With regard to the conditions that surfaced in this multiple-case analysis, the role of previous experience was explored in relation to teacher motivation and success in delivering the curriculum with high fidelity and quality. For some teachers, their experience and passion for teaching SEL motivated them to learn about and teach mindful awareness practices as part of CSP. For another, in the absence of a priori passion, the job requirement of attending the PL workshops motivated the teacher enough to participate in the PL experience. Although in an ideal world, teachers would not be asked to deliver programs without initial buy-in, in reality this scenario happens, especially with SEL programs (e.g., Reyes et al., 2012). Regardless of the reasons, researchers and program developers generally agree that initial teacher buy-in is critical to SEL program success (Greenberg et al., 2005). However, the case of Ms. Jennifer presents a counterexample, showing that an initially resistant teacher can become a successful and passionate implementer. One condition that the results showed to be especially pertinent to changing Ms. Jennifer's orientation toward mindfulness was her positive experience with the initial training component of the program (e.g., CARE/CSP PL).

Professional development workshops can provide a powerful means of motivating teachers to deliver a program successfully (Greenberg et al., 2005; Turnbull, 2002). The trainings were experienced by all teachers as motivating to practice and teach mindfulness. For the initially resistant teacher, the trainings, especially the CARE portion of the PL workshops, which was presented before any implementation occurred, provided an opportunity for her to experience the personal impact of mindfulness and thus realize the need for mindfulness for herself and her students. This result led us to question the suggestion by Reyes et al. (2012) (based on the outcomes of their study on an SEL program) to refrain from training low-buy-in teachers and concentrate instead on teachers who initially bought into the program. However, it is also important to consider the differences between the PL these teachers experienced and the typical SEL PL. Because the CSP teachers were expected to practice mindfulness themselves, their PL was very experiential and mindfulness-based, providing the opportunity for them to experience firsthand the positive impacts of mindful awareness practices and possibly motivating them to want to share them with others. Although teacher SEL has been increasingly considered important for teaching students SEL (Jennings & Greenberg,

2009), the preparatory PL for SEL curricula typically focus more on how to teach SEL, rather than on helping the teachers develop their own social–emotional skills and providing experiential opportunities for them to experience the benefits.

Delivering the curriculum was another condition that motivated teachers' commitment to practicing and teaching CSP. Teacher beliefs relating to the personal need for mindfulness practice and a belief that students need and benefit from mindfulness practice were strengthened through the experience of actually delivering the content. These cases provide support for teachers who have minimal training in mindfulness to effectively teach the practice while learning and practicing it alongside their students.

Curriculum flexibility was also found to be motivating for teachers. Curriculum flexibility is important to teaching mindfulness, because of the expectation that the teacher is responsive to the present moment needs of students (Broderick et al., 2018; Crane et al., 2012). Our study shows that curriculum flexibility, or teacher control over classroom implementation, adds enjoyment to teachers' experiences in teaching mindfulness. This aligns with the association reported between teacher enthusiasm and teaching autonomy (see Keller et al., 2016) and between teacher control over program implementation and teacher buy-in (Turnbull, 2002). Teachers in the present study were motivated to teach mindfulness, because they had a large degree of freedom as to how and when to integrate practices depending on their personal strengths and perceptions of student needs.

In alignment with previous research, we found that it was essential that teachers and students experience the impact of the practices in order for teachers to recognize the need and to believe in the potential benefit of mindfulness for themselves and students, as well as enjoy the process of teaching this content (Keller et al., 2016; Turnbull, 2002; Vallerand et al., 2003). However, unlike the other conditions, "impact" is not something that can be controlled or adjusted by program developers. Although we can provide the opportunities for teachers and students to experience impact, trainers of mindfulness-based PL may have to rely on what Crane et al. (2012) call "trust and confidence in the process" (p. 21)—that the practice will lead to individuals experiencing the benefits.

Limitations and Implications

There are several limitations to this research. Using interviews as the only method of data collection does not allow for triangulation of the results, and thus forces the researchers to rely on the memories, perceptions, and thoughts shared by the teachers. Additionally, interviewing the teachers at several points throughout the time they delivered the curriculum would have helped to obtain a more in-depth understanding of the process by which teachers cultivated passion. Further, these three teachers do not necessarily represent all the high-fidelity teachers delivering CSP, and thus, the results herein cannot necessarily be generalized to all these teachers or others delivering mindfulness-based interventions to elementary school students. The study also does not include teachers with low and middle levels of implementation fidelity, which could have deepened our understanding of the relationship between passion and implementation.

At the same time, the study generates several useful considerations for school-based mindfulness program development and implications for future research aimed at better understanding how to foster teacher passion for delivering mindfulness-based interventions. For one, the study confirms that it is possible for elementary school teachers with no background in mindfulness, and even no initial buy-in to the program, to become empassioned about practicing mindfulness and teaching it with high fidelity and quality. It provides a preliminary conceptual framework that illustrates the mechanisms (internal processes) that were found to promote the participants' passion for teaching mindfulness along with the conditions that enabled those processes to occur.

Some of the more notable results related to the mechanisms include the beneficial role that teachers' passion for personal practice can play in motivating them to share mindfulness with their students. With regard to conditions, this study shows that PL workshops, especially ones focused on teacher mindfulness, such as CARE (Jennings et al., 2017), and curriculum delivery can be potent methods for getting teachers enthusiastic about mindfulness.

However, a more rigorous grounded-theory study of a larger number of teachers could help develop a more robust model. Qualitatively interviewing more teachers could help refine the mechanisms to the ones that are most salient and effective in motivating teachers. Additionally, a more thorough analysis of the conditions could help program developers adjust their recruitment decisions and adapt the conditions they can control to make them more transformative for teachers. For example, it could help elucidate what characterizes a quality mindfulness PL experience and how much of it is needed to influence teachers' buy-in. Further, future research could also explore quantitatively which proposed mechanisms and conditions are predictive of being a high-fidelity and high-quality teacher.

Conclusion

This case study is a starting point for improving our understanding about how teachers with little formal experience in mindfulness become passionate about sharing mindfulness with their students. The study also emphasized the importance of paying attention to teachers' voices and experiences when implementing mindfulness-based curricula. The hope is that by listening to teachers tell us about their experiences we may learn to introduce mindfulness in ways they find meaningful and personally beneficial. Then, their "heart [may overflow] with the need to express what the individual personally experiences as liberating and valuable in the practice" (Brandsma, 2017, pp. 208–209), and they can become motivated to effectively share the practice with their students.

References

Brandsma R. (2017). *The mindfulness teaching guide: Essential skills and competencies for teaching mindfulness-based interventions.* Oakland, CA: New Harbinger.

Broderick, P. C., Frank, J. L., Berrena, E., Schussler, D. L., Kohler, K., Mitra, J., ... Greenberg, M. T. (2018). Evaluating the quality of mindfulness instruction delivered in school settings: Development and validation of a teacher quality observational rating scale. Retrieved from *https://link.springer.com/article/10.1007%2Fs12671-018-0944-x#citeas.*

Buchanan, R., Gueldner, B. A., Tran, O. K., & Merrell, K. W. (2009). Social and emotional learning in classrooms: A survey of teachers' knowledge, perceptions, and practices. *Journal of Applied School Psychology, 25*(2), 187–203.

Carbonneau, N., Vallerand, R. J., Fernet, C., & Guay, F. (2008). The role of passion for teaching in intrapersonal and interpersonal outcomes. *Journal of Educational Psychology, 100*(4), 977–987.

Collaborative for Academic, Social, and Emotional Learning (CASEL). (2013). *2013 CASEL guide: Effective social and emotional learning programs—Preschool and elementary school edition.* Chicago: Author.

Collaborative for Academic, Social, and Emotional Learning (CASEL). (2018). What is SEL? Retrieved from *https://casel.org/what-is-sel.*

Compassionate Schools Project. (2017). *Curriculum overview.* Unpublished training document.

Compassionate Schools Project. (n.d.). Program. Retrieved from *www.compassionschools.org/program.*

Corbin, J., & Strauss, A. (2015). *Basics of qualitative research: Techniques and procedures for developing grounded theory* (4th ed.). Thousand Oaks, CA: SAGE.

Clawson, J. G. (2011). *Level three leadership: Getting below the surface* (5th ed.). Upper Saddle River, NJ: Prentice Hall.

Crane, R. S., Soulsby, J. G., Kuyken, W., Williams, J. M. G., Eames, C., ... Silverton, S. (2012). The Bangor, Exeter and Oxford Mindfulness-based Interventions Teaching Assessment Criteria. Retrieved from *www.mindfulnessbergamo.net/documenti/Mindfulness_Teaching_Assessment_Criteria.pdf.*

Durlak, J. A., & DuPre, E. P. (2008). Implementation matters: A review of research on the influence of implementation on program outcomes and the factors affecting implementation. *American Journal of Community Psychology, 41,* 327–350.

Elias, M. J., Bruene-Butler, L., Blum, L., & Schuyler, T. (2000). Voices from the field: Identifying and overcoming roadblocks to carrying out programs in social and emotional learning/emotional intelligence. *Journal of Educational and Psychological Consultation, 11, 253–272.*

Frenzel, A. C., Goetz, T., Lüdtke, O., Pekrun, R., & Sutton, R. E. (2009). Emotional transmission in the classroom: Exploring the relationship between teacher and student enjoyment. *Journal of Educational Psychology, 101*(3), 705–716.

Greenberg, M. T., Domitrovich, C. E., Graczyk, P. A., & Zins, J. E. (2005). *The study of implementation in school-based preventive interventions: Theory, research, and practice.* Rockville, MD: Center for Mental Health Services, Substance Abuse and Mental Health Services Administration.

Hunzicker, J. (2004). The beliefs-behavior connection: Leading teachers toward change. *Principal, 84*(2), 44–46.

Jennings, P. A., Brown, J. L., Frank, J. L., Doyle, S., Oh, Y., Tanler, R., . . . Greenberg, M. T. (2017). Impacts of the CARE for Teachers program on teachers' social and emotional competence and classroom interactions. *Journal of Educational Psychology, 109,* 1010–1028.

Jennings, P. A., & Greenberg, M. T. (2009). The prosocial classroom: Teacher social and emotional competence in relation to student and classroom outcomes. *Review of Educational Research, 79,* 491–525.

Kabat-Zinn, J. (1990). *Full catastrophe living: Using the wisdom of your body and mind to face stress, pain and illness.* New York: Dell.

Kabat-Zinn, J. (2003). Mindfulness-based interventions in context: Past, present, and future. *Clinical Psychology: Science and Practice, 10,* 144–156.

Kabat-Zinn, J. (2010). Foreward. In D. McCown, D. Reibel, & M. S. Micozzi (Eds.), *Teaching mindfulness: A practical guide for clinians and educations* (pp. ix–xxii). New York: Springer.

Keller, M. M., Woolfolk Hoy, A., Goetz, T., & Frenzel, A. C. (2016). Teacher enthusiasm: Reviewing and redefining a complex construct. *Educational Psychology Review, 28*(4), 743–769.

Kunter, M., Frenzel, A., Nagy, G., Baumert, J., & Pekrun, R. (2011). Teacher enthusiasm: Dimensionality and context specificity. *Contemporary Educational Psychology 36,* 289–301.

Kuyken, W., Weare, K., Obioha, C., Ukoumunne, R. V., Motton, N., Burnett, R., . . . Huppert, F. (2013). Effectiveness of the mindfulness in schools programme: Non-randomised controlled feasibility study. *British Journal of Psychiatry, 203*(2), 126–131.

Lamaze International. (n.d.). About Lamaze. Retrieved from *www.lamaze.org/AboutLamaze.*

Lawlor, M. S. (2016). Mindfulness and social emotional learning (SEL): A conceptual framework. In K. A. Schonert-Reichl & R. W. Roeser (Eds.), *Handbook of mindfulness in education* (pp. 65–80). New York: Springer.

Maloney, J. E., Lawlor, M. S., Schonert-Reichl, K. A., & Whitehead, J. (2016). A mindfulness-based social and emotional learning curriculum for school-aged children: The MindUP program. In K. A. Schonert-Reichl & R. Roeser (Eds.), *Handbook of mindfulness in education* (pp. 313–334). New York: Springer.

Polly, D., McGee, J. R., Wang, C., Lambert, R. G., Pugalee, D. K., & Johnson,

S. (2013). The association between teachers' beliefs, enacted practices, and student learning in mathematics. *The Mathematics Educator, 22*(2), 11–30.

Reyes, M. R., Brackett, M. A., Rivers, S. E., Elbertson, N. A., & Salovey, P. (2012). The interaction effects of program training, dosage, and implementation quality on targeted student outcomes for the RULER approach to social and emotional learning. *School Psychology Review, 41*(1), 82–99.

Schonert-Reichl, K. A., Oberle, E., Lawlor, M. S., Abbott, D., Thomson, K., Oberlander, T. F., & Diamond, A. (2015). Enhancing cognitive and social-emotional development through a simple-to-administer mindfulness-based school program for elementary school children: A randomized controlled trial. *Developmental Psychology, 51*(1), 52–66.

Schonert-Reichl, K. A., & Roeser, R. W. (2016). Mindfulness in education: Introduction and overview of the handbook. In K. A. Schonert-Reichl & R. Roeser (Eds.), *Handbook of mindfulness in education* (pp. 3–16). New York: Springer.

Smith, T. W., Baker, W. K., Hattie, J., & Bond, L. (2004). Chapter 12: A validity study of the certification system of the National Board for Professional Teaching Standards. In R. E. Stake, S. Kushner, L. Ingvarson, & J. A. C. Hattie (Eds.), *Assessing teachers for professional certification: The first decade of the National Board for Professional Teaching Standards* (pp. 345–378). Oxford, UK: Elsevier.

Thibaut, L., Knipprath, H., Dehaene, W., & Depaepe, F. (2018). The influence of teachers' attitudes and school context on instructional practices in integrated STEM education. *Teaching and Teacher Education, 71*, 190–205.

Turnbull, B. (2002). Teacher participation and buy-in: Implications for school reform initiatives. *Learning Environments Research, 5*(3), 235–252.

Vallerand, R. J., Blanchard, C., Mageau, G. A., Koestner, R., Ratelle, C. F., Leonard, M., & Gagné, M. (2003). Les passions de l'âme: On obsessive and harmonious passion. *Journal of Personality and Social Psychology, 85*, 756–767.

Yin, R. K. (2014). *Case study research: Design and methods* (5th ed.). Thousand Oaks, CA: SAGE.

Zenner, C., Herrnleben-Kurz, S., & Walach, H. (2014). Mindfulness-based interventions in schools: A systematic review and meta-analysis. *Frontiers in Psychology, 5*, 1–20.

CHAPTER 7

The School Counselor

Change Agent and Collaborator
for Holistic Student Well-Being

REBECCA L. TADLOCK-MARLO
MEGHAN DAMLER

As collaborators, leaders, and system change agents, school counselors are ideally positioned to spearhead the integration of mindfulness into schools. This chapter explores the roles of school counselors and identifies how they are equipped with unique competencies and skills to situate them as leaders in building bridges across stakeholders to facilitate the entry of mindfulness into schools. This chapter clarifies the role of the school counselor as an instrument of mindful practice and discusses the inimitable skills school counselors can contribute to the transformation of school culture. We include case examples using specific mindfulness exercises within schools and conclude with collaboration initiatives that engage various stakeholders in unifying the integration of mindfulness strategies. Because mindfulness-based programing in elementary, middle, and high schools is an intervention that may simultaneously prevent and remediate student issues, it is a technique school counselors can use to help students achieve academic, personal and/or social, and college and career readiness and success (Deringer, 2017; Klingbeil et al., 2017). Through the use of mindfulness techniques, students can increase their awareness of themselves and others, providing a context of understanding, respectfulness, and valuing both themselves and others, which is central to the vision and mission of school counselors (American School Counselor Association [ASCA], 2014).

The School Counselor's Role

According to the American School Counselor Association (2014), school counselors are change agents and advocates for students, harnessing a belief in the synergistic development of the whole self. Through the roles of advocacy, leadership, collaboration, consultation, and counseling, school counselors foster a constructive learning environment that addresses the needs of all students through programs that are culturally sensitive, comprehensive in design, and developmental in nature, and focus on both prevention and intervention (ASCA, 2012; Lee, 2001).

As critical stakeholders of the educational team, school counselors are charged with helping all students become productive, well-adjusted adults (ASCA, 2018). To safeguard students within this charge, school counselors support students in the areas of academic achievement, personal and social development, as well as college and career readiness. In addition, developing a sense of empathy, respect, and acceptance in students is integrated within this call to action for the work of a school counselor (ASCA, 2014). To be adequately prepared to meet this need, school counselors must be able to implement multifaceted approaches to their roles.

Mindfulness may be one way to satisfy this need within schools, as the techniques offer multifaceted preventative and remedial interventions for student issues. Students can cultivate a more robust ability to meet, manage, and surmount challenging issues as they learn to engage and apply mindfulness practices (Klingbeil et al., 2017). Through the use of mindfulness, students can take ownership of their lives, make sound choices, develop enhanced academic abilities, cultivate stronger social skills, and develop acceptance and appreciation for college and career readiness (Hamiel, 2005; Thompson & Gauntlett-Gilber, 2008).

The Role of Mindfulness

Mindfulness can be comprehensively described as a multidimensional, present-moment awareness intervention that develops self-awareness and compassion (Gehart & McCollum, 2007; Whitfield, 2006). Through this perspective, the personal view of self and the perception of reality are relational, rather than being distinct entities (Nanda, 2009). In this perspective, life struggles that students face are viewed as opportunities to yield personal growth by altering one's relationship between the self and the situation (Cleveland, 2016). Students who face struggles or life stressors are challenged to view the situation from a different perspective, one in which they have greater awareness, and thus greater control over and responsibility for their own responses to the stressors. Through the use of mindfulness, students can suspend judgment of the presenting issue and its consequences and their personal reactions to the issue. By learning to step back from the situation, students can recognize the essence of the problem as distinct from their personhood.

Therefore, students' internal reactions can be conceptualized as the common root of the issues expressed to the school counselor (Whitfield, 2006). Mindfulness practice can be used with students as a model of empowerment, giving them the tool to accept personal responsibility for life situations they can control and to accept events that are beyond their control. Students are taught to confront problems with mindful awareness. Rather than being a static observation, this awareness is a wakeful sensitivity to the experience and internalization of, and reaction to, the presenting issue (Langer & Moldoveanu, 2000). By facilitating self-awareness and acceptance, school counselors help students take ownership of their thoughts, feelings, and actions through the use of tailored mindfulness interventions (Gehart & McCollum, 2007; Nanda, 2009). These mindfulness practices, then in turn, help students understand, embrace, and control their reactions to the issues they face (Cleveland, 2016). This ownership empowers students to self-manage cognitions and feelings rather than be driven in their actions by these thoughts and emotions.

Elementary, middle, and secondary schools are a superlative environment in which to implement and practice mindfulness. School settings are places for learning and development, so it follows that this environment would also be an excellent arena for teaching mindfulness techniques that can enhance everyday life. Since mindfulness practices are recognized as resting within the individual, the interventions are intrinsically portable, pertinent, and applicable to the school context (Kostanski & Hassed, 2008). Mindfulness may be used in schools as both preventative and remediation measures. If students learn mindfulness techniques early in life, they can acquire concentration abilities that advance academic skills, and develop into self-reflective individuals who are appreciative of others' circumstances, and who can fully engage in the college- and career-readiness process. When these students are presented with issues that seem insurmountable, mindfulness can be applied to help them gain centeredness, confidence, self-awareness, and self-control.

Academic Success

A primary role of a school counselor is to support the academic development and success of all students (ASCA, 2014). Many students are often pressed by environmental circumstances at home, in the community, and at school, and find themselves marginalized and unable to adequately cope.

Life stressors, such as parental strife, peer conflicts, or socioeconomic burdens, are brought to the classroom, thereby affecting concentration, initiative, and academic achievement (Harpin, Rossi, Kim, & Swanson, 2016). Now that education systems are zeroing in on closing achievement gaps, mindfulness training may be one way in which students can begin to learn coping and centering techniques to help navigate angst and decrease distractions to more fully engage in academic achievement.

Executive functions, such as concentration, attention, focus, memory, and impulse control, are compulsory for academic success in today's classroom (Thompson, 2018). While students are asked to "pay attention" in classrooms, perhaps more so than in any other environment, they are frequently left without systematic training on how to engage in this practice. Mindfulness has been found to enhance attention, cognitive flexibility, and self-awareness (Moore & Malinowski, 2009). Therefore, if students are taught how to start each day and each class, moment by moment, as balanced, centered, focused, and clear-minded individuals through mindfulness practice, then they can begin to regain control over their lives, choices, connections, and directions. If society seeks students with more cognitive flexibility, or the ability to fluidly and readily switch between different concepts to generate appropriate behavioral responses (Dajani & Uddin, 2015), then they must be instructed in attention training and given opportunities to practice. Because mindfulness is dependent on the channeling of attention on a moment by moment basis, mindfulness training can be seen as directly enhancing cognitive flexibility (Moore & Malinowski, 2009). This enriched cognitive flexibility allows for the mental and emotional freedom to detect incorrect, unbalanced, and unwholesome thoughts that typically leads to mistaken attitudes and emotions, thereby influencing thoughts, behaviors, and actions.

Through the use of mindfulness techniques, such as breathing exercises, present moment awareness, and concentration exercises, students become more mentally focused (Parker, Kupersmidt, Mathis, Scull, & Sims, 2014), resulting in cognitive flexibility, increased academic engagement, and focused performance (Dajani & Uddin, 2015). Currently, mindfulness has been integrated into classroom curricula to advance academic achievement, reduce test anxiety, increase concentration, decrease boredom, promote emotion regulation and prosocial behavior, and reduce mental health problems (Harpin et al., 2016; Parker et al., 2017; Sibinga, Webb, Ghazarian, & Ellen, 2017; Talathi & Mhaske, 2017). When implemented with fidelity, mindfulness has also been found to increase student creativity, bolster student engagement, help students draw innovative conclusions in problem solving, and develop students' ability to self-manage (Deringer, 2017; Talathi & Mhaske, 2017; Thompson, 2018). By advocating for the implementation of mindfulness into the academic curriculum, school counselors help students learn academic material with greater depth, intensity, insight, and application, thereby providing the foundation for academic success (Cleveland, 2016; Deringer, 2017; Flook et al., 2010).

If school counselors extended this training into individual counseling sessions, classroom guidance curricula, and small groups, as well as help teachers infuse mindfulness into the daily curriculum, students could repetitiously engage in mindful awareness practices, which is the ideal recommendation for implementing the practice (Nanda, 2009). Integrating mindfulness practices into both counseling sessions and the classroom fosters collaboration between the counselor and teacher. By providing a leadership role in this collaborative approach and implementing mindfulness in a schoolwide domain, a new path to helping students overcome academic barriers is constructed, providing a gateway to academic success.

Social and Emotional Development

School counselors are social justice advocates who strive to foster the symbiotic social and emotional development of students for unmitigated well-being. Through their multifaceted roles and responsibilities, school counselors help students bolster resiliency, develop coping skills, improve decision-making abilities, and enhance interpersonal relationships to further cultivate a salubrious learning environment for all (ASCA, 2014). Using counseling, collaboration, leadership, and advocacy skills, counselors often use the social–emotional learning (SEL) curriculum to create a welcoming, involved, and compassionate environment for all stakeholders. Mindfulness and social–emotional learning are highly complementary tools that can be integrated by counselors when fostering student well-being in the social and emotional development domain (Lawlor, 2016).

Developmentally, schoolchildren of all ages confront physical, social, emotional, and psychological challenges. In these life-stage transitions, students often face intense emotions from dealing with complex layers of decisions that require advanced coping skills. To navigate this terrain most effectively, school counselors can help students with the use of mindfulness-based interventions infused within the social– emotional curriculum.

The SEL curriculum contains explicit instruction on self-management, social awareness, problem solving, perseverance, and collaboration with others (Harpin et al., 2016). The attention to and application of SEL is burgeoning in the field of education, driven by the ambition to construct a positive environment within school systems. By promoting reflection on thoughts, feelings, and actions, SEL promotes prosocial behaviors that encourage the holistic well-being of students, schools, and society (Velsor, 2009). Because school counselors are specifically trained in social–emotional domains (ASCA, 2014), they have the counseling, leadership, advocacy, and collaboration skills that are paramount in implementing SEL. From this perspective it follows that they can simultaneously use mindfulness as a path to personal and social development through the SEL curriculum.

Having self-compassion and acceptance for the self during the unfolding awareness of emotions, thoughts, and physical reactions are critical elements in mindfulness practice (Carmody, 2009; Gehart & McCollum, 2007). Through mindfulness, individuals learn to practice removing self-judgment in an effort to recognize actual thoughts, feelings, emotions, and physical reactions nonjudgmentally, rather than as intrinsically good or bad (Deringer, 2017; Whitfield, 2006). Therefore, as an individual becomes aware of an emotion, thought, or response, it is vital that she be unautocratic to these aspects of awareness so that personal safety in reflection can be developed (Nanda, 2009). Honoring, recognizing, and unconditionally accepting these aspects of the self help to preclude the intensification of negative thoughts and feelings in behavioral patterns (Deringer, 2017; Harpin et al., 2016). Students may then use mindfulness practices to foster both personal acceptance and compassion for others' situations, which is the very basis of SEL. Learning how to recognize and accept cognitions, emotions, and reactions in an unprejudiced way can help students to develop a sense of appreciation and respect for both the self and others, consequently enriching the school community.

A kind of decentering, or shift in perspective, results for students who cultivate an increased awareness of internal feelings, thoughts, and physical reactions (Lebois et al., 2015; Whitfield, 2006). Decentering is viewed as a process in which individuals step back from an event, reaction, or situation. This process is known as meta-awareness (Bernstein et al., 2015). Creating psychological space from reflexes enables students to not identify as the response, but rather as a person who is feeling the response, which is known as disidentification from experience (Bernstein et al., 2015). By separating one's sense of self from one's emotions, students can be empowered to discontinue rumination and actively minimize the physical stress responses in a previously disconcerting situation, known as reducing reactivity (Bernstein et al., 2015; Talathi & Mhaske, 2017). For example, a student who is angry with a peer after a verbal altercation visits a school counselor, and is clearly emotionally and physically upset. The school counselor can guide the student through the reflection process to identify the triggers that led to the verbal altercation. Once the triggers are identified, the emotions can be labeled and understood by the student. This process allows the student to separate personal emotions from the situation and focus on the underlying emotional triggers that may affect him or her in other life situations. Through this process, the school counselor also teaches students to mindfully respond rather than instantaneously react, further developing students' abilities to self-manage and reflect before acting (Talathi & Mhaske, 2017). The self-reflective loop can help students achieve social and emotional balance.

The SEL curriculum functions to cultivate a safe learning environment for all stakeholders, and mindfulness has been found to help both students and teachers analytically assess social structures and standards (Harpin et al., 2016; Deringer, 2017). By mindfully examining power structures that surround them, students can begin to strive for deeper learning experiences that promote social justice, appreciation, and understanding (Deringer, 2017). To be mindful is to learn to reject prescribed social categories and evaluate constructs on a personal level (Langer, 1992). Helping students learn to mindfully critique socially imposed values, assumptions, and norms is a first step that school counselors can take to promote a more socially just learning environment. Mindfulness practice can cultivate cultural awareness in students by allowing them to be mindful in certain social situations where they can assess social structures. By being mindful in practice toward other cultures, students can see others' viewpoints in highly charged emotional situations. Rather than acting out as a first step, students learn to center, focus, and reflect on another's experience, thereby helping promote social justice and appreciation.

College and Career Readiness

Being college and career ready means that students graduate from rigorous programs that promote the acquisition of both the knowledge and skills necessary to be successful in their postsecondary educational endeavors or career journeys (U.S. Department of Education, 2017). Ensuring that students are prepared for college and the workplace is an increasing concern of school counselors in all grades (Hines & Lemo, 2011). In fact, school counselors are charged with advocating for the success of all students in a course of study that helps ready them for successful college and career ventures (ASCA, 2012). While these entities may be seemingly distinct, the importance of integrating mindfulness into the college and career readiness domain within schools cannot be discounted.

For instance, "soft skills," such as collaboration, self-management, problem solving, teamwork, and perspective taking are highlighted as integral components of career readiness that are not often explicitly taught in higher education that prepares students for the workforce (Handley & Earls, 2014; Ramasubramanian, 2017). The practice and integration of mindfulness into the K–12 curriculum may be an efficient and effective way to bolster these skills for students. Mindfulness is expressed as generating nonjudgmental mind–body awareness in the present moment (Kabat-Zinn, 1990). By bringing attention to a current experience, with an accepting stance, students can learn coping and calming skills that simultaneously build these soft skills (Handley & Earls, 2014; Harpin et al., 2016). Therefore, the need to learn these skills at an earlier age is heightened, so that students may be better equipped for both college and career experiences.

At the primary and middle school levels, college and career readiness is commonly overlooked (Parker & Diaz, 2018). However, this domain is an undeniably crucial area that helps safeguard the development of behaviors and skills required for postsecondary success (Parker & Diaz, 2018). Mindfulness integrated at the elementary level is a preventative measure that school counselors can use in helping students develop the self-compassion, healthy interpersonal relationships, and conflict management strategies needed to be successful in either attending college attendance or in entering the workforce.

Students must graduate high school with the ability to self-regulate, reflect, and be present to be successful in the workplace environment. In fact, research notes that new employees are most commonly dismissed from their jobs owing to poor interpersonal skills, lack of self-management, and underdeveloped conflict-resolution abilities (Handley & Earls, 2014). Teaching, practicing, and helping students implement mindfulness is a way school counselors can address the soft-skill gaps that students face when they transition into the world of work. Through mindfulness training, students can build a steadfast connection among values, beliefs, hopes, dreams, thoughts, and behaviors (Stickler, 2016). By acknowledging the need for these attributes, students can more readily align their future career to the core of their personhood. When a school counselor helps students practice mindfulness, students can acknowledge and develop the hard skills, or training and experiences, needed for success in their chosen vocation, because the soft skills are able to be practiced more readily. For instance, mindfulness provides the mental focus and attention needed for increased cognitive flexibility (Dajani & Uddin, 2015; Moore & Malinowski, 2009). This cognitive flexibility, in turn, allows students to engage in creative thinking, problem solving, self-management, and openness to new ideas, all of which are critical skills needed for career readiness (Stickler, 2016; Talathi & Mhaske, 2017; Thompson, 2018). Students can be more comprehensively prepared for the demands of both college and career by creating and honoring the synergistic balance of both hard and soft skills.

Mindfulness can create a connection between the search for the self and what is a good fit in terms of preparation for college and careers. Mindfulness can offer students a time of deliberate stillness and silence, in which they quiet their mental noise and examine themselves as persons (Ramasubramanian, 2017). By knowing themselves better, students can more readily understand their aspirations, choices, and life directions (Handley & Earls, 2014). In addition, by practicing mindfulness, students are better equipped to cope with academic disappointments in the college search process and bolster the resiliency needed in future careers (Ramasubramanian, 2017).

The convergence of personal, social, academic, college, and career demands and pressures often results in stress and anxiety for students

(Deringer, 2017; Klingbeil et al., 2017). As these demands accumulate for students of all ages, the needs for research-based, flexible, multifaceted skills are needed. When school counselors help students use mindfulness as an instrument to moderate stress, students can develop coping skills, academic resilience, positive and adaptive responses to change, and emotional regulation skills, all of which are needed for college and career success.

Models of Practice

Schools by their nature are institutions for formal education, but they also are an environment in which personal development needs and well-being in individuals are cultivated (Zenner et al., 2014). The social–emotional needs of individuals in schools have driven educators to seek methods of improving school-based learning, while recognizing how social–emotional experiences are largely connected to learning objective outcomes. School counselors are change agents who can assist students in exploring the power of emotion regulation through mindfulness techniques, which will result in students being self-aware, successful adults.

Common Mindfulness Exercises

Concentrated Breathing

There are several mindfulness exercises that can be implemented in the school environment. One prevalent mindfulness exercise is concentrated breathing. This practice brings attention to the breath, observing the breath, and perceiving whether attention has drifted, and if the mind drifts, brings attention back to breath. Mindful breathing can create inner awareness for stronger concentration, deeper self-acceptance, and appreciation for circumstances by being aware of how to be in the present moment without judgment (Flook et al., 2010). School counselors can implement mindful breathing exercises with individual students, small groups, or classroom guidance.

The primary objective in concentrated breathing is to center one's focus on the physical sensation of breathing. The activity starts with students sitting or lying down with their eyes closed; then they are instructed to pay attention to their breath. Students are asked to intentionally feel the movement of their breath. The school counselor asks the students to not alter or adjust their breath but simply to take notice of how it feels. The school counselor then asks them to consider the three parts of breathing: inhaling, exhaling, and the pause in between each breath. There are several different questions to ask during this exercise, such as the following (adapted from Flook et al., 2010):

- "How does your breath feel as you inhale? Is it warm, cold, smooth, choppy, fast, or slow?"
- "Where do you feel this breath in your body? In your nose, belly, chest, or somewhere else?"
- "When exhaling, do you feel relaxed or tense?"
- "How does your exhale breath feel? Is it warm, cold, smooth, choppy, fast, or slow?"
- "What do you notice in the pause taken between your breaths?"
- "Follow the flow and movement of your breath through your whole body and see where it goes and how it feels."

It is recommended that the school counselor discuss the practice with students once the centered breathing exercises are complete. If students are not comfortable verbalizing their experience, they can either draw a picture of or write down how they felt during the exercise.

As students become comfortable in attending to their neutral breath, an awareness of personal control develops, helping them to feel empowered (Deringer, 2017). To practice this breathing exercise with students, it is important to educate them about using the breathing exercise effectively to self-regulate. For instance, first there is a stressor; after recognizing the stressor, the student concentrates on his or her breath. While focusing on breathing, students can check internal feelings and thoughts so they can intentionally deescalate their thoughts and emotions, improving their ability to not automatically react. A student's ability to control his or her emotional reactions creates a sense of empowerment, enabling the student to recognize and diffuse future stressful situations (Deringer, 2017; Harpin et al., 2017; Talathi & Mhaske, 2017).

CASE EXAMPLE

Teachers commonly ask students to meet with their school counselor to work on different techniques for coping with the stress they face, both in and outside the classroom. Students use the deep breathing exercises when dealing with recurring traumatic events that happen in their daily lives. In a specific instance, a middle school student used deep breathing when faced with a situation that triggered her anxiety because of her past experiences of trauma. She struggled with male teachers because of past abuse, but after training in deep breathing she was able to work through this trauma and subsequent anxiety. Focusing on her breath helped this student be mindful of her emotional stability in those moments and helped her to be more self-aware of her triggers.

In another example, a high school student was referred to the school counselor in the beginning of the year for social anxiety. In class, she would get anxious about tests because she felt her peers were judging her. Working together, the school counselor and the student concluded she would need a new tool in her repertoire to use before testing. This student had no previous experience with concentrated breathing. The school counselor walked the student through the concentrated breathing exercise, teaching and modeling the process. The counselor also modeled focusing on the breath with intentionality and mindfulness. Both the student and the school counselor worked together to develop a 2-minute script of 10–12 breaths that she could do at her desk before taking any test. The student started practicing mindful breathing just before taking math tests, and described feeling more present in the moment and more focused on her test and did not worry about her peers. The counselor and student agreed to integrate concentrated breathing before going to the lunchroom and during passing periods as well since she also felt anxiety peak during unstructured settings. Each week, they met to talk about how she used the breathing, and what her reactions were after the concentrating breathing, and to practice in-session so she was ready to use it again in the upcoming week. The student expressed that she immediately saw the difference in her ability to concentrate and a decrease in her felt social anxiety. This student experienced an increase in academic achievement, as she integrated concentrated breathing before exams, and more fulfilling peer relationships as a result of decreased anxiety in unstructured situations.

Progressive Muscle Relaxation

Progressive muscle relaxation (PRM) is a mindfulness practice that involves tensing and relaxing muscles. The school counselor guides students to take deep breaths while tensing muscles for a few seconds and then releasing them (Rausch, Gramling, & Auerbach, 2006). The students focus on the difference between tensed and relaxed states within the body. This exercise has been found to help reduce anxiety, regulate emotions, processes trauma, and provide a sense of self-management in students (Deringer, 2017; Rausch et al., 2006). School counselors can use this mindfulness technique specifically to work with students who have high anxiety related to academics. This technique is specifically useful before standardized testing when student anxiety can be high.

The exercise reduces anxiety by calming the mind and body and can be easily introduced in the classroom, in individual counseling, or at home. For instance, students can tense their muscles at many different times during the day when feeling anxious without causing distractions to other students. This exercise can be practiced at their desks right before taking a test by making a fist under their desks, relaxing, concentrating on their breath, and focusing on their thoughts.

During classroom guidance time, a school counselor can invite students to find a place on the floor to lie down, or they can remain seated. The lights are turned off, and relaxing music is played in the background. Once the students are ready, the school counselor slowly leads them through PMR, reading a script, or reciting it from memory. An example of a script that can be read (adapted from Bourne, 2011) includes:

"Take a deep breath, filling up your belly, and hold it for a few seconds [count out loud slowly, 1, 2, 3]. Now exhale slowly [count out loud, 1, 2, 3]. Let's do that again, inhale; exhale. This time when we breathe, notice how your stomach rises as your lungs fill up with air. When you breathe out, envision the tension and stress in your body flow out on the air. Feel how your body relaxes as the tension floats away on the exhale breath. As we go through each step, remember to keep breathing deeply. Now raise your eyebrows as high as possible. [Hold for 3 seconds.] Let your eyebrows release and relax; feel that tension float away. Now give a big smile, making your mouth and cheeks as tense as you can. [Hold for 3 seconds.] Let your smile relax and fade, feeling the ease in your face. [Pause for about 5 seconds.] Now squint your eyelid shut tight, [hold for 3 seconds], and relax your face. Gently and smoothly bring your head back like you were looking at the ceiling. [Hold for 3 seconds.] Now bring your head back to where it was and feel the stress release from your neck. Let's take a second to feel the relaxed weight of your head and neck. Breathe in, 1, 2, 3; and breathe out, 1, 2, 3. Any stress you notice breathe it in and collect it, and breathe it out. Now, clench both fists firmly and without straining. [Hold for 3 seconds.]. Slowly release both hands and allow the tension to be let go. [Pause for 6 seconds.] Flex both biceps and allow the tension to build up in the muscles. [Hold for 3 seconds.] Release both arms, and feel the limpness of the muscles as the strain leaves your body. Let's tighten the triceps now by slowly and smoothly extending both arms out and locking your elbows. [Hold for 3seconds.] Let's take a second to feel the relaxed weight of your arms and hands. Breathe in, 1, 2, 3; and breathe out, 1, 2, 3. Any stress you notice breathe in and collect it, and breathe it out."

Through the tension and relaxation of muscles, students can focus attention on their body and help to bring a sense of calm over their emotions. Students tend to use the fist clenching at their desks because it is not usually noticeable, but it allows them to feel both tension and relaxation, become self-aware of their emotions, and take the time needed to control their reactions and emotional outbursts.

CASE EXAMPLES

In elementary classrooms, teachers are constantly tasked with working with students who have difficulty paying attention. In one case, the school counselor met individually with a kindergartner who had a hard time paying attention without fidgeting, getting out of his seat, and showing high levels of impulsivity. There are several interventions for students who fidget, many involving physical items, such as fidget spinners, that often cause disputes with other students in the classroom. For this child, the fidget spinner and other tools were not effective in helping to him self-regulate and focus, so the counselor tried something different. Once a week, he came to the school counselor's office, and they worked through a PMR practice focusing on the tension and relaxation of his hands and his feet, the areas he struggled with regulating. The practice was short and age appropriate, tailored to his need to focus. However, each week the school counselor made the practice a little longer, and she added modeling of concentrated breathing to the practice to help extend his focus time. When the counselor saw the student in guidance lessons, she reminded him of their "tension in our hands," "feet stand still," and "we take deep breaths" exercises. As the year progressed and the student continued practicing, the teacher observed a marked decline in his fidgeting behavior and an increase in the time he stayed in his seat without reminders. For this student, PMR was used as a foundation for success in his future years in school.

In another instance, with the support of a school counselor, a group of junior high girls were able to learn, practice, and implement PMR to become more self-aware and gain empowerment over their emotions. Together the group set a goal of becoming mindful of their words and actions in response to situations with their peers to promote healthier social relationships. During the group check-in, each member shared experiences from that week, including how they were able to control their reactions in situations by using PMR. After the discussion, the school counselor led members through a new PMR practice. She dimmed the lights, put on relaxing music, and instructed the members to focus on the experience as she led the practice. At the end of the exercise, each student reflected on how she felt through the PMR and how using it helped calm her anger, build stronger social relationships, and understand her emotional reactions to social situations. The students' teachers also noted that these girls had less need for conflict mediation.

Reoccurring Experiential Descriptions

Throughout the year, school counselors meet with students who have continuous negative thoughts, such as self-criticism and rumination on perceived personality flaws.

Given that such continuous negative thoughts can lead to serious emotional disturbance and mental health issues, helping students to become more self-aware of these thoughts and corresponding emotions and to focus instead on character strengths and positive qualities could help them achieve well-being. An exercise called "reoccurring experiential descriptions" helps students process their thoughts and emotions in a mindful way. A school counselor asks the student to describe his or her thoughts and emotions that arise any time an emotion-evoking experience occurs (Kerr, Josyula, & Littenberg, 2011). Through the use of reoccurring experiential descriptions, students can develop a more accepting sense of self by desensitizing the power and influence of such reactions (Tadlock-Marlo, 2011). By teaching students to observe experiences without impulsively reacting or engaging in negative self-talk, a reoccurring experiential description exercise may decrease everyday negative reactivity (Kerr et al., 2011).

This exercise allows students to simply observe themselves in certain experiences and to remember that they can control their impulsive reactions to these experiences. It can be described as "reperceiving," which involves a shift in perspective (Lebois et al., 2016; Shapiro, Carlson, Astin, & Freedman, 2006). Instead of being drawn into a situation that cannot be controlled and reacting emotionally, the individual can withdraw and objectively witness the situation, which changes the way she or he reacts. Reperceiving allows students to observe the situation, discriminate the self from his or her emotions, and simply be with the emotions instead of being controlled by them. Unlike the concept of decentering, reperceiving focuses on dis-identifying from thoughts, feelings, and reactions as they come about, and not necessarily on reducing emotional reactivity in the moment (Bernstein et al., 2015). In school counseling, reperceiving can be used to help students identify problems they can and cannot control and focus instead on how to stand back from the situation to gain an awareness of self.

Reoccurring experiential descriptions and reperceiving can be useful for school counselors who work with students who have experienced trauma (Boyd, Lanius, & McKinnon, 2018; Hamiel, 2005). These individuals often have a myriad of symptoms, including cognitive intrusions, distorted perceptions of reality, negative alterations in cognitions and mood, inattention, and decreased self-regulation (Boyd et al., 2018; Dass-Brailsford, 2007; Hamiel, 2005). When students are not able to regulate their emotions as a result of experiencing triggers to traumatic experience, they often react in problematic ways, which can cause disciplinary issues within the classroom. Specifically, younger students often do not understand their emotions, and when compounded with a trauma mindset, they can react to situations very differently from a student who has not experienced trauma (Boyd et al., 2018; Hamiel, 2005). For instance, when a nonthreatening event is experienced, such as a teacher raising his or her voice to get the attention of the class, a student who has experienced trauma will be mobilized to either run from or fight the threat by hiding under the desk, leaving the classroom without permission, or yelling at the teacher. This reaction can seem out of place, over the top, or rude when taken out of the context of the trauma. For a traumatized child, something as simple as the teacher raising his or her voice can trigger his or her problematic emotional reaction

School counselors are afforded the opportunity to meet with students who have experienced an adverse response to a situation. Reoccurring experiential descriptions can be implemented with students who have current or past concerns or situations to which they strongly react, including those focusing on traumatic issues. When meeting one on one, the school counselor asks the student to share exactly how he or she felt in the moment to cause the behavioral reaction in order to give the student an opportunity to practice mindfully accepting the feelings involved with the reaction. After the student expresses both the feelings and the negative thoughts he or she experienced, the school counselor works with the student to interrupt automatic maladaptive emotions. This interruption allows the student to become less controlled by the emotions and thoughts that arise in that moment and then, in turn, be less likely to impulsively react as a result of the emotion (Shapiro et al., 2006).

Diving deep into these moments with a student allows him or her to recognize that there can be a lack of control over certain situations, but that the student can have full control over his or her reactions (emotions) by taking time to practice reperceiving. This time also allows for strength building with the student to create self-awareness. The school counselor facilitates the process of the student taking him- or herself out of that moment, so the individual can see it from an experiential viewpoint. Therefore, the next time the situation arises, the student is able to better understand the emotions associated with the situation and control or moderate his or her reactions.

CASE EXAMPLES

Reoccurring experiential descriptions is a versatile exercise that can be used with students of all ages. Using this technique with elementary and middle school students can be difficult because they have not yet developed the ability to consistently observe themselves creating negative self-talk and may react automatically without thinking about what is happening. However, with the skillful guidance of a counselor, even young students can begin to develop this skill, as evidenced by the following example.

A school counselor worked individually with an elementary student who struggled with negative thoughts and reactions to both peers and teachers. He had an extensive history of abuse and family violence in the home. When he received consequences in class for inappropriate behavior, he lashed out and then hid under his desk and cried. Through the use of the reoccurring experiential descriptions exercise, the school counselor and child worked on processing what he was thinking in the moments in which he lashed out at the teacher. The school counselor asked him to step out of the moment and look at it from an experiential standpoint. Using developmentally appropriate language that he could relate to, the school counselor walked through the experience together with him to discuss his thoughts during those heightened emotional moments. Rather than telling him that his feelings were not valid, the school counselor discussed with the student how he can control his reactions by understanding the trigger. Over time, using mindful breathing combined with reoccurring experiential descriptions, the counselor and the student worked through the residual effects of the abuse and how it played a role in his reactions when he received consequences in the classroom. Through this practice, he processed how he could control his emotional reactions and understand that the consequences were not meant to harm him, but to help him grow as a student.

The reoccurring emotional descriptions exercise was introduced to a small group of fifth-grade students who struggled with controlling emotional reactions owing to negative self-talk and a lack of self-awareness. Each student was allowed the opportunity to share the "moment" when he or she reacted negatively during the previous week. The school counselor and students then examined the event to determine what the student could and could not control in the situation. Students then described what it would be like to simply observe without reacting and discussed what other outcomes might be possible. Throughout the group session, students reported that the practice resulted in personal empowerment. Through personal observations, these students built resilience and expressed greater self-worth after learning and applying mindfulness in this way.

Mindfulness Programs for K–12 Students

Recently, several mindfulness-based curricula for students have been developed. These curricula include mindfulness foundations with conjoint recommendations from both educators and researchers who are proficient in the field of mindfulness (see Baelen, Esposito, & Galla, Chapter 2, this volume, for a review of programs). Mindfulness-based curricula should be age appropriate and strive to increase focus, social competencies, and emotional regulation (Meiklejohn et al., 2012). The age range and length of each program are different and can be implemented within the classroom or schoolwide. Before implementations, school counselors should research the mindfulness-based curriculum program that best fits the holistic needs of the school. Once the program is approved by the administration, school counselors play a pivotal role in delivering the curriculum, in training the teachers in classroom implementation, and in providing ongoing support and supplements to the program. Throughout the school year, school counselors hold staff meetings to discuss the program, provide ongoing training, and collect data that correspond with program objectives. At the end of the year, school counselors assemble the data and report back results to the staff, ensuring the accountability and efficacy of the program. School counselors are key to the success of a mindfulness-based program, promoting greater student success in academic, career, and personal and/or social domains.

Collaboration

As systems-change agents, school counselors are called upon to identify student needs, act as a liaison among stakeholders, assess barriers to growth and potential, and provide leadership (ASCA, 2014, Dahir & Stone, 2009; Dollarhide & Saginak, 2012; Ratts, DeKruyf, & Chen-Hays, 2007). School counselors and administration alike ensure that all students receive access to high-quality and appropriate curricula to support the needs of the student body and bolster success (Dahir & Stone, 2009; Ratts et al., 2007). As leaders in advocacy and systemic change, school counselors are summoned to be champions for students, enabling and empowering healthy student learning and development (Dahir & Stone, 2009; Dollarhide & Saginak, 2012). To champion the integration of mindfulness trainings in schools, counselors cannot work in isolation, but must harness their collaborative efforts to integrate a mindfulness-based curriculum and lifestyle into the students' worldview.

The ASCA National Model (2012) emphasizes the importance of school counselors as members of the educational unit who commence systematic change. Through their leadership, advocacy, and collaboration skills, school counselors work to promote academic achievement, social–emotional wellness, and college and career readiness for all students. Administrators, teachers, and other stakeholders may struggle to understand the use of mindfulness in the classroom. Teachers may struggle to understand the connection or usefulness of mindfulness to success in the core curriculum, they may be reluctant to attend additional training for implementing mindfulness, and they may be disinclined to take on additional commitments due to busy schedules (Dariotis et al., 2017). Administrators may be hesitant to provide funding for training, space for implementation, or resources for programs (Dariotis et al., 2017; Meiklejohn et al., 2012). In addition, the school board and administration face challenges in determining who is considered highly qualified to teach mindfulness to students and teachers alike (Meiklejohn et al., 2012). In these cases, the school counselor can be an advocate for mindfulness practices and educate others about the power of mindfulness as an effective intervention beyond a trend or fad (Cleveland, 2016).

For instance, when principals and school counselors amalgamate their professional skills, they can help effectively and efficiently serve students in developing holistic wellness and positive academic outcomes (McCarty, Wallin, & Boggan, 2014). When principals and counselors collaborate, a more robust academic atmosphere can be developed, creating a healthy space for teaching and learning to occur. Mindfulness can provide the means through which these two leaders support one another, manage their responsibilities, and care for themselves, so that they can better care for others (Thompson, 2018). School principals provide leadership and direction within the school, creating and sustaining a school climate that fosters high expectations for all students. In turn, school counselors possess the distinct skills to reinforce this vision by helping all students attain rigorous academic preparation, personal and social wellness, and navigate the course of college and career readiness. When introducing mindfulness into the schools, school counselors and principals must form a united front in integrating the curriculum. Once principals understand mindfulness practice and its benefits to the school, students, and stakeholders, they are more likely to provide the required support and staff training (McCarty et al., 2014; Thompson, 2018).

Administrators of a school often set its emotional tone and climate, similar to what parents do in the family (Thompson, 2018). When school counselors collaborate with administrators to practice, integrate, and model mindfulness practice, the two parties create a synergy that enriches student development (McCarty et al., 2014; Rock, Remley, & Range, 2017). With a shared vision and clear collaboration, administrators and school counselors generate a team approach that positively influences the school environment and creates a solid alliance that perpetuates student success. For instance, after choosing a mindfulness curriculum that meets the needs of a school population, the school counselor and administrators must continually collaborate and communicate about the vision, goals, and data related to student outcomes. An example vision statement may include:

The vision of this program is that, over time, all members of the school will be

- Trained and empowered to implement mindfulness and life-long learning strategies.
- Grounded in current best practice mindfulness research.
- Able to demonstrate awareness of self and others, show cognitive flexibility, and exhibit the capacity to self-regulate.
- Socially and emotionally healthy individuals who incite solicitous inter- and intrapersonal communication, while promoting a sense of acceptance and community.

School counselors and administrators collaborate to collect, evaluate, and report program data in an effort to adjust the program to fit the needs of the school. When collaboration is used in assessing data, both parties can work to strengthen the program and meet the needs of students. Working together, the power of mindfulness can be harnessed, further encouraging teachers, staff, parents, guardians, and other stakeholders to value and engage in mindfulness.

When mindfulness is practiced and modeled by school counselors and administrators, teachers may find it easier to integrate such practices into their classrooms (Harpin et al., 2016; Rock et al., 2017; Thompson, 2018). School counselors can collaborate with teachers, helping to design mindfulness practice, and model and implement it into daily class activities. In addition, this collaboration helps teachers to develop social–emotional competence, which improves educational effectiveness and personal well-being (Dorman, 2015; Roeser, Skinner, Beers, & Jennings, 2012). Counselors can help teachers by modeling their own social–emotional competence and mindfulness practice and giving them mindfulness exercises to complete on their own. Achieving personal well-being can help teachers prevent burnout, recognize student issues earlier, and collaborate more effectively with other stakeholders (Dorman, 2015; Roeser et al., 2012). As mindful collaborators, teachers and school counselors can further enhance the school environment, increase student engagement, and bolster student resiliency.

As school counselors collaborate with parents and guardians to help them practice mindfulness at home, they build the necessary home–school bridge that is recommended for successful implementation of mindfulness interventions (Nanda, 2009). For instance, school counselors can provide workshops for parents to teach and practice mindfulness at home. They can send parents resources, such as video links, handouts, practice exercises, scripts, or books, to use with their children. School counselors are well positioned to support this critical link between home and school. When school–family partnerships are strengthened, students experience greater academic achievement, personal resilience, and a stronger sense of self-identity (Bryan & Henry, 2012; Cox, 2005). Successful home–school partnerships are formed intentionally and infused with principles, such as advocating for personal empowerment; reflecting on personal values, skills, and goals and adjusting behavior to achieve those goals; using a strengths-based approach; and advocating for social justice, each of which is a critical component of mindfulness practice (Bryan & Henry, 2012; Cox, 2005; Singh et al., 2010).

Making mindfulness practices part of the collaboration with parents and guardians allows school counselors to be champions for change and support both parent and student well-being. When practiced at home, parents and guardians find that mindfulness promotes familial bonds, more effective parent–child communication, and stronger psychological well-being for both the caregiver and the child (Duncan, Coatsworth, & Greenberg, 2009; Singh et al., 2010). School counselors who collaborate with parents and guardians, model mindful awareness practices, and teach mindfulness to parents help empower caregivers to develop positive interactions with their children and build a needed bridge between home and school.

Conclusion

Equipped with unique competencies and skills, school counselors are ideally situated to integrate mindfulness into school systems. As a result of their leadership, advocacy, counseling, and collaboration skills, school counselors are well equipped to be the bridge between practicing mindfulness and transforming school cultures. By engaging various stakeholders in the process, school counselors can use mindfulness to concurrently prevent and remediate student concerns. Mindfulness techniques help facilitate growth in the self and awareness of others for students of all developmental levels. This awareness promotes academic achievement, personal and social development, and college and career readiness. Through the implementation of mindfulness and collaboration with stakeholders, school counselors work to provide a school environment that respects, values, and appreciates students of all walks of life, thereby promoting holistic student well-being.

References

American School Counselor Association. (2012). *ASCA National Model*. Alexandria, VA: Author.

American School Counselor Association. (2014). *Code of ethics*. Alexandria, VA: Author.

American School Counselor Association. (2018). Role of the school counselor. Retrieved from *www.schoolcounselor.org/asca/media/asca/Careers-Roles/RoleStatement.pdf*.

Bernstein, A., Hadash, Y., Lichtash, Y., Tanay, G., Shepherd, K., & Frescon, D. M. (2015). Decentering and related constructs: A critical review and metacognitive process model. *Perspectives on Psychological Science, 10*, 599–617.

Bourne, E. J. (2011). *The anxiety and phobia workbook*. Oakland, CA: New Harbinger.

Boyd, J., Lanius, R. A., & McKinnon, M. C. (2018). Mindfulness-based treatments for posttraumatic stress disorder: A review of the treatment literature and neurobiological evidence. *Journal of Psychiatry Neuroscience, 43*, 7–25.

Bryan, J., & Henry, L. (2012). A model for building school-family-community partnerships: Principles and process. *Journal of Counseling and Development, 90*, 408–420.

Carmody, J. (2009). Evolving conceptions of mindfulness in clinical settings. *Journal of Cognitive Psychotherapy: An International Quarterly, 23*, 270–280.

Cleveland, R. E. (2016). Mindfulness in K–12 education: School counselor connections. *ACA VISTAS, 79*, 1–16.

Cox, D. D. (2005). Evidence-based interventions using home–school collaboration. *School Psychology Quarterly, 20,* 473–497.

Dahir, C. A., & Stone, C. B. (2009). School counselor accountability: The path to social justice and systemic change. *Professional School Counseling, 87,* 12–20.

Dajani, D. R., & Uddin, L. Q. (2015). Demystifying cognitive flexibility: Implications for clinical and developmental neuroscience. *Trends in Neurosciences, 38,* 571–578.

Dariotis, J. K., Mirabal-Beltran, R., Cluxton-Keller, F., Gould, L. F., Greenberg, M. T., & Mendelson, T. (2017). A qualitative exploration of implementation factors in a school-based mindfulness and yoga program: Lessons learned from students and teachers. *Psychology in the Schools, 54,* 53–69.

Dass-Brailsford, R. (2007). *A practical approach to trauma: Empowering interventions.* Thousand Oaks, CA: SAGE.

Deringer, S. A. (2017). Mindful place-based education: Mapping the literature. *Journal of Experiential Education, 40,* 333–348.

Dollarhide, C. T., & Saginak, K. A. (2012). *Comprehensive school counseling programs: K–2 delivery systems in action* (2nd ed.). Upper Saddle River, NJ: Prentice Hall.

Dorman, E. (2015). Building teachers' social-emotional competence through mindfulness practices. *Curriculum and Teaching Dialogue, 17,* 103–120.

Duncan, L., Coatsworth, J. D., & Greenberg, M. T. (2009). Pilot study to gauge acceptability of a mindfulness-based, family-focused preventive intervention. *Journal of Primary Prevention, 30,* 605–618.

Flook, L., Smalley, S. L., Kitil, M. J., Galla, B. M., Kaiser-Greenland, S., Locke, J., . . . Kasari, C. (2010). Effects of mindful awareness practices on executive functions in elementary school children. *Journal of Applied School Psychology, 26,* 70–95.

Gehart, D., & McCollum, E. (2007). Engaging in suffering: Towards a mindful revisioning of family therapy practice. *Journal of Marital and Family Therapy, 33,* 214–226.

Hamiel, D. (2005). Children under stress and trauma: The use of biofeedback, cognitive behavioral techniques and mindfulness for integrated and balanced coping. *Biofeedback, 33,* 149–152.

Handley, M., & Earls, J. (2014). Minding the gap: Incorporating mindfulness to facilitate students' soft-skill development. *National Association of Colleges and Employers Journal, 75,* 25–29.

Harpin, S., Rossi, A., Kim, A. K., & Swanson, L. (2016). Behavioral impacts of a mindfulness pilot intervention for elementary school students. *Education, 137,* 149–156.

Hines, P. L., & Lemo, R. (2011). Poised to lead: How school counselors can drive college and career readiness. *The Educational Trust, 12,* 2–8.

Kabat-Zinn, J. (1990). *Full catastrophe living: The program of the stress reduction clinic at the University of Massachusetts Medical Center.* New York: Delta.

Kerr, C. E., Josyula, K., & Littenberg, R. (2011). Developing an observing attitude: An analysis of meditation diaries in an MBSR clinical trial. *Clinical Psychology and Psychotherapy, 18,* 80–93.

Klingbeil, D. A., Renshaw, T. L., Willenbrink, J. B., Copek, R., Chan, K. T., Haddock, A., . . . Clifton, J. (2017). Mindfulness-based interventions with youth:

A comprehensive meta-analysis of group-design studies. *Journal of School Psychology, 63,* 77–103.

Kostanski, M., & Hassed, C. (2008). Mindfulness as a concept and a process. *Australian Psychologist, 43,* 15–21.

Langer E. J. (1992). Matters of mind: Mindfulness/mindlessness in perspective. *Consciousness and Cognition, 1,* 289–305.

Langer, E. J., & Moldoveanu, M. (2000). The construct of mindfulness. *Journal of Social Issues, 56,* 1–9.

Lawlor, M. S. (2016). Mindfulness and social emotional learning (SEL): A conceptual framework. In K. A. Schonert-Reichl & R. W. Roeser (Eds.), *Handbook of mindfulness in education* (pp. 65–80). New York: Springer.

Lebois, L., Papies, E. K., Gopinath, K., Cabanban, R., Quigley, K. S., Krisnamurthy, V., . . . Barsalou, L. W. (2015). A shift in perspective: Decentering through mindful attention to imagined stressful event. *Neuropsychologia, 75,* 505–524.

Lee, C. (2001). Culturally responsive school counselors and programs: Addressing the needs of all students. *Professional School Counseling, 4,* 163–171.

McCarty, D., Wallin, P., & Boggan, M. (2014). Shared leadership model for 21st century schools: Principal and counselor collaborative leadership. *National Forum of Educational Administration and Supervision Journal, 32*(4), 1–9.

Meiklejohn, J., Phillips, C., Freedman, M. L., Griffin, M. L., Biegel, G., Roach, A., . . . Isberg, R. (2012). Integrating mindfulness training into K–12 education: Fostering the resilience of teachers and students. *Mindfulness, 3,* 291–307.

Moore, A., & Malinowski, P. (2009). Meditation, mindfulness and cognitive flexibility. *Consciousness and Cognition, 18,* 176–186.

Nanda, J. (2009). Mindfulness: A lived experience of existential phenomenological themes. *Existential Analysis, 20,* 147–162.

Parker, A. E., Kupersmidt, J. B., Mathis, E. T., Scull, T. M., & Sims, C. (2014). The impact of mindfulness education on elementary school students: Evaluation of the Master Mind program. *Advances in School Mental Health Promotion, 7,* 184–204.

Parker, L., & Diaz, J. (January, 2018). College and career readiness in elementary school: Beginning with the end in mind. Retrieved from *www.schoolcounselor.org.*

Ramasubramanian, S. (2017). Mindfulness, stress coping and everyday resilience among emerging youth in a university setting: A mixed methods approach. *International Journal of Adolescents and Youth, 22,* 308–321.

Ratts, M., DeKruyf, L., & Chen-Hays, S. F. (2007). The ACA advocacy competencies: A social justice framework for professional school counselors. *Professional School Counseling, 11,* 90–97.

Rausch, S. M., Gramling, S. E., & Auerbach, S. M. (2006). Effects of a single session of large-group meditation and progressive muscle relaxation training on stress reduction, reactivity, and recovery. *International Journal of Stress Management, 13,* 273–290.

Rock, W., Remley, T., & Range, L. (2017). Principal–counselor collaboration and school climate. *NASSP Bulletin, 101,* 23–35.

Roeser, R., Skinner, E., Beers, J., & Jennings, P. (2012). Mindfulness training and teachers' professional development: An emerging area of research and practice. *Child Development Perspectives, 6,* 167–173.

Shapiro, S. L., Carlson, L. E., Astin, J. A., & Freedman, B. (2006). Mechanisms of mindfulness. *Journal of Clinical Psychology, 62,* 373–386.

Sibinga, E. M., Webb, L., Ghazarian, S. R., & Ellen, J. M. (2016). School-based mindfulness instruction: An RCT. *Pediatrics, 137,* 1–8.

Singh, N. N., Sign, A. N., Lancioni, G., Singh, J., Winton, A., & Adkins, A. (2010). Mindfulness training for parents and their children with ADHD increases the children's compliance. *Journal of Child and Family Studies, 19,* 157–166.

Stickler, T. (2016). How to set a career compass. *Central Penn Business Journal, 32*(49), 10–12.

Tadlock-Marlo, R. L. (2011). Making minds matter: Infusing mindfulness into school counseling. *Journal of Creativity in Mental Health, 6,* 220–233.

Talathi, M., & Mhaske, M. S. (2017). Effect of mindfulness on emotional liability among adolescents. *Indian Journal of Positive Psychology, 8,* 654–658.

Thompson, E. (2018). Mindfulness for students and the adults who lead them. *Leadership, 47*(3), 28–32.

Thompson, M., & Gauntlett-Gilbert, J. (2008). Mindfulness with children and adolescents: Effective clinical application. *Clinical Child Psychology and Psychiatry, 13,* 396–408.

U.S. Department of Education. (2017). College and career ready standards. Retrieved from *www.ed.gov/k-12reforms/standards.*

Velsor, P. (2009). School counselors as social–emotional learning consultants: Where do we begin? *Professional School Counseling, 13,* 50–58.

Whitfield, H. (2006). Towards case-specific applications of mindfulness-based cognitive-behavioral therapies: A mindfulness-based rational emotive behavior therapy. *Counselling Psychology Quarterly, 19,* 205–217.

Zenner, C., Herrnleben-Kurz, S., & Walach, H. (2014). Mindfulness-based interventions in schools: A systematic review and meta-analysis. *Frontiers in Psychology, 5,* 603–623.

CHAPTER 8

Creating Mindful and Compassionate Schools

Including Parents as Partners

J. DOUGLAS COATSWORTH
MELISSA W. GEORGE
AIMEE KLEISNER WALKER

It felt so good to be listened to . . . as a parent, and as a
person. I immediately felt connected to her and the school.
—PARENT OF KINDERGARTENER ABOUT TEACHER'S
GREETING ON THE FIRST DAY OF SCHOOL

All human beings have a basic need to connect in deep, meaningful,
and nurturing relationships with other human beings and to feel a sense
of belonging to social groups, including families, peers, schools, and other
socially constructed relationships (Biglan, 2015). These individual and
group relationships are central to all human development and learning
across the life span. Furthermore, we know that high-quality relationships
and attachments are central to healthy human development (e.g., Bowlby,
1983). We also know that high-quality early care and education contributes
significantly to children's long-term positive development (Vandell, Belsky,
Burchinal, Steinberg, & Vandergrift, 2010), and may be particularly beneficial to children from vulnerable populations (Espinosa, 2013). Given that
children spend a significant amount of time during their formative years of

development in both the family and school contexts, scientists, educators, and practitioners have devoted considerable effort to designing and implementing programs that support strong families and schools to help promote healthy and positive development (Bosworth, 2015; Van Ryzin, Kumpfer, Fosco, & Greenberg, 2015).

Two broad areas of empirical research and current social change efforts that have significant potential for informing each other are school transformation efforts and mindfulness research and practice. Although these areas have been integrated mainly by training teachers and administrators in mindfulness and compassion practices that influence the quality of the classroom (e.g., Jennings et al., 2017), there may be additional areas of mutual influence. For example, parent and family training programs that include mindfulness and compassion practices can significantly alter relationship quality within the family (e.g., Coatsworth et al., 2014). Combining family- and school-based programs may have a synergistic effect on developmental outcomes (e.g., Herman, Borden, Reinke, & Webster-Stratton, 2011; Reinke, Splett, Robeson, & Offutt, 2009). However, mindfulness-based programs for students, teachers, and administrators and mindfulness-based programs for families have not been applied widely in an integrative approach that might influence how parents and schools together create a high-quality partnership that benefits the child's development. We propose that combining these kinds of programs would be a fruitful avenue for application and research. In this chapter, we present such an integrative approach, through the Mindfulness-enhanced Strengthening Families Program (MSFP; Coatsworth et al., 2014), which addresses mindfulness in parenting for students' caregivers, and the Cultivating Awareness and Resilience in Education program (CARE; Jennings et al., 2017), which trains mindfulness in educators.

One critical feature of these converging areas is their emphasis on a developmental viewpoint. The school transformation movement has expanded beyond an approach that examines only how schools contribute to academic achievement (although it necessarily remains a primary goal for schools) to include a broader focus on social and emotional development as well (Elias, Zins, Graczyk, & Weissberg, 2003). The integration of social–emotional learning (SEL) programs into the academic curricula is one example of this expansion. These programs can address different developmental needs of children and adolescents (Elias et al., 2003). The literature on parenting within families also follows a developmental perspective that reflects the changing needs of children and youth and how parents can provide the nurturing environment that meets those specific needs. Similarly, mindfulness and compassion in parenting has been used with parents of children at different ages to address specific developmental and parent–child relationship issues (e.g., Bögels & Restifo, 2013; Coatsworth et al., 2014). Although some programs for transforming schools have adopted approaches emphasizing mindfulness and/or compassion training of school personnel, programs that create successful and sustainable school–family partnerships generally have not. Again, we propose that programs and activities that teach mindfulness skills to parents, teachers, and administrators, could be used as models for developing new programs to strengthen school–family partnerships.

School transformation efforts have also broadened the typical view of education from being solely a school and/or teacher's responsibility to a responsibility shared between educators and families (e.g., Weiss, Lopez, Kreider, & Chatman-Nelson, 2013). The strategy of transforming schools through teaching students SEL skills (Bridgeland, Bruce, & Hariharan, 2013) has also expanded the boundaries of the school. Research has demonstrated that both educational and SEL programs in schools become more powerful when they extend into the home (Albright & Weissberg, 2010). Over the past decade, as SEL programs have gained prominence, it is becoming increasingly evident that reinforcing and aligning school efforts with children's at-home experience helps maximize the effectiveness of the programs (Patrikakou & Weissberg, 2007).

Despite a compelling rationale for partnerships between schools and families, there is no consensus on a definition of, or agreement about, the best practices for creating successful school–family partnerships. Educators have conceptualized and cultivated parental or family involvement in diverse ways, and families participate in school activities and governance to varying degrees and with varying effectiveness. Parental involvement models tend to highlight parental efforts to support what schools do to promote learning, but family–school partnership models are broader and are defined by how parents and professionals cooperate, coordinate, and collaborate to increase opportunities and accomplishments related to children's and adolescents' social, emotional, behavioral, and academic development (Albright & Weissberg, 2010). Not surprisingly, the vast majority of work in this area is done by the administrators and the personnel of the school, which places a greater burden on that side of the school–family partnership equation. However, shifting the focus to include parents, who contribute their own skills or competencies, can also shed new light on how to improve these important relationships.

School–Family Partnerships

It is clear that both schools and families play essential roles in promoting children's positive SEL development and academic performance. It is also clear that when educators and parents work together as partners, the synergy creates new and expanded opportunities to help children develop healthy social, emotional, and academic skills. When parents are involved in their children's education, children have higher rates of attendance, homework completion, and school graduation, as well as elevated grades and test scores (Jeynes, 2005). Family involvement also facilitates children's self-esteem, behavior, and positive attitudes toward school (Christenson & Reschly, 2010).

Successful school–family partnerships are based on the underlying beliefs that *all* families (regardless of parents' level of education, socioeconomic status, and race or ethnicity) can contribute to children's learning and development, and that parents and teachers share responsibility for nurturing and educating children. Moreover, successful partnerships are flexible and diverse, reflecting and incorporating the needs and characteristics of the particular school community in which they are based (Christenson & Reschly, 2004). While the nature of a school–family partnership varies across the educational and developmental spectrum, particularly in terms of the types of communication and involvement that are appropriate and effective, these partnerships continue to be critically important as children progress through school (Patrikakou, 2008).

Models of School–Family Partnerships

Central to all models of school-family partnerships is the cultivation of caring learning environments across contexts of development that promote student, family, educator, school, and community successes (Epstein, Coates, Salinas, Sanders, & Simon, 1997). These caring learning environments result from cooperation, coordination, and collaborations that scaffold substantively meaningful interconnections among educators and families. Programs that cultivate mindful practices across a student's microsystems facilitate caring, constructive, and bidirectional connections among educators and families. These connections provide the foundation of school–family partnerships through the promotion of cross-system supports and continuities intended to enhance the quality of learning opportunities and enrich student outcomes.

Epstein's Overlapping Spheres of Influence Model

Guided by Bronfenbrenner's ecological systems theory, Epstein (1995) identified *family, school,* and *community* as critical contexts that interact to influence student learning and success. The greater the overlap among these spheres of influence, the stronger the partnership. The overlap representing genuine partnerships between schools and families is established through reciprocal mesosystemic interactions among these microsystemic spheres of influence (Epstein, 1995). Dependent on the characteristics, philosophy, and practices within and across these microsystems, reciprocal interactions can either enrich or thwart genuine school–family partnerships that promote positive student outcomes. Epstein's theoretical model of school–family partnerships provides an organizational framework for examining the barriers and supports that contribute to the cultivation of caring learning communities that promote student success.

Using this theoretical model, Epstein and colleagues (2009) identified "six types of caring" in the extant research on parental involvement that provide a typology of the key developmental opportunities for reciprocal interactions essential to promoting genuine school–family partnerships: parenting, communicating, volunteering, learning at home, decision making, and collaborating with the community.

- Type 1: *Parenting*—establishing a home environment conducive to successful learning.
- Type 2: *Communicating (two-way)*—implementing effective bidirectional strategies for successful communication about the student, family, and school progress.
- Type 3: *Volunteering*—fostering opportunities for direct involvement of families within the school context to help and support learning.
- Type 4: *Learning at home*—providing guidance about how to help students with homework and other curriculum-related learning opportunities within the home context.
- Type 5: *Decision making*—including parents in partnership processes with school personnel to develop shared vision and actions to accomplish shared goals.
- Type 6: *Collaborating with the community*—identifying and capitalizing on community resources and services.

These caring activities provide shared opportunities, grounded in mutual respect and shared goals, that empowers partners and mobilizes the resources needed to cultivate caring learning environments across the overlapping spheres of influence. However, Mapp and Kutner (2013) suggest that the individuals and systems represented in Epstein's overlapping spheres may not have the requisite capacities needed to capitalize on the developmental opportunities represented within Epstein's "types of caring." As such, the effectiveness of many school–family partnership interventions is quite variable, because it is contingent on the baseline requisite capacities (Lawson, Alemeda-Lawson, Lawson, Briar-Lawson, & Wilcox, 2014).

The Dual Capacity-Building Framework

The dual capacity-building framework (Mapp & Kutner, 2013) expands on Epstein's work in that it examines the requisite capacities of students, caregivers, and schools that contribute to both the decision to engage and the *quality* of engagement across Epstein's typology of caring. Most notably, the framework suggests that programs designed to enhance partnership capacity should target four areas: capabilities, connections, cognition, and confidence. *Capabilities* are the requisite skills, knowledge, and human capital needed to effectively engage in partnerships across the spheres of influence. Social capital needed for partnership engagement is cultivated through respectful and trusting *connections* between the stakeholders and systems surrounding the student. Programs should also target participants' *confidence* or self-efficacy related to engagement in Epstein's "types of caring," because believing that they can be competent and capable will support their ability to connect and successfully engage. Finally, participants need to develop *cognitions,* or assumptions and beliefs, that allow them to successfully construct roles for engaging in partnership. Specifically, Mapp and Kuttner (2013) identified seven roles for parents' partnerships: supporter, encourager, monitor, model, advocate, decision maker, and collaborator. When these theoretical models are coupled with mindfulness research, it becomes clear that interventions that include mindfulness and compassionate practices have the potential to scaffold the development of the requisite capacities for school–family partnerships.

Mindfulness and School–Family Partnerships

The literature on teacher and parent mindfulness has developed partially along a similar trajectory, with research groups identifying core aspects of mindfulness and "mindful relating" as central constructs on which to focus conceptual and intervention models (Duncan, Coatsworth, & Greenberg, 2009a; Jennings & Greenberg, 2009). Central to these models is the cultivation of an engaged presence or "attunement" with others. When applying this concept to school–family partnerships, cultivating this kind of interpersonal relating can be effective if done with either parents or teachers separately, but it may be most effective when done conjointly. Cultivating these capacities in both partners may enhance the relationship between them, allow them to see each other through a different lens, and enable them to interact with each other in a more peaceful and compassionate manner. Our model and our intervention work with mindfulness applied specifically to parenting is described next.

Mindfulness in Parenting

Mindful parenting has become a popular way of viewing effective parenting practices, although it has been conceptualized in many different ways. Influenced by the seminal work of Jon and Myla Kabat-Zinn in their book *Everyday Blessings: The Inner Work of Mindful Parenting* (Kabat-Zinn

& Kabat-Zinn, 1997), a variety of authors in the popular and academic literature have defined this way of relating to how parents think and feel about their own parenting as mindful parenting (Bögels & Restifo, 2013; Coatsworth et al., 2014); as conscious parenting (Lozowick, 2010; Tsabary, 2014), as positive parenting (Eanes, 2016); and as parenting with presence (Stiffleman, 2015). These approaches are similar in the way they describe how the daily practices of mindfulness are readily applicable to parenting (Kabat-Zinn & Kabat-Zinn, 1997).

Five Dimensions of Mindful Parenting

Duncan et al. (2009a) described five dimensions that are characteristic of mindful parenting and used them as foundational mindfulness skills that can be taught in conjunction with basic parenting skills (Coatsworth et al., 2014). This model has influenced the thinking and research that study mindful parenting and the interventions designed to influence it. Based on the conceptual model, we created a program called the Mindfulness-Enhanced Strengthening Family Program 10–14 (MSFP; Coatsworth et al., 2014, 2015). Although the original model focused on mindful parenting for parents of adolescents, the five dimensions, which we describe in the following sections, are easily translatable to parenting of youth of other ages.

LISTENING WITH FULL ATTENTION

Clear attention and receptive awareness to the experiences of the present moment are central aspects of mindfulness (Baer, Smith, Hopkins, Krietemeyer, & Toney, 2006) and also of effective parenting (Steinberg, 2004). For parenting, we emphasized pairing attention with listening, because it is by directing their full attention to their child that parents convey that they are truly listening to him or her. This dimension of mindful parenting goes beyond simply hearing words that are said to sensitively attending to the emotions behind the words and developing an internal representation of the child's perspective, which is critical in forming a secure parent–child attachment (Ainsworth, Blehar, Waters, & Wall, 1978; Siegel, 2001). As children age, mindful parents are sensitive both to the content of conversations as well as to their child's tone of voice, facial expressions, and body language. Attention and attunement to these affective and behavioral cues help parents detect the child's underlying needs. In adolescence, listening with full attention is particularly important, because parents need to monitor their youth, and monitoring is done more often through adolescents' disclosure rather than through direct observation (Smetana, Campione-Barr, & Metzger, 2006). By bringing their full attention to these interactions, parents may perceive their adolescents' thoughts and feelings more accurately, reduce conflict and disagreement (Turpyn & Chaplin, 2016) and promote more self-disclosure by the adolescent (Smetana et al., 2006).

NONJUDGMENTAL ACCEPTANCE OF SELF AND CHILD

Mindful parenting involves being aware of the attributions and expectations that may influence how parent–child interactions are perceived. Parental perceptions of their children's attributes influence their expectations, values, interactions with their child, and ultimately their child's behavior (Jacobs, Chhin, & Shaver, 2005). Parents may directly or indirectly communicate beliefs about their child's attributes that are biased by their own desires for their child, even if they are unrealistic (Goodnow, 1985). The goal of nonjudgmental acceptance is that of helping parents see their youth as they are and not how parents want them to be. Nonjudgmental acceptance involves parents' recognizing that youth have their own thoughts, feelings, desires, and goals, which may or may not align with what parents perceive or want. Nonjudgmental acceptance also entails seeing beyond outward conditions in a way that recognizes and supports a child's true nature. Seeing one's child clearly, without judgment, helps parents develop a fuller understanding of their children's internal lives and a more compassionate view of their experiences. Parents connect how their desires and expectations for their child or their worries about their own parenting influence the quality of their relationships with their teens. Avoiding these evaluative thoughts can lead to parenting that is supportive and nurturing rather than critical and censoring.

Nonjudgmental acceptance also means bringing a sense of curiosity to one's experience and accepting that parenting can be very challenging, that both parents and children struggle at times, and that today's world can be difficult for children. Acceptance does not mean that mindful parents blindly approve of disruptive or aggressive behavior, but that they learn to acknowledge what they can and cannot control. For example, they cannot immediately control their child's present disruptive behavior or something that the child did in the past. They can, however, bring a genuine curiosity to the conditions and factors, including their own actions, that may support and reinforce their child's aggression, and consciously work to change them. They can use then use this heightened awareness to provide clear standards and expectations for behavior that are culturally, developmentally, and situationally appropriate. Being able to accept one's experience in the present moment reduces avoidance of uncomfortable thoughts or feelings, which instead may lead to reappraising those uncomfortable experiences in more positive ways. Related to nonjudgmental acceptance is a concept that others have termed *reperceiving* (Shapiro, Astin, & Freedman,

2006). *Reperceiving* involves a fundamental shift in one's perspective that arises from a sense of clear awareness and an ability to understand one's own personal experiences and those of others in an objective way. It means that the stories we create to define our lives can be viewed as just stories, rather than as something that we identify with so strongly (Shapiro & Carlson, 2017).

EMOTIONAL AWARENESS OF SELF AND CHILD

Mindfulness theories emphasize individuals' capacities for focusing attention on internal states such as cognitions and emotions. Mindful parenting, in turn, emphasizes parents' capacity for an awareness of their own and their children's emotions. To truly be able to listen with full attention and to do so nonjudgmentally requires parents to also have the capacity for correctly identifying emotions within themselves and their child. Strong emotions trigger automatic evaluative processes (Bargh & Williams, 2007) that lead to specific behaviors. Virtually all aspects of parenting are influenced by parents' affective activation, engagement, and regulation (Dix, 1991). Parents may experience intense negative and positive affect during parenting that can ignite automatic cognitive processes and behaviors that are likely to undermine parenting practices. Mindfulness skills can help redirect these processes. Cultivating emotional awareness helps parents identify both their own and their child's emotions by bringing a mindful awareness to the interaction. In turn, they are better able to make conscious choices about how to respond, rather than reacting automatically to these experiences. Years of emotional parent–youth exchanges can lead to ingrained patterns of interaction that shape the cognitive schemas and behaviors of both parents and youth. Mindfulness training can help reduce the influence of these interaction patterns.

Key to this process is helping parents perceive emotions as transient states, or as "comfortable" and "uncomfortable" feelings they have while parenting, that are neither "good" nor "bad." Parents who can develop a recognition and acceptance that emotions are unavoidable parts of one's experience that signal the need to refocus their attention to the present behave less reactively.

SELF-REGULATION IN THE PARENTING RELATIONSHIP

In addition to full attention, nonjudgmental acceptance, and emotional awareness, mindful parenting implies a certain degree of self-regulation. Mindful parenting involves developing a low reactivity to normative child behavior. It does not imply that negative affect, anger, or hostility are not experienced, but it does involve pausing before reacting in order to exercise greater self-regulation and choice in how to react. The ways in which parents respond to their child's emotions and express their own emotions have an important socializing effect (Eisenberg, Cumberland, & Spinrad, 1998). Parents who are tolerant and supportive of their child's emotional displays and do not dismiss or meet their child's displays of negative affect with their own negative affect promote more emotionally and socially competent youth (Katz, Wilson, & Gottman, 1999). Mindful parenting may also promote parenting practices, such as teaching children how to label, express, and talk about their feelings, that can promote youth's own self-regulation abilities (Gottman, Katz, & Hooven, 1997). Mindful parenting helps parents discern that automatic behavioral reactions usually are preceded by strong, uncomfortable emotions that may overwhelm their cognitive processes and leave them less able to parent intentionally. To gain some conscious control over automatic reactions, parents can become aware of and label feelings as they are arising, which provides the opportunity to pause and reflect before responding. By increasing self-awareness and noticing one's feelings right away, parents can perceive situations more clearly, respond in ways that are aligned with their parenting goals, and prevent highly charged and potentially relationship-damaging emotional interactions with their children.

COMPASSION FOR SELF AND CHILD

In addition to having an open and accepting stance, mindful parenting includes active empathic concern for one's child and for oneself as a parent. *Compassion* is defined as an emotion representing the "desire to alleviate suffering" (Lazarus & Lazarus, 1994). In having compassion for one's child, a mindful parent will feel a desire to meet the child's appropriate needs and to comfort a child who might be distressed. Children of mindful parents may feel a greater sense of positive affection and support from their parents. In addition to compassion for others, mindfulness also includes self-compassion.

Self-compassion partially comprises a sense of common humanity (Neff, 2003), which, when applied to parenting, may allow parents to take a less harsh, more forgiving view of their own parenting efforts. Self-compassion in parenting involves avoiding self-blame when one's parenting falls short and reduces harsh self-evaluations. Parental self-evaluations can have considerable influence on parenting (Teti & Gelfand, 1991) and on parent–child interactions. A mindful approach may lead to greater acceptance of one's efforts in the process, rather than focusing on specific outcomes of parenting. When parents can replace harsh self-judgment with a compassionate approach to their parenting missteps, they are better able to be present for their children and are better able to repair relationship disconnections.

Mindfulness-Enhanced Strengthening Families Program 10-14

To create MSFP (Coatsworth et al., 2014), we developed activities around core mindfulness practices that were common to other interventions, but made them appropriate for a parent-training context and consistent with our conceptual model. We then integrated these practices into an evidence-based family prevention program—the Strengthening Families Program: For Parents and Youth 10–14 (SFP 10–14; Molgaard, Kumpfer, & Fleming, 2001). We selected SFP 10–14, because of its underlying philosophy of building new and enhancing existing individual and family strengths, and because the evidence for improving parenting practices, enhancing youth development, and preventing problem behavior is strong (Spoth, Shinn, & Redmond, 2006). MSFP includes seven didactic and interactive training activities in highly structured 2-hour sessions, in which parents and youth meet separately for the first hour and conjointly for the second. Throughout the program, we added "mindfulness" language by using words such as *presence, attention,* and *compassion.* MSFP is a school-delivered program, in which the advertising and delivery of the program and outreach to families are coordinated with school administrators and teachers.

Each of the seven parenting session begins and ends with a 1- to 5-minute reflection in which parents practice specific skills, such as focused attention and deep breathing, intention setting for their experience in the program, and cultivating a kind attitude toward themselves and their children. Breath awareness is used throughout MSFP with the dual purpose of helping parents learn to focus their attention on the present moment and of reducing stress. Specific activities are used to train parents in the skills reflecting the five dimensions of mindful parenting: listening with full attention, nonjudgmental acceptance of self and child, emotional awareness of self and child, self-regulation in the parenting relationship, and compassion for self and child. Activities targeting these dimensions are sequenced and sometimes repeated across the seven sessions to help parents acquire skills successively and in an integrated way. A more complete description of the program activities can be found in Coatsworth et al. (2014).

Research and Case Studies on MSFP

Results from empirical evaluations of MSFP have shown that the training improves mindfulness in parents, reduces parental stress, and creates a closer, more supportive bond between parent and child (Coatsworth, Duncan, Greenberg, & Nix, 2010; Coatsworth et al., 2014). Other programs that have trained parents in mindfulness have found similar effects and also changes in youth behaviors (Bögels & Restifo, 2013).

Parents have found the MSFP training useful and enjoyable (Duncan,

Coatsworth, & Greenberg, 2009b). But even more noteworthy, parents report how it changes their mindfulness (in all dimensions) and the way they interact with their children. A father in one of our studies told us:

> [Since participating] I find that the more I can remove the anger that I'm feeling from the situation, the more productive the solution becomes, and I can stop and think and feel and express not only how I am feeling, but it gives her [my daughter] a chance to express how she's feeling and gives me time, that's the important thing, gives me some time to understand how she's feeling and remember how old she is and that no matter what it is, it's not the end of the world. Usually it's a pretty minor thing, in the big scheme of things. (in Duncan et al., 2009b, p. 614)

Moreover, our work with parents has shown that they take the teachings from the parenting program and apply it to situations outside the parent–child relationship. Parents have told us that they have used the techniques with colleagues, employees, and bosses. The application of mindfulness to the work context is a growing development, and shows that even parents who learn these skills in one context can apply it in another. It suggests to us that training parents in mindfulness, even in an MSFP program, could facilitate important relationships in the school–family partnership. Indeed, we have some personal experience that illustrates this point. A parent who was working with one of us (J. Douglas Coatsworth) to cultivate mindfulness skills relayed the following story about her interaction with a teacher and a principal:

> "My son, who is a very good student [sixth grade] and received mostly A's, was caught at school one day breaking a rule about when he could enter specific rooms in school when they were not occupied. I got a call from the principal a little after noon asking me to pick up my son, because he was going to be suspended. My reaction was immediate and strong—I was angry. Angry at my son, angry at the principal, and angry that I had to leave work so early and go pick him up. I carried that anger with me for the entire drive from my job to the school. My thoughts whirled around inside my head. I was not told what he had done specifically, but I imagined all the awful, terrible things he might have done and imposed on him all sorts of evil motives. Those thoughts helped fuel the anger I was feeling. My anger was so strong that I forgot all the mindfulness skills that you had taught me. When I entered the principal's office, the principal and my son's homeroom teacher were sitting there with him, [and] MSFP the anger on their faces rivaled what I was feeling in my body. But when I turned to see the frightened look on the face of my son, my thoughts suddenly shifted and I began to look at the situation in a different way. I was able to

calm myself, and asked the principal and teacher to let me know what had happened. Both launched into a tirade of descriptions of horrible things that my son had done and accusations of what an awful student he had become. It shocked me, but I was able to stay calm and listen intently. When they stopped, I acknowledged their anger and how upsetting it must be for them to have to address this with a student and a parent. I then asked them a question they did not seem ready for. In a calm voice I asked, 'What kind of student and person has my son been these past 5 years, and how do you see him now?' I asked this question, because in my work with you on mindfulness in parenting I have found that when I am able to step back and reflect on how I am perceiving the moment, I can see my judgments and how those are influencing how I am behaving. I was hoping that these people, who have always seen my son as a good student and person would see him in this situation as that same person, who had made a mistake and perhaps to whom they were attributing some characteristics that he did not have. My thought was that they were stressed and fed up with students doing these kinds of things—perhaps students who caused them more trouble than my son ever had, and perhaps they were projecting some characteristics onto him. I am not sure if it was my calm demeanor or their own reflectiveness at that point, but it broke the ice and the tension and we could have a calm, clear discussion where we listened to each other respectfully and come to a reasonable solution (in my mind and theirs) that upheld school rules and acknowledged the true character of my son while not dismissing his misdeed."

Teachers' Mindfulness for Effective School–Family Partnerships

Models that are similar to Duncan and colleagues' mindful parenting model have also been used to promote effective mindfulness/compassion skills for teachers. Cultivating Awareness and Resilience in Education (CARE; Jennings et al., 2017) and SMART (Roeser et al., 2013) are two examples. More complete descriptions of these interventions are available elsewhere, so only a brief summary is given here only for the purpose of illustrating similarities to mindful parenting and of describing the utility of enhancing similar skills in parents and teachers as a means for fostering more effective school–family partnerships.

CARE

CARE (Jennings et al., 2017) uses a model of mindfulness skills that is similar to the model of mindful parenting (Duncan et al., 2009a) and that is organized around three superordinate sets of skills: (1) emotional skills,

(2) mindfulness-based stress reduction skills, and (3) caring and listening skills (Jennings, 2016).

1. *Emotional skills.* Within the broad domain of emotional skills, CARE helps teachers develop emotional skills that help reduce teacher burnout. Using reflective practice and role plays, CARE introduces exercises that help teachers recognize and explore their habitual emotional patterns, learn self-regulation skills and cultivate a calmer emotional climate for the classroom. These practices are similar to those taught in MSFP, although they are contextualized to the school classroom and the teacher's interactions with students.

2. *Mindfulness-based stress reduction.* Within this area, CARE uses a variety of techniques, such as standing, walking, listening, and being in front of a group, to help develop mindful awareness in a variety of situations. Once these skills are practiced individually, teachers role-play applying them to different challenging scenarios they might experience at school. These scenarios might include students, colleagues, or parents.

3. *Caring and listening.* The third broad domain of skills taught in CARE include caring practices and mindful listening. These skills, similar to those in MSFP, are intended to generate feelings of empathy and compassion and to help teachers develop the ability to listen with deep awareness, and to respond with greater sensitivity to students and others.

CARE has been tested in both smaller pilot studies and large randomized trials (Jennings, Frank, Snowberg, Coccia, & Greenberg, 2013; Jennings et al., 2017). Findings from these studies reveal that CARE increases teachers' mindfulness, improves adaptive emotional regulation, and decreases teachers' psychological distress. In addition, it helps teachers create a more supportive and organized classroom.

SMART in Education

SMART in Education (Benn, Akiva, Arel, & Roeser, 2012) is a mindfulness-based education program for teachers that is derived from the model of mindfulness-based stress reduction. The program content concentrates on emotion regulation, forgiveness, kindness, and compassion, and how they are applied in the context of both teaching and parenting. Activities include helping parents and teachers think about stress, focus on their breathing and sounds to develop greater awareness, engage in stretching and body scans to develop greater awareness of bodily sensations, and reflect and meditate on their emotions and mental states. It is interesting to note that this training included ways that these activities could be applied to parents as well.

Results of empirical tests of SMART indicate that the intervention helps to alter the ways that teachers respond to the cognitive, social, and emotional demands of teaching. It fosters teachers' mindfulness and self-compassion, which, in turn, reduces their experience of stress and distress (Benn et al., 2012; Roeser et al., 2013).

Most of our work has been with parents and families, but we have also worked directly with schools that have trained their teachers in mindfulness techniques. Although those programs were meant specifically for teachers' application of mindfulness in the classrooms, our discussion with teachers allowed us to ask about their interactions with parents following their training. One seventh-grade teacher told us how she applied what she learned to working with parents of her students.

"I mostly used my skills of mindful listening. In the past I usually started right in with discussing how the student was doing in my class. I always felt so rushed in those parent–teacher conferences and wanted to make sure that I had time to say everything I needed to say and the parent had time to ask all the questions she had. What I have realized that is when I slow down, pause, and engage in a more mindful conversation, we have enough time, there is no sense of pressure, and we both enjoy it much more than we might have before. I now start all my conferences with asking the parent how her day has been going, [and] we usually engage in some chit chat the eases us into the conversation. I find that it relieves a little of the pressure if I have not met that parent before, and I think it also lets her know that I am interested in her as a person, not just as the parent of "my student." When I find that I have to have a hard conversation with a parent about a student's behavior or work habits or something like that, if I am able to take a moment before that parent comes in to gather my thoughts and make sure I am seeing this student in his or her entirety and not just looking at the few aspects I might see in the classroom, I can have a fuller, more meaningful, and more authentic conversation with her. I also find that I can control my own emotions more easily. The same kinds of skills that I use with my students in the classroom are effective in working with parents. I find that I can more easily create a working relationship with parents now, they are more likely to reach out to me with questions, and we can have better conversations that make it more enjoyable for the student too, I think."

The research evidence clearly shows that teachers and children benefit from training teachers in mindfulness. Yet, the effects may also involve changed interactions with parents. It is possible that when both teachers and parents receive training in mindfulness skills, the effects on parent–teacher interactions and on effective school–family partnerships would be even more significant.

These examples of teaching parents and teachers mindfulness skills illustrate that incorporating mindful awareness into the way we think about school–family partnerships may allow parents and teachers to fundamentally shift their awareness in order to view their present-moment experiences differently, shift how they think about working with each other, and alter the relationships between teachers, parents, and students in a positive way. When parents and teachers bring the practices of mindfulness and compassion to their interactions, they are likely to engage in calmer and more generally positive interactions that can engender greater trust and support. Mindful and compassionate interactions can disrupt destructive cycles of negativity and disengagement that can become entrenched and almost "automatic" for some parents who have experienced difficulties with schools in their past, either as a student or as a parent.

As we have discussed, mindful and compassionate practices have the potential to strengthen the requisite capacities needed to support successful school–family partnerships. The dual capacity-building framework advocates for school–family partnership programs that improve participants' capacity for partnership through the cultivation of capabilities, connections, cognitions, and confidence. Mindfulness programs develop skills, such as listening with attention, that reinforce our social networks (connections) and provide frameworks for shared beliefs and values (cognition). Indeed, many of the programs archived as "promising partnerships practices" (e.g., Our Mindful School, Conscious Discipline) incorporate the dimensions of mindful parenting and teaching models. For example, the school–family partnership program, Our Mindful School, is identified as a successful endeavor that cultivates the second type of caring within Epstein's model, that of communication (Thomas, Greenfeld, Ames, Hine, & Epstein, 2015). Our Mindful School promotes "habits of the mind" (e.g., listening with understanding and empathy, managing impulsivity of parents and children) among elementary school students and their parents and teachers. In doing so, Our Mindful School also cultivates the individual and system capacities identified by Mapp and Kutner (2013) that are needed to stimulate heathy communication patterns within school–family partnerships. Specifically, through the promotion of mindful and compassionate practices for all stakeholders in school–family partnership processes, Our Mindful School strengthens the requisite capacity needed to allow stakeholders to establish and maintain healthy communication patterns within the mesosystemic interactions between home and school.

Barriers to Engaging Parents in School–Family Partnerships

Research has identified several distinct barriers to engaging parents fully in school–family partnerships, including demographic, economic, and time constraints; logistical difficulties; cultural differences; and narrow definitions of parental roles (e.g., Christenson, Godber, & Anderson, 2005). This research flies in the face of the traditional view that parents who are not involved are disinterested and unconcerned. The biggest set of barriers for parental involvement revolves around mismatched demographics and logistical concerns and/or resources. Some families may not be able to spend time at their child's school and may feel unwelcome there because of cultural and language differences. Teachers and school personnel can use mindfulness and compassion skills to ensure a warm and welcoming environment for parents who may be unfamiliar with the "typical" school–family partnership expectations. The key is interpersonal presence (Carreón, Drake, & Barton, 2005), meaning being able to bring mindful attention and awareness to an interaction with others. Often parents and school personnel may simply misread how one another are feeling about being engaged, and those thoughts and feelings may linger but go unexpressed or unexplored, shutting down open communication.

Another barrier to full and meaningful parental engagement may involve negative attitudes and perceptions held by either the parents or the school staff. This barrier is related to the first barrier and to the lack of mindful awareness of either the parents and/or the teacher. Parents who have a history of disliking school when they were students, or have had difficulty dealing with school personnel as an adult, may maintain that perspective and avoid engaging in school–family partnerships as a result. The notion of reperceiving is relevant here, as mindfulness and compassion approaches can facilitate an openness to engaging purposefully in the moment and can help parents and school personnel remain willing to understand what is occurring in the present and not rely on perceptions and beliefs that are framed from past experiences.

Often, parents may experience stress and distress that influence their ability to meet with teachers and engage in school activities. Mindfulness practices with parents has been shown to reduce their levels of stress and increase their well-being (Coatsworth et al., 2014), which may facilitate better connections to schools. But beyond this, when teachers meet parents with a perspective of empathy and compassion for what is happening in their lives, it alters the quality of the relationship. Family engagement models tend to emphasize "relational engagement" (Virmani, Wiese, & Mangione, 2016), noting that relationships are central to learning and development and also that information alone is unlikely to change the behavior of either parents or teachers. It also emphasizes reflective practices, including observation, listening, and wondering, which are skills consistent with a mindfulness approach to cultivating staff skills that can guide meaningful interactions with parents.

Parents' and children's states of mental health and well-being can also influence engagement. Parents with mental health issues may be less able to organize themselves to fully engage. When children are experiencing mental health problems, parents may feel stigmatized or that their concerns and needs are not being met. In this situation, it is critical that school personnel bring their full awareness to the specific needs and abilities of the student. Teachers (and parents) must be able to discern these needs with clarity and bring a nurturing and compassionate approach to how they engage with children. It is important for both parents and school personnel to develop an openness to expressing and receiving concerns in an effort to work together collaboratively.

Conclusion

We continue to learn more about how to effectively engage families and build strong family–school partnerships. Simultaneously we have started to learn more about how mindfulness and compassion approaches can help parents and teachers develop skills to facilitate supportive, collaborative, and nurturing interpersonal relationships. If we adopt the perspective that children's learning emerges from high-quality parent–child and teacher–child relationships, then we might change what we attend to regarding building quality school–family partnerships. Even the most researched model of "parental involvement" focuses more on what parents do at home and at school, rather than on the quality of the relationships between parents, children, and teachers, which are stronger predictors of student outcomes (Jeynes, 2005). Programs that develop parents' mindfulness skills and programs that develop teachers' similar skills show promise for altering qualities that promote healthy school–family partnerships. Perhaps it is time to investigate more programs that incorporate training for both. The effect on student development and learning may be substantial.

References

Ainsworth, M. D. S., Blehar, M. C., Waters, E., & Wall, S. (1978). *Patterns of attachment*. Hillsdale, NJ: Erlbaum.

Albright, M. I., & Weissberg, R. P. (2010). School-family partnerships to promote social and emotional learning. In S. L. Christenson & A. L. Reschly (Eds.), *Handbook of school–family partnerships* (pp. 246–265). New York: Routledge.

Baer, R. A., Smith, G. T., Hopkins, J., Krietemeyer, J., & Toney, L. (2006). Using self-report assessment methods to explore facets of mindfulness. *Assessment, 13*, 27–45.

Bargh, J. A., & Williams, L. E. (2007). The nonconscious regulation of emotion. In J. J. Gross (Ed.), *Handbook of emotion regulation* (pp. 429–445). New York: Guilford Press.

Benn, R., Akiva, T., Arel, S., & Roeser, R. W. (2012). Mindfulness training effects for parents and educators of children with special needs. *Developmental Psychology, 48*(5), 1476–1487.

Biglan, A. (2015). *The nurture effect: How the science of human behavior can improve our lives and our world*. Oakland, CA: New Harbinger.

Bögels, S., & Restifo, K. (2013). *Mindful parenting: A guide for mental health practitioners*. New York: Springer Science & Business Media.

Bosworth, K. (Ed.). (2015). *Prevention science in school settings: Complex relationships and processes*. New York: Springer.

Bowlby, J. (1983). *Attachment and loss: Vol. 1. Attachment*. New York: Basic Books.

Bridgeland, J., Bruce, M., & Hariharan, A. (2013). *The missing piece: A national teacher survey on how social and emotional learning can empower children and transform schools*. Chicago: Civic Enterprises.

Carreón, G. P., Drake, C., & Barton, A. C. (2005). The importance of presence: Immigrant parents' school engagement experiences. *American Educational Research Journal, 42*(3), 465–498.

Christenson, S. L., Godber, Y., & Anderson, A. R. (2005). Critical issues facing families and educators. In E. N. Patrikakou, R. P. Weissberg, S. Redding, & H. J. Walberg (Eds.), *School-family partnerships for children's success* (pp. 21–39). New York: Teachers College Press.

Christenson, S. L., & Reschly, A. L. (Eds.). (2010). *Handbook of school–family partnerships*. New York: Routledge.

Coatsworth, J. D., Duncan, L. G., Berrena, E., Bamberger, K. T., Loeschinger, D., Greenberg, M. G., & Nix, R. L. (2014). The mindfulness-enhanced strengthening families program: Integrating brief mindfulness activities and parent training within an evidence-based prevention program. *New Directions in Youth Development, 142*, 45–58.

Coatsworth, J. D., Duncan, L. G., Greenberg, M. T., & Nix, R. L. (2010) Changing parents' mindfulness, child management skills, and relationship quality with their youth: Results from a randomized pilot intervention trial. *Journal of Child and Family Studies, 19*, 203–217.

Coatsworth, J. D., Duncan, L. G., Nix, R. L., Greenberg, M. G., Gayles. J. G., Bamberger, K. T., . . . Demi, M. A. (2015). Integrating mindfulness with parent training: Effects of the mindfulness-enhanced strengthening families program. *Developmental Psychology, 51*, 26–35.

Dix, T. (1991). The affective organization of parenting: Adaptive and maladaptive processes. *Psychological Bulletin, 110*, 3–25.

Duncan, L. G., Coatsworth, J. D., & Greenberg, M. T. (2009a). A model of mindful parenting: Implications for parent-child relationships and prevention research. *Clinical Child and Family Psychology Review, 12*, 255–270.

Duncan, L. G., Coatsworth, J. D., & Greenberg, M. T. (2009b). Pilot study to gauge acceptability of a mindfulness-based family-focused preventive intervention. *Journal of Primary Prevention, 30,* 605–618.

Eanes, R. (2016). *Positive parenting: An essential guide.* New York: Penguin.

Eisenberg, N., Cumberland, A., & Spinrad, T. L. (1998). Parental socialization of emotion. *Psychological Inquiry, 9,* 241–273.

Elias, M. J., Zins, J. E., Graczyk, P. A., & Weissberg, R. P. (2003). Implementation, sustainability, and scaling up of social-emotional and academic innovations in public schools. *School Psychology Review, 32*(3), 303–319.

Epstein, J. L. (1995). School/family/community partnerships. *Phi Delta Kappan, 76*(9), 701.

Epstein, J. L., & Associates. (2009). *School, family, and community partnerships: Your handbook for action* (3rd ed.). Thousand Oaks, CA: Corwin Press.

Epstein, J. L., Coates, L., Salinas, K., Sanders, M., & Simon, B. (1997). A comprehensive framework for school, family, and community partnerships. In *School, family, and community partnerships: Your handbook for action* (pp. 1–25). Thousand Oaks, CA: Corwin Press.

Espinosa, L. M. (2013). *Early education for dual language learners: Promoting school readiness and school success.* Washington, DC: Migration Policy Institute.

Goodnow, J. J. (1985). Change and variation in ideas about childhood and parenting. In I. E. Sigel (Ed.), *Parental belief systems: The psychological consequences for children* (pp. 235–270). Hillsdale, NJ: Erlbaum.

Gottman, J. M., Katz, L., & Hooven, C. (1997). *Meta-emotion: How families communicate emotionally.* Mahwah, NJ: Erlbaum.

Herman, K. C., Borden, L. A., Reinke, W. M., & Webster-Stratton, C. (2011). The impact of the Incredible Years parent, child, and teacher training programs on children's co-occurring internalizing symptoms. *School Psychology Quarterly, 26*(3), 189–201.

Jacobs, J. E., Chhin, C. S., & Shaver, K. (2005). Longitudinal links between perceptions of adolescence and the social beliefs of adolescents: Are parents' stereotypes related to beliefs held about and by their children? *Journal of Youth and Adolescence, 34,* 61–72.

Jennings, P. A. (2016). CARE for Teachers: A mindfulness-based approach to promoting teachers' well-being and improving performance. In K. A. Schonert-Reichl & R. W. Roeser (Eds.), *Handbook of mindfulness in education: Emerging theory, research, and programs* (pp. 133–148). New York: Springer.

Jennings, P. A., Brown, J. L., Frank, J. L., Doyle, S., Oh, Y., Tanler, R., . . . Greenberg, M. T. (2017). Impacts of the CARE for Teachers program on teachers' social and emotional competence and classroom interactions. *Journal of Educational Psychology, 109*(7), 1010–1028.

Jennings, P. A., Frank, J. L., Snowberg, K. E., Coccia, M. A., & Greenberg, M. T. (2013). Improving classroom learning environments by cultivating awareness and resilience in education (CARE): Results of a randomized controlled trial. *School Psychology Quarterly, 28,* 374–390.

Jennings, P. A., & Greenberg, M. (2009). The Prosocial Classroom: Teacher social and emotional competence in relation to child and classroom outcomes. *Review of Educational Research, 79,* 491–525.

Jeynes, W. H. (2005). A meta-analysis of the relation of parent involvement to urban elementary school student academic achievement. *Urban Education,* *40*(3), 237–269.

Kabat-Zinn, M., & Kabat-Zinn, J. (1997). *Everyday blessings: The inner work of mindful parenting.* New York: Hachette Books.

Katz, L. F., Wilson, B., & Gottman, J. M. (1999). Meta-emotion philosophy and family adjustment: Making an emotional correction. In M. J. Cox & J. Brooks-Gunn (Eds.), *Conflict and cohesion in families: Causes and consequences* (pp. 131–165). Mahwah, NJ: Erlbaum.

Lawson, H., Alameda-Lawson, T., Lawson, M., Briar-Lawson, K., & Wilcox, K. (2014). Three parent and family interventions for rural schools and communities. *Journal of Education and Human Development, 3*(3), 59–78.

Lazarus, R. S., & Lazarus, B. N. (1994). *Passion and reason: Making sense of our emotions.* New York: Oxford University Press.

Lozowick, L. (2010). *Conscious parenting.* Chino Valley, AZ: Hohm Press.

Mapp, K. L., & Kuttner, P. J. (2013). Partners in education: A dual capacity-building framework for family–school partnerships. Retrieved from *www. sedl.org/pubs/framework/FE-Cap-Building.pdf.*

Molgaard, V., Kumpfer, K. L., & Fleming, E. (2001). *The strengthening families program: For parents and youth 10–14: A video-based curriculum.* Ames: Iowa State University Extension.

Neff, K. (2003). The development and validation of a scale to measure self-compassion. *Self and Identity, 2,* 223–250.

Patrikakou, E. N. (2008). *The power of parent involvement: Evidence, ideas, and tools for student success.* Lincoln, IL: Center on Innovation and Improvement.

Patrikakou, E. N., & Weissberg, R. P. (2007). School-family partnerships and children's social, emotional, and academic learning. In R. Bar-On, J. G. Maree, & M. J. Elias (Eds.), *Educating people to be emotionally intelligent* (pp. 49–61). Westport, CT: Greenwood.

Patrikakou, E. N., Weissberg, R. P., Redding, S., & Walberg, H. J. (2005). School–family partnerships: Enhancing the academic, social, and emotional learning of children. In E. N. Patrikakou, R. P. Weissberg, S. Redding, & H. J. Walberg (Eds.), *School–family partnerships for children's success* (pp. 1–17). New York: Teachers College Press.

Reinke, W. M., Splett, J. D., Robeson, E. N., & Offutt, C. A. (2009). Combining school and family interventions for the prevention and early intervention of disruptive behavior problems in children: A public health perspective. *Psychology in the Schools, 46*(1), 33–43.

Roeser, R. W., Schonert-Reichl, K. A., Jha, A., Cullen, M., Wallace, L., Wilensky, R., . . . Harrison, J. (2013). Mindfulness training and reductions in teacher stress and burnout: Results from two randomized, waitlist-control field trials. *Journal of Educational Psychology, 105*(3), 787–804.

Shapiro, S. L., & Carlson, L. E. (2017). *The art and science of mindfulness: Integrating mindfulness into psychology and the helping professions.* Washington, DC: American Psychological Association.

Shapiro, S., Carlson, L. E., Astin, J. A., & Freedman, B. (2006). Mechanisms of mindfulness. *Journal of Clinical Psychology, 62*(3), 373–386.

Siegel, D. (2001). Toward an interpersonal neurobiology of the developing mind:

Attachment relationships, "mindsight," and neural integration. *Infant Mental Health Journal, 22*(1–2), 67–94.

Smetana, J. G., Campione-Barr, N., & Metzger, A. (2006). Adolescent development in interpersonal and societal contexts. *Annual Review of Psychology, 57,* 255–284.

Spoth, R. L., Shin, C., & Redmond, C. (2006). Long-term effects of universal preventive interventions on methamphetamine use among adolescents. *Archives of Pediatrics and Adolescent Medicine, 160,* 876–882.

Steinberg, L. (2004). *The 10 basic principles of good parenting.* New York: Simon & Schuster.

Stiffleman, S. (2015). *Parenting with presence: Practices for raising conscious, confident, caring kids.* Novato, CA: New World Library.

Teti, G. M., & Gelfand, D. M. (1991). Behavioral competence among mothers of infants in the first year: The mediational role of maternal self-efficacy. *Child Development, 62,* 918–929.

Thomas, B. G., Greenfeld, M. D., Ames, R. T., Hine, M. G., & Epstein, J. L. (2015). *Promising Partnership Practices 2017.* Baltimore: National Network of Partnership Schools at Johns Hopkins University.

Tsabary, S. (2014). *The conscious parent: Transforming ourselves, empowering our children.* London: Hachette.

Turpyn, C. C., & Chaplin, T. M. (2016). Mindful parenting and parents' emotion expression: Effects on adolescent risk behaviors. *Mindfulness, 7,* 246–254.

Van Ryzin, M. J., Kumpfer, K. L., Fosco, G. M., & Greenberg, M. T. (Eds.). (2015). *Family-based prevention programs for children and adolescents: Theory, research, and large-scale dissemination.* New York: Psychology Press.

Vandell, D. L., Belsky, J., Burchinal, M., Steinberg, L., & Vandergrift, N. (2010). Do effects of early child care extend to age 15 years?: Results from the NICHD Study of Early Child Care and Youth Development. *Child Development, 81*(3), 737–756.

Virmani, E. A., Wiese, A. M., & Mangione, P. L. (2016). Pathways to relational family engagement with culturally and linguistically diverse families: Can reflective practice guide us? In J. A. Sutterby (Ed.), *Family involvement in early education and child care* (pp. 91–115). Bingley, UK: Emerald Group.

Weiss, H. B., Lopez, M. E., Kreider, H., & Chatman-Nelson, C. (Eds.). (2013). *Preparing educators to engage families: Case studies using an ecological systems framework.* Thousand Oaks, CA: SAGE.

PART III

LOOKING TO THE FUTURE

CHAPTER 9

Finding Peace in Chaos
Mindfully Prepared Public School Teachers

RICHARD C. BROWN
ELIZABETH GRASSI

At a time like this, when there's so much chaos and suffering in the world, individuals who are willing to wake up and make friends with themselves are actually needed, because they can work with others, they can hear what people are saying to them, they can come from the heart and be of use.
—PEMA CHÖDRÖN (IN WELWOOD, 1992, P. 223)

Teaching is a stressful, chaotic field. Owing to increasing demands on students and teachers, persistent low salaries, and overcrowded schools, teacher retention is at an all-time low. Studies have found that mindfulness-based practices help reduce student stress and increase academic achievement even within the high-paced environments found in most public schools today (Ahmed, Trager, Rodwell, Foinding, & Lopez, 2017). And because students spend a great deal of time in schools, teachers who practice mindfulness with students are in a position to positively influence student well-being, including a reduction in stress, anxiety, and depression (Stuart, Collins, Toms, & Gwalla Ogisi, 2017).

In this chapter, we describe the development of a contemplative state-approved teacher licensure program, in which we prepare teachers in mindfulness-based contemplative practices, alongside traditional teacher education, to better prepare them for the classrooms of today. We describe this process in detail, from vision to development. Particular attention is given to our integration of contemplative disciplines and pedagogies into standards-based state licensure requirements. While this process involved a team of five people, this chapter arises from the experience and perspectives of two of those members—Richard C. Brown and Elizabeth [Liz] Grassi—who are the authors of this chapter.

Contemplative Education

It is important to consider what we mean by contemplative education and how it may be distinctive. To contemplate means to deeply consider one's connection to a subject or discipline in unbiased, selfless, compassionate, and holistic ways. For centuries Western education has prioritized cognitive learning and suppressed the wisdom of the body, manifested in its senses and emotions. This legacy has unnecessarily isolated teachers and learners from the foundational roots of knowing and caring. Contemplative education seeks to restore the natural ways of knowing and pair them with contemporary methods, skills, and knowledge.

Naropa University's approach to contemplative education is secular, yet spiritually inspired—similar to other mindfulness-based programs that value and engage the inner lives of students and teachers. At its best, it uses a broad array of practices, including mindfulness, awareness, compassion, and embodied presence to develop inclusive and life-affirming methods of teaching and learning. By mixing contemplative practices with a full range of human capacities and areas of study, students and teachers make personalized and sustainable connections to skills and subject content. This synthesis results in a genuine empathetic presence, a deeply felt relationship to content, agile thinking, and enlivened learning cultures. Contemplative education at Naropa prepares its graduates to benefit the world and have a meaningful personal life.

The activation and clarification of the inner resources of the teacher become the primary basis for the meaningful holistic instruction of students. When experienced through the practices of mindfulness and awareness, the teacher's life is stabilized and enriched through nonjudgmental acceptance of present-moment experiences.

Compassion practice builds on the teacher's foundation of mindfulness and awareness, activating empathy and interdependence with students. Compassionate relationships with students are deepened by the teacher's self-compassion and emotional regulation of his or her own feelings and thoughts. The teacher balances empathy for students with an awareness of the classroom culture and curricular requirements. Compassionate learning cultures organically emerge through disciplined interdependence.

Contemplative classrooms are not as easily recognizable as some other spiritually inspired approaches, such as Waldorf and Montessori, because contemplative approaches are readily applicable to any holistic method or setting. Contemplative pedagogy can be used at any level of instruction from PreK through higher education and in any area of study. Contemplative learning environments support reflective rhythms in class activities, creating spacious, yet focused atmospheres. As in other social–emotional learning (SEL) environments, contemplative learning communities are based on co-created guidelines, empathy, and genuine personal connections, rather than on prescriptive norms. Contemplative teachers are often indistinguishable from other skilled teachers, because contemplative teaching is at its essence a natural and caring intragenerational exchange that is not reliant on fixed techniques. Teachers are typically nonreactive, yet engaged; they are empathetic, yet disciplined in their relationships with students. Another feature that contemplative learning has in common with the best SEL environments is the teacher's ability to accommodate and transform the strong emotional experiences that can arise from students making deep personal connections with the material they are studying, as well as from the emotional complexities of students' personal lives. The teachers are able and willing to meet the students where they are, developing a feeling of trust that begins to chip away at students' limiting or harmful styles of relating and learning. With a settled, yet lively presence, teachers and students engage with the curriculum in genuine, effective, and creative ways. Through ongoing practice, teachers and learners become calmer, more creative, and better able to sustain themselves in a demanding enterprise.

How We Got Here: Obtaining State Approval for Licensure

In 2017 Naropa University gained approval from the state of Colorado to develop the first Contemplative Elementary Teacher Licensure with an added endorsement in Culturally and Linguistically Diverse (CLD) Education. State approval was easier to secure than it might have been in the past because the mindfulness in education movement and SEL had begun to take root in the educational field across much of the country. In addition, contemplative education has gained recognition because it provides teachers with the tools and practices needed to flourish and sustain themselves while working in the demanding field of education. School systems are recognizing that supporting the mental and emotional health of their teachers can lead to less turnover and increased student learning, and new research on mindfulness in education supports the benefits of contemplative practices for teachers and students. (Ahmed et al., 2017; Maynard, Solis, Miller, & Brenden, 2017).

Finding the Team for the Licensure Program

The development of a state-approved contemplative teacher licensure required the creation of a strong team. The team consisted of five members from the Contemplative Education Department, two of whom are the authors of this chapter. Because of our diverse backgrounds as educators, we both contributed important dimensions to the task of creating the first state-approved contemplative teacher licensure program.

I (Richard) offered the contemplative lens to the process. After 9 years of public and private K–12 teaching, I founded the Contemplative Education Department at Naropa University in 1990. I developed a BA in Early Childhood Education (ECE) and the low-residency MA in Contemplative Education. My approaches drew heavily from Buddhist principles and practices, while remaining nonsectarian. Over the years of training preservice and inservice teachers, I have refined my methods, making them more applicable to public and private classrooms.

I (Elizabeth [Liz]) came to Naropa after spending 12 years as a K–12 public school teacher and 14 years as a university professor, during which time I developed and taught courses aligned with state teacher accreditation standards. I had experience working with the State Department of Education on teacher licensure and had successfully achieved state approval for higher-education endorsement programs previously.

The first challenge the team faced was developing an understanding of the different "languages" team members used to communicate and of the different cultures from which everyone operated. For example, while Liz spoke in terms of teacher quality standards, CLD strategies, licenses, and endorsements, Richard spoke in terms of presence, awareness, emotional fluency, and rhythms. While Liz operated from a fast-paced, action-oriented culture, Richard worked from a contemplative, reflective culture. Both addressed assessment, but from very different perspectives. Bridging our diverse perspectives was a challenge on its own, but was integral to the development of a working team and a licensure program that deeply incorporated both perspectives. We started with baby steps. Liz took a class in the Naropa MA program to begin to understand the aspects of contemplative teaching. She also worked with a meditation mentor at Naropa and started a practice of her own. Richard gradually learned from Liz about state standards and CLD strategies and endeavored to see how contemplative practices and methods could be woven into the required state curriculum.

In department meetings Liz worked to embody and express her feelings, while the rest of the team worked to regulate their own feelings in a tense environment of initial misunderstandings. In each meeting, Richard explained the contemplative perspective, while Liz explained the standards perspective. Gradually over the first year, the team began to grasp contemplative teaching practices, and understand and speak in terms of standard-based practices. This process required patience, openness, and an eagerness on everyone's part to learn. While this process would have been simplified by adopting a "business model" in which Liz was hired to develop the standards-based aspect of the licensure and Richard was in charge of developing the contemplative aspect, thereby never truly blending or acquiring a deeper understanding of the two, we wanted to collaborate in our learning, and develop a richly integrated, contemplative licensure. We needed to find a way to understand and work closely together.

From the outset, we all believed that the development of a contemplative state licensure was the correct path on which to proceed. We believed deeply in our work, and that the future of education would benefit from contemplatively prepared teachers. This common belief held us together, regardless of the situation, but we still established norms to help us better work as a team. We scheduled weekly 2- to 3-hour meetings with team members. We always started with a check-in to get a read on people's feelings and any issues they were dealing with. We set an agenda each week, which involved Liz discussing the standards-based aspect and Richard discussing the contemplative-based aspect. We then left time to create and build. Co-creation of syllabi and classes is a difficult task, and while the task was not seamless, it gave us all an opportunity to practice mindful listening and speaking and checking in with oneself around triggers. By consistently meeting, checking in, and coming together on a meaningful task, we found a way to work closely on developing a licensure program wherein contemplative practices were front and center in teacher preparation.

From Past to Present: The Legacy of the Naropa Inservice and Preservice Program's Philosophical Foundations and Early Years

"The teacher is an anchor whose presence in body, voice, and mind empowers students, themselves, to become fully immersed in the learning process. Having such presence, an embodied teacher brings together the students' collaborative energies in a circle of mutual discovery, where the outcomes may surprise both teacher and students and lead to an excitement for life and learning."
—BROWN, SIMONE, AND WORLEY (2016, P. 210)

The contemplative foundations for our education programs were derived from several sources. The primary source was Buddhist practices and principles, which have been adapted for Western education at Naropa since 1974. This source has primarily affected our approach to the personal and relational development of the teacher, regarding mindfulness, awareness, compassion, sensory embodiment, and artistic expression. However, there was another Buddhist-inspired source that deeply influenced our approach, particularly in the graduate program. The 10 *vidyas*, which were part of the curriculum of Nalanda University of Medieval India, involved the teaching of content— language, logic, creativity, and so forth—using methods that imbued this content with profound depth. This became an increasingly relevant part of our inservice training since many of our instructors were teaching content that was prescribed by their schools. Adapting the 10 vidyas, or Aspects of Knowledge, to contemporary teaching and learning proved to be a key bridge in beginning a state-approved licensure program.

The foundations of our state-approved licensure were put in place in 1990 when Naropa University established a BA in ECE that trained early educators and certified preschool administrators. At Naropa's lab school, Alaya, our ECE students were able to observe and intern at a preschool setting with exceptional contemplative teachers. In the beginning, the preservice contemplative dimensions of our teacher training focused on presence and relationship skills. Students were taught mindfulness, awareness, embodiment, and compassion skills so they could sustain themselves and thrive in the classroom. Next, they learned to integrate these skills into their teaching relationships with children. Early on in our program, pedagogical skills were learned largely from supervising teachers in contemplative internship placements at the Alaya Preschool. Fortunately, the teachers had experience with compatible teaching traditions, primarily Waldorf and Montessori. Starting in 1978, Alaya's preschool teachers had begun to introduce these traditions into their curriculum. As more of our ECE graduates started centers in Boulder, our contemplative placement sites grew and also offered a variety of educational approaches, including the arts-centered Reggio approach. This diversity reflects a basic approach of contemplative education: contemplative principles, practices, and pedagogies can be integrated into virtually any educational approach because the emphasis is more on the presence of the teacher and how content is taught, rather than on what is being taught.

In 2001 Naropa expanded by launching a low-residency inservice MA in Contemplative Education for teachers of all subjects and at all levels of instruction from PreK through higher education. Over the previous 10 years in the ECE program, we had developed contemplative methods and pedagogies involving mainly personal presence and relationship skills. In the 2-year MA program, we began more explicitly to develop classroom management and pedagogy training.

The 3-week summer retreat that begins the first year of the MA program allowed our students to focus intensively on their own contemplative development, to create compassionate relationships, and to experience a carefully crafted contemplative learning climate. Each summer program is followed by two semesters of online courses during which the students return to their teaching roles and practice applying what they had learned for themselves in their own classrooms. The application of contemplative skills in the program is carefully sequenced, so that the teachers first learn how to nurture and sustain themselves before they begin implementing contemplative relationships, classroom management, compassionate community building, and curricular transformational approaches. Because our online students report back every week on their progress in contemplative development and pedagogy, we are able to refine and improve our approaches. We can assess how our students are adapting the practices they learn and are integrating them into their classrooms around the country and abroad. For example, our students reported that contemplative observation practice (Brown, 1998–1999) was an important method for integrating their inner experiences into observational and instructional processes. As a result, we began to sequence and practice the necessary observation skills throughout the courses in the MA program. This ongoing emphasis better established students' abilities to infuse their inner experiences with their teaching presence.

The powerful learning communities that take shape during the two summer programs and in the online courses are another key element in the success of the program. The students who returned for their second summer program become mentors for the first-year students. The same close community has developed among our devoted program faculty, who often co-teach, collaborate, and mentor newer faculty. During the summer programs, our faculty meet almost daily to plan and improve what we are doing. Since the faculty is drawn from different contemplative disciplines (arts, performance, psychology, and education), the exchanges are extremely generative and create an integrated multidisciplinary program. These advantages also carry over into the online courses, which are frequently co-taught, as are the summer courses. Over the years our mutual understanding of effective contemplative practices and pedagogy has broadened and deepened. Every year the pedagogies and sequences are refined, and their scope is expanded.

While the programs we have mentioned had an impact on practicing teachers and ECE teachers, they did not include the licensure to teach in public schools. We knew that if Naropa were to make a significant impact on the preparation of K–12 teachers, we needed to be approved for state teacher licensure. The contemplative state-approved licensure would be tied to two programs: a BA in contemplative education (which includes licensure) and a contemplative Graduate Teacher Licensure 1-year program.

Developing a State-Approved Contemplative Curriculum

Developing a state-approved contemplative teacher licensure program involved addressing two integral questions:

1. How do we incorporate nonsectarian contemplative practices into a standards-based state-approved curriculum?
2. How do we translate contemplative practices and pedagogies in such a manner that the department of education would understand our vision?

Because state approval of licensure depended heavily on our alignment with state-required teacher standards, we first needed to learn what
they were. What undergraduate courses that already existed at Naropa met
these standards, and what courses needed to be developed or revised to
meet them? As a group, we examined the required standards and started
work on curriculum development.

The key distinction between state teacher quality standards and a
contemplative approach is that the quality standards are mainly outer
directed. They are designed to fully develop teaching strategies that help
children access the curriculum and thrive academically. These standards
do not take into account the natural interface that exists between a teacher's inner resources and students' learning processes. While they are integral to our teacher preparation program, they need to be linked to contemplative practices and pedagogies to give teachers the skills of meaningful
self-sustainability, genuine contact with students, and creative teaching.
Our experience in the Contemplative Education Department at Naropa
over the last 28 years has led us to believe that teachers needed both the
teacher quality standards that help them develop the seminal strategies to
effectively teach children and contemplative competencies to develop the
resilience, presence, inner reflection, and insight needed to thrive.

We realized early on that the contemplative component could not be
an "add-on" to traditional courses. We had to consider the contemplative
practices as foundational to the standards-based curriculum. Readings and
practices in contemplative education had to be fully integrated into every
aspect of the curriculum. We also realized that all of the contemplative
aspects of the program needed to be presented and taught using nonsectarian terms and methods, considering that our teachers would be working in
the public school system. Not only was this strategy necessary for broader
acceptance of contemplative education, but it also reflected its essentially
nonreligious nature. In order to create a nonsectarian program, the education faculty collaborated in developing appropriate syllabi. We began with
traditional standards-based syllabi by looking at the topics presented (e.g.,
student engagement) and offered readings and practices from the contemplative field for each topic.

However, this process still seemed disjointed and tended to reflect an
"add-on" perspective, rather than a truly integrated process. We needed to
step back and select the seminal contemplative skills that we wanted every
teacher to employ, and these skills needed to be woven throughout our curriculum. We required a series of nonsectarian contemplative exercises that
were carefully sequenced through students' 4 years of preservice education.
These activities or practices would move from the teacher's inner awareness
to mindful engagement with instructional activities and be correlated with
courses. This approach, we felt, would give rise to individualized versions
of contemplative competencies for each preservice teacher.

Because the contemplative elements of the program were to be infused into already densely packed state-mandated course syllabi, we did not want to overwhelm students and faculty with the many contemplative practices and pedagogies that had become part of the Contemplative Education program over 28 years. After many iterations, we created a list of core Contemplative Teaching Competencies that would help us gauge the development of the skills expected of all our preservice teachers. Contemplative teaching competencies are developed over time as teachers incorporate contemplative practices, like mindfulness, awareness, embodiment, and compassion, into their teaching lives. The competencies are the synthesis of best teaching practices with contemplative approaches to learning relationships within the culture of particular environments.

While all iterations of the contemplative competencies were incredibly valuable and encouraged rich, deep discussions in department meetings, our fear was that the State Department of Education would be unable to fully appreciate the Trajectory of Competencies (shown in Figure 9.1), unless they were presented in an organized fashion as the outcomes of the program. The Competencies are cultivated through bridge exercises within which are imbedded the practices tied to each course.

Trajectory for Contemplatively Prepared Teachers

The Contemplative Teaching Competencies we develop in each preservice teacher involve a multistep process that we illustrate using the backward design method (Wiggins & McTighe, 2005) shown in Figure 9.1.

The Naropa Contemplative Teaching Competencies[1]

The Contemplative Teaching Competencies represent the integration of effective instructional practices with contemplative capacities. They are divided into four areas: Presence, Relationship, Environment, and Pedagogy, which represent a progression from inner to outer capacities. The Presence competencies are the basis for the Relationship, and Environmental competencies. In combination the Presence, Relationship and Environment competencies constitute the foundation of the Pedagogical competencies.

The Competencies are articulated in nonsectarian terms for use in all educational settings, from PreK through college and beyond. They are

---

[1]We are calling these "*Naropa* Contemplative Competencies" because they are being used widely at Naropa University. Originally developed by Richard, he refined this version with Naropa's Center for the Advancement of Contemplative Education (CACE). It is the basis for the Contemplative Development section of the Naropa Faculty Handbook for the Faculty Promotion Review process.

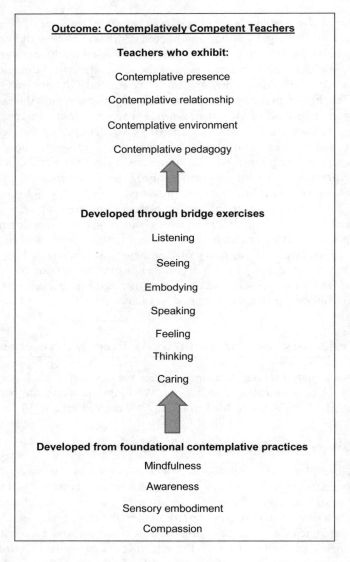

FIGURE 9.1. Trajectory of Competencies.

stated in general terms to allow for their natural emergence in individual teachers in diverse situations. A teacher may be proficient in a particular competency one minute and not in another. Because the competencies are dynamically interconnected, individual variations occur. Because of differences in individual dispositions, teachers may be effective in some areas and not in others. Partial proficiency can be sufficient, because the competencies constitute an interdependent whole and reinforce each other. While it is not necessary to master them all, relating to the foundational practices cultivates wholeness and fosters any undeveloped competencies. In ideal learning environments, co-teaching compensates for variations in the individual competencies of teachers. The sum of the teachers' strengths and skills creates greater wholeness, and teachers have the opportunity to learn from each other's competencies.

The Contemplative Teaching Competencies were abstracted from numerous, mainly Buddhist, sources and adapted to Naropa's Western liberal arts model. The main sources include the 10 *vidyas,* or *"fields of knowledge,"* from the Indo-Tibetan monastic curriculum; the Five Buddha Families of Tibetan Buddhism; and Richard's experiences teaching in contemplative schools from PreK through the graduate level over the past 40 years.

Throughout our program, the Contemplative Teaching Competencies are not only the "standard" we want all preservice and inservice teachers to develop, but they provide the evaluation tools for supervisors observing the contemplative aspects of teaching.

Presence Contemplative Competencies

Presence competencies are based on the development of the inner foundational practices of mindfulness, awareness, sensory embodiment, compassion, and contemplation, and are learned through the Bridge Exercises. Presence practices sustain and nurture teachers and liberate a fuller range of instructional abilities, which are the basis of contemplative teaching competencies. In this competency the teacher:

1. Is mindful and aware of inner experiences and how they change.
2. Understands that complex factors contribute to any given moment of experience.
3. Values inner and somatic responses without indulging or repressing them.
4. Appreciates the fundamental goodness and workability of all experiences.
5. Experiences moments of "not-knowing" as potential sources of insight.
6. Is kind and forgiving toward oneself.
7. Cultivates grace and authenticity in movement and speech.

Relationship Contemplative Competencies

Relationship competencies extend the teacher's contemplative presence skills into meaningful and effective relationships with students and others.

Relationship competencies enhance interactive communication skills that deeply engage both teacher and student in the context of the instructional climate. In this competency the teacher:

1. Recognizes and softens feelings of separation between oneself and others.
2. Experiences embodied presence as an aspect of communication.
3. Collaborates and communicates with authenticity, empathy, and compassion.
4. Fosters honest and compassionate relationships with and among others.
5. Is open to creative and playful elements in communication and creativity.
6. Engages with what is offered, pleasurable or painful, without defensiveness.
7. Authentically engages with all who are suffering, or may be perceived as different, marginalized, or underrepresented.

Environmental Contemplative Competencies

The learning environment, an essential dimension of contemplative teaching and learning, includes the space within and beyond the immediate classroom. An awareness of spacious inner and outer environments with defined, yet flexible boundaries cultivates relaxed and challenging teaching. In this competency the teacher:

1. Creates welcoming, clean, and uplifted learning environments.
2. Creates open environments that facilitate movement and creativity.
3. Accommodates immediate student needs within the existing curricular sequence.
4. Engages environmental elements within and beyond the classroom, including the seasons, the natural world, and **the rhythms, rituals, and celebrations that connect** to the seasons and natural world.
5. Cultivates disciplined subjectivity, synchronizing spacious inner experience with outer and global occurrences.
6. Develops respect and genuine appreciation for diverse cultures, races, ethnicities, genders, and sexualities, including one's own,
7. Supports the well-being and safety of all, and opposes harmful actions.

Pedagogical Contemplative Competencies

Pedagogy refers to contemplative approaches and holistic methods that are based on the previous Presence, Relationship, and Environmental skills.

Contemplative pedagogies transform existing or newly created curricula, and improve classroom management at any level and in any subject discipline. In this competency the teacher:

1. Practices mindfulness, awareness, embodiment, and compassion during instruction.
2. Appropriately infuses personal emotional, cognitive, and somatic-based inspirations into instructional activity.
3. Personalizes subject content, and encourages direct experience and creativity.
4. Creates pauses during instruction and transitions to encourage participation, self-care, and insight.
5. Promotes accountability by setting clear, appropriate, yet flexible boundaries.
6. Values mistakes as opportunities for learning, and is able to be critical and caring without praise or blame.
7. Cultivates a climate of curiosity and openness that accommodates ambiguity, competing ideas, and strong emotions.

Bridge Exercises

Selected specifically for teacher education, each set of exercises connects the foundation practices to the Contemplative Teaching Competencies, or the skills and attitudes teachers need to become contemplatively competent educators. The Bridge Exercises are sequenced and distributed throughout the curriculum to connect inner capacities, such as mindfulness, with outer practical classroom applications. The Exercises are resources that can be integrated into each course syllabus. Specific exercises from different areas (Listening, Seeing, Speaking, Embodying, Feeling, Thinking, and Caring) can be tailored, adapted, and added in order to meet the focus of a particular course. Later we give examples of different Bridge Exercises that are appropriate for different courses.

Bridge Exercises are intended to "bridge" foundational practices with traditional teacher practices. We selected Listening Exercises as an example here because listening skills are fundamental to responsive teaching. Other bridge exercises include speaking, seeing, embodying, thinking, and caring.

> The first stage, which lays the groundwork, is listening, listening, listening, and listening. Listening to your own thoughts and to your heart before you speak, so that you know what you really want to say; listening attentively with open mind and heart to what others are saying and encouraging others to listen to their own hearts and to others in the same way. Listening is perhaps the most important aspect of working together in a group. (Hayward, 1995, p. 253)

Listening Bridge Exercises

In early preservice courses, the Listening Bridge Exercises are woven together with other exercises to develop the Contemplative Competencies. In the next sections, we provide a few examples of one of the Listening Bridge Exercises, and how they work within a traditional teacher education program to help teachers acquire specific competencies.

Developing the Presence Competency through Listening Exercises

   1. *Mindfully receiving sounds as pure sense perception.* This basic exercise involves preservice teachers hearing a simple sound, such as a bell ringing. While listening, they keep their attention on the sound itself. They mindfully notice their emotional, cognitive, and somatic responses to the sound and bring their attention back to just hearing the sound. This exercise can be expanded to include self-compassion when the preservice teacher experiences self-judgment. It is applicable to the classroom, because it helps teachers separate the actual sounds and voices in the classroom from the reactions they produce within the teacher—allowing for more effective responses.

   2. *Pausing while listening, tuning into oneself, and coming back to deep listening.* Preservice teachers place a hand on their chest while listening to simple sounds. The use of the hand is a reminder to notice their inner experiences, honor them, set them aside, and return to listening from the heart. This activity prepares teachers to include their inner experiences and caring practices while listening to students. When teachers' inner experiences are nonjudgmentally noticed, they can be regulated and then become sources for personalized and creative communications. Self-compassion is essential in this and virtually all exercises, because of the tendency toward self-judgment.

   3. *Creating space around and within sounds.* This advanced-awareness exercise involves preservice teachers listening to a sound and noticing that the sound has space around and within it. At first, space awareness exercises like this challenge one's abilities and understanding. But with practice, using a variety of methods and applications, the space-awareness competency becomes an almost indispensable skill. This exercise is directly applicable to the classroom, because sound can be overwhelming and exhausting. With a spaciously aware mind, the teacher can relax within an often chaotic classroom soundscape. When lessened anxiety is lessened, the teacher can appreciate the aliveness of sounds and can respond more effectively and creatively. He or she learns to experience the context and

natural openness of sounds, which otherwise may only be flat, meaningless conveyers of information.

4. *Listening to an audio of a voice and experiencing it as simple sounds.* The instructor plays an audio of someone reading or telling a story. As before, the preservice teacher practices alternately listening from both the heart and the head to the content and the sounds by practicing deep holistic listening to a human voice. Additions to this exercise can include self-compassion and compassion for the reader when the teacher notices that judgments arise.

Developing the Relationship Competency through Listening Exercises

1. *Mindful listening in pairs with no somatic response.* Preservice teachers are not only encouraged to mindfully listen, without giving a response, but also to notice any reaction within the body while listening. They pair–share afterward. Often preservice teachers are triggered by what they hear their students say, and their bodies react by flinching, for example. If the teacher can pause, really listen to students, and notice their own somatic responses, then they can learn to regulate, rather than react to them. The preservice teacher's relationship with the student will become calmer and more resonant.

2. *Listening from the heart and head to a classmate describe a meaningful experience.* Preservice teachers mindfully listen to a classmate without preparing a response. They are prompted to notice any feelings or emotions that arise, honor them without reacting, and return to deep listening. When this exercise is used in the classroom, the result is that students feel thoroughly heard, and preservice teachers can wait and respond more effectively after a pause.

3. *Deep listening with somatic resonance, then with a simple verbal response.* This exercise requires pausing after mindfully embodied listening in pairs, and sharing a short, authentic verbal response. Then the pair discusses their experiences. A more-advanced level of the exercise involves being authentic *and* finding a caring way to genuinely respond. When applied in the classroom, the exercise involves being able to give feedback to students, which is both honest and kind.

4. *Deep listening to a variety of role-played scenarios.* The preservice teachers themselves suggest challenging scenarios drawn from their classroom experiences to role-play. The instructor should select the suggestions

in order to provide for increasing levels of challenge and to eliminate the highly charged ones. It is important not to suggest instructional strategies to "fix" the scenarios. It is more effective for developing contemplative competencies to have preservice teachers imagine how to refine their Presence and Relationship listening skills in order to shift the dynamics of the situation.

Developing the Environmental Competency through Listening Exercises

1. *Mindfully listening to the natural sounds of wind and water.* Begin by having preservice teachers listen to louder natural sounds, like strong winds or rushing water, at the source or by listening to audio recordings. Use mindful listening techniques: letting go of thoughts or returning to the sounds themselves, for example. Then decrease the volume or move farther away from the source, and repeat the exercise. In this case, in addition to the natural sound have the teachers notice other ambient noises, including human-caused sounds. Practice regarding all the sounds as "natural" by using mindfulness techniques. In other variations, notice the space between the sounds, the rhythm among the sounds, or the creative thoughts or images that may occur to the listener. These exercises can develop the preservice teacher's ability to experience previously jarring or discordant classroom sounds as more natural, thus relieving stress.

2. *Symphony of place.* Preservice teachers sit grounded on the earth beside a busy street, without looking at the vehicles. They mindfully listen—letting go of naming and judging the sounds. After listening, they record the symphony of sounds, using letters, syllables, or invented words. Alternatively, they can use pencil, pen, paintbrush, or charcoal, to interpret the sounds. As the practice develops, they can interpret the sounds through movement, song, or simple musical instrumentation. In the classroom, this exercise could help develop creative or somatic resonance with classroom sounds that could affect how they move through the classroom or their on-the-spot expressions.

3. *Mindfully aware listening to an audio of a busy classroom.* Sequence the previously practiced deep listening skills to listen on different levels to a busy or chaotic classroom or lunchroom. Using an audio recording or observation, preservice teachers practice finding space within the sounds or within their own emotional responses, offering kindness to the students affected by the chaos, and regarding the sounds as natural.

4. *Extending an awareness of sounds beyond the classroom.* Include the sounds heard beyond the classroom by inviting the preservice teachers

to listen for those more distant sounds. This exercise can be done during classroom observations or in a moment during student teaching, and cultivates the teacher's awareness that is not limited to the classroom walls. It can help the preservice teacher point out resonances in the outside world, such as a passing thunderstorm during a difficult lesson.

Developing the Pedagogy Competency through Listening Exercises

1. *Practicing wait time.* Use wait-time techniques, such as allowing a few seconds before responding, while participating in a discussion or engaged in practice teaching. During the 3-second pause, the preservice teachers tune in to their body as a way of grounding themselves in the present moment. They notice their emotional field to see whether it needs regulating or whether it can be a vehicle for a meaningful personal contribution. Waiting allows for greater cognitive precision to emerge through contemplation, thereby producing more articulate instruction. They may also notice any anxiety that arises around the thought that they might not have a chance to contribute to the discussion, or any feeling of insecurity as a teacher, because they are not taking the lead role.

2. *Being mindfully aware while teaching or presenting material to the class.* Preservice teachers pause a moment to tune into the soundscape of the class before they begin teaching. They take some time to look around at the students, not individually, but as a class body. While speaking, they allow for pauses and are mindful of the sound and feel of their own voice. They pause when arriving at an important idea. They may try expressing it in a slightly new way. They stop briefly to see how that idea lands with the students. They notice if anyone looks befuddled or has checked out—then they empathize with and gently question them.

3. *Practicing empathetic listening to an emotionally charged student.* Preservice teachers can practice role-play situations based on staged encounters with emotionally charged students. These could begin with relatively tame scenarios, then progress to more difficult ones. During the role play, the preservice teachers focus on the sounds of the students' words. They practice pausing and silently offering kindness. While listening during the staged encounters, preservice teachers apply their knowledge of how to experience their own emotions, such as respecting or noticing the emotion, but not indulging it. When preservice teachers practice teaching, they could identify students who trigger their emotions, then role-play those encounters in education courses. These teachers could further strengthen their empathetic connections with challenging students by bringing them to mind during their personal compassion practice sessions. Doing so would

make it easier to remember to offer kindness to those students during their actual student teaching experiences.

Foundational Contemplative Practices

Foundational practices (mindfulness, awareness, sensory embodiment, and compassion) are the central basic inner practices that give teachers the capacities to sustain themselves, teach effectively, and enhance their students' creativity and insight. In a sense, the foundational practices are the roots of the Bridge Exercises distributed throughout the curriculum. The Bridge Exercises listed previously are sequenced so as to give rise to the Contemplative Teaching Competencies.

Infusing the Contemplative Trajectory throughout the Teacher Licensure Courses

In order to integrate the Naropa Contemplative Teaching Competencies into the developmental sequence of our teacher education courses, we implemented a three-step process:

1. We agreed that the Contemplative Competencies would be an integral part of our program and incorporated it as part of our application for teacher licensure and as part of our evaluation process.
2. We examined the pedagogical skills or theoretical topics pertinent to each teacher education course.
3. We aligned the contemplative Bridge Exercises with each class, noting in which areas Contemplative Teaching Competencies are developed and ensuring that all competencies are addressed and assessed throughout the program.

A teacher licensure program requires several layers of preparation, and as we looked to incorporate the three-step process throughout these layers, we needed to examine the appropriate developmental contemplative skills for each course level. We categorized all teacher preparation classes into three levels: introductory, middle, and upper. We then concurrently developed contemplative Bridge Exercises for each level and aligned them with the Contemplative Teaching Competencies.

Although this process presented a linear sequence that often satisfied the state evaluators, the practice of learning and implementing contemplative skills is anything but linear. For example, although we would like students to practice advanced self-care skills in upper-level courses, the stress and confusion of teaching in real time often has our students returning to the basic self-care skills, such as grounding oneself in one's body, to make it through the day. The use and practice of contemplative skills are cyclical in nature, and students will naturally alternate between basic and advanced skills depending on the situation and the stress levels.

In order to give our undergraduate instructors greater freedom to select specific Bridge Exercises that would correspond more precisely to the emergent needs of a particular class day, we created a Resource Guide for Contemplative Pedagogy that provides optional exercises for listening, speaking, seeing, embodying, thinking, and caring, as well as other information.

Aligning Contemplative Exercises with State Standards

The second approach we took was to examine the pedagogical skills required for the development of the State Teacher Quality Standards in each course and to develop contemplative activities that would enhance these pedagogical skills. We looked at each Teacher Quality Standard and aligned specific contemplative practices with that standard. To better illustrate this process, we examine Teacher Quality Standard 8.02(2)(b): *Plan and implement differentiated instructional strategies that address stages of individual development; personal traits and interests; language diversity; exceptionality.*

Teacher Quality Standard 8.02(2)(b) can be more broadly interpreted as "knowing your students" and developing lessons that meet the varied needs of diverse learners in the classroom. In order to develop contemplative skills that emphasize the "knowing of students," we utilized the Bridge Exercises (listening, seeing, feeling, speaking, thinking, embodying, and caring) that develop the Presence, Relationship, Environmental, and Pedagogical competencies. We demonstrate how this process works by examining three education courses: an introductory course, a middle-level course, and an upper-level course.

Introductory-Level Course: EDU 150—Foundations of Education

This course emphasizes the traditional teacher standard of "knowing your students." We ask our students, "What do we need to do as teachers to get to know your interests, traits, language diversity, and exceptionalities?" We explore the different facets of students' lives that we must know in order to be effective teachers. At the same time, we introduce the Bridge Exercises as a way of getting to know ourselves as teachers as well. We purposefully introduce the inner-teacher presence perspective, and practice becoming confident in ourselves as teachers so that we can contribute our inner resources and wisdom. In an introductory course such as this one, we set the stage for our preservice teachers to develop the inner capacities needed to take the time to "know their students" as they concurrently recognize and integrate themselves into the teaching and learning relationship.

In this introductory course, we focus particularly on the development of mindfulness, awareness, and embodiment practices experienced through numerous Bridge Exercises in the areas of listening, seeing, and speaking. As the instructor lays out a progression of these exercises, he or she can select from a number of options that are detailed in our Resource Guide for Contemplative Pedagogy.

In the words of Thich Nhat Hanh: "You listen without giving advice or passing judgment. You can say to yourself about the other person, 'I am listening to him just because I want to relieve his suffering.' This is compassionate listening" (2009, p. 85). To deepen preservice teachers' knowledge of their students, we develop their listening skills, as the earlier examples illustrate. Generally speaking, we have the teachers mindfully decouple listening to sounds from making associations with sounds in order to help teachers reconnect with the information available to them from the simple sounds of their students' voices. When teachers can listen to the sounds *and* the meaning of students' words, then they have more resources from which to draw. For example, a student might say that he understands what a teacher is saying, but the sound of his voice may convey uncertainty.

A listening exercise that cultivates this basic skill is listening to a stream of water or the sound of the wind. As presented earlier, preservice teachers are first reminded that their sense of hearing conveys information on a purely sensory level, apart from any labels or interpretation they may associate with the sound. They are given the basic mindfulness instruction to simply receive the sound of the stream—by just allowing their ears to function on their own. Whenever thoughts arise, they are noticed, and then set aside. Thoughts are not rejected, just distinguished from the direct experience of hearing. This mindfulness skill of distinguishing thoughts from other experiences is fundamental to all contemplative experience.

Listening to sound itself can relieve teachers' stress. By experiencing sound apart from evaluation or judgment, the mind may be freed from the constant monitoring of or feeling bombarded by classroom noise. A mid-level activity that develops this skill is listening to audiotapes of classroom sounds. By listening to recordings of various classroom sounds that run the gamut from the gentle humming of a smoothly running classroom to more raucous levels— think enthusiastic group work—teachers gradually learn to use awareness practices to relax their emotional stress level and become more effective in listening, communicating, and decision making.

Self-compassion, a skill that is part of the caring activity thread, intersects with the development of the competency of deep listening. Two successive courses in the preservice teacher's first year as an undergraduate are devoted to learning a nonsectarian version of compassion practice. Practicing self-forgiveness and being kind to oneself are absolutely essential, because training the ways we process what we hear can be quite challenging. We support these practices by teaching self-care techniques, which lessen teachers' stress. As teachers learn to mindfully notice self-judging thoughts and generate true kindness for themselves, their inner dynamics become more straightforward and manageable. As the BA courses unfold, compassion practice is further developed so that the preservice teacher learns to generate true kindness for students, parents, colleagues, and others.

Middle-Level Course: EDU 375—Linguistics for CLD Students

One of the biggest challenges we face when preparing teachers to work with CLD students is the inherent, and oftentimes, unconscious bias that all teachers bring with them to the classroom. When a teacher encounters a child who has a different language and/or cultural background, teachers will most often fall back on their own cultural norms as a measurement for "the classroom norm." Thus, when a child acts, speaks, behaves, or "does school" from his own cultural norms, the teacher may assume that the child is "rude" or "badly behaved," because he is not conforming to the teacher's cultural expectations. However, the child may be acting perfectly normal for the culture and language from which he/she hails. Because the teacher is in a position of power, the child usually loses in these cases of cultural mismatch and is expected to conform to the teacher's and school's culture and language, rather than being respectfully allowed to conform to his own.

Today, the majority of teachers are white, English-speaking, middle-class females (U.S. Department of Education, 2016), who bring certain cultural expectations for school behavior, social behavior, ways of showing respect, and ways of interacting with the teacher and others. When a child behaves in a way that is appropriate for his or her own culture, but not that of the teacher, the teacher can be triggered into enacting learned, and perhaps unconscious, biases and prejudice. Research shows that white teachers in particular discipline children of color much more often than white children (Heitzeg, 2016). These disciplinary actions can, in turn, contribute to the increasingly alarming rates of children being pushed into "the school-to-prison pipeline" (Alexander, 2012; Heitzeg, 2016).

In traditional teacher preparation, we address this situation by having teachers examine their own biases through the reading of culturally relevant pedagogy and white-privilege literature; through the practice of developing lessons that "shelter instruction" for emerging bilinguals and differentiate instruction for diverse learners; and through class discussions, service projects with cultures other than the teachers, and immersion in culturally diverse schools. Although these activities can be effective, they are also outer directed and do not require teachers to pause and feel what is happening inside themselves when they notice bias and discrimination.

Traditionally, we do not ask teachers to feel their triggers, notice what the trigger is, and notice their emotional reaction to the trigger. Teachers are often not taught to look at a situation with a "beginner's mind," noticing the thoughts and stories they attribute to the situation, and try to start anew. But when dealing with students who are different from themselves, it is imperative that teachers notice their thoughts (which could be learned bias and prejudice), feelings, and emotions (which could be based on learned biases and prejudice), and look at the child simply as she is in this moment. It is imperative that we work with teachers to help the teachers sift through their learned thoughts and emotions and see children as the beautiful beings they are.

Contemplative education broadens our approach to dealing with bias beyond that of using our educated intellect to manage our experiences of discrimination. In contemplative teaching, we also notice our thoughts and feelings without judgment before we act. Pausing and reflecting help keep us from being blindsided by our habitual biases and prejudice while in the presence of the multifaceted diversity present in all classrooms. It requires discipline and practice for teachers to learn to create pauses and transitional moments that interrupt their own harmful feelings of bias or discrimination. Then they can discover more peaceful compromises in which they neither overreact nor are overly accommodating that open avenues for respectful exchange.

SEEING BRIDGE EXERCISE FOR WORKING WITH BIAS

This more advanced exercise involves showing preservice teachers a series of slides. When each slide is shown, they write about their immediate feeling and thinking reactions. First they are shown slides with a red rose, a while rose, and a yellow rose. Immediately following are three more slides of students' faces: a white student, an African American student, an Asian student, and a Latino student. This exercise invites preservice teachers to use awareness practices to notice their emotional and conceptual experiences of latent racism and to lessen their habitual reactions to the different faces and to bring awareness of any latent racist reactions they may feel. By noticing these reactions without judgment, latent racism gradually dissolves.

MULTIDIMENSIONAL BRIDGE EXERCISE FOR WORKING WITH BIAS

We eventually apply these exercise to a real classroom. We ask preservice teachers to enter a classroom with children from diverse cultures and languages—some of whom are from the same background as the teacher, and some from backgrounds different from the teacher. We then ask preservice teachers to observe the children and notice and record any emotions or thoughts that arise. When a preservice teacher is triggered, or has a strong emotion or biased thought, we ask him in that moment to deeply dive into a contemplative observation of the child. We ask the teacher to actively notice and separate his thoughts, judgments, and emotions from the direct observation of the student's action. What is the child really doing? Is the child squirming at his desk, and if so, is this really misbehavior, or is the child simply moving? And when a child from the same background as the teacher is doing the same thing, what is the teacher's emotional reaction? Is the child speaking to the teacher in a way that triggers a reaction? Is the child actually being rude, or is the tone of voice and words used just different from the way the teacher might articulate the thought? Is the child exhibiting physical behavior that is really threatening, or is the child trying to express an emotion? Along the same lines, when a child from the teacher's same cultural background is physically active, what is the teacher's reaction?

We feel deeply obligated to uproot the stereotypes, bias, and prejudice teachers bring to the classroom, and an integral first step is to help teachers separate their learned stereotypes and biases from the actual, describable actions and words of the child. As more and more students are being punished for behaviors that are within the normal spectrum of frustrated, emotional, or angry child and adolescent behavior, we need our teachers to recognize what this behavior is really trying to convey. We then ask teachers to notice their different emotional reactions to children who express emotions in a cultural manner that mimics that of the teacher, and children who express emotions in a cultural manner that differs from the teacher. No longer can we prepare teachers who enter the classroom by giving them one cultural lens. Rather, we need to prepare teachers who are comfortable with the uncomfortable, who notice their differing reactions to different student behavior, and are able to regulate and respond, rather than react.

In the same course, we dig deeply into the levels of language proficiency of students, and ascertain how to make the content relevant by "knowing our students." In this course, teachers learn to listen carefully, not only to their own immediate experiences of CLD students, but also to the way their students express themselves. When CLD students are learning a new language, they will use body language, gestures, and imprecise grammar and pronunciation to get their point across. The teacher needs to notice these clues, and listen deeply, to learn about the student's level of proficiency and what lessons would be most beneficial. Above all, the teacher needs to ensure that the student feels safe. When emerging bilingual learners use inappropriate language (a very common occurrence), teachers need to regulate their own emotional and cognitive responses and listen to the student's speech from the standpoint of "what does the student know," and "what is the student trying to produce." The traditional teacher's approach is to examine the child's language systematically, noting the grammar errors first, and perhaps, noting the emotion behind the language second. From the perspective of the Contemplative Teacher Competencies, we ask teachers to notice, modulate, and liberate their own habitual responses to students.

EMBODIMENT BRIDGE EXERCISE TO ASSIST IN SOMATIC
AWARENESS OF OTHERS

In the Linguistics for CLD course preservice teachers observe their class-mates who are walking and moving in very simple ways. After establishing themselves in their own authentic movement patterns, the preservice teachers are instructed to notice how the movements of others resonate within their own bodies and what sensations and feelings arise in the course of observa-tion. This requires the ability to move with self-awareness while observing others and to respond with simple movements from self-regulated somatic and emotional inner experience as much as possible. At more advanced levels of embodied movement practice somatic awareness is developed between and among the preservice teachers who are moving together in pairs, in groups, or in role plays. Over time, such practices improve teachers' somatic and emotional sensitivity and fluency in their ability to synchronize with their own students' body language and gestures in class.

Upper-Level Courses: EDU 400—Methods of Social Studies, Science, Math, and EDU 475—Student Teaching

These courses ask our preservice teachers to implement strategies that are developmentally appropriate, that make the content comprehensible to all learners, that address the interests of all learners, and that meet the needs of culturally and linguistically diverse students and students with special needs. In traditional teacher preparation, students practice research-based strategies to increase comprehension of the content for everyone. From a contemplative perspective there are several teacher competencies that com-bine to "make the content comprehensible to all learners."

Within our contemplative trajectory, these upper-level BA courses represent the culmination of the contemplative education of the preser-vice teacher. At this point in their 4-year journey preservice teachers are familiar with an array of inner and outer contemplative skills. They have been encouraged to incorporate contemplative methods for inner practices that seem most natural to them individually. For instance, some preservice teachers may feel most at home with compassion practices, while others function best within the broader context of awareness practice. The same applies to pedagogical methods—some find it natural to use wait-time techniques, while others use contemplative observation.

SPEAKING EXERCISES TO ENHANCE CLARITY OF SPEECH

The purpose of these exercises is to improve the effectiveness of communication with students in the present moment, rather than repeating time-worn phrases or lectures. One speaking exercise involves teachers listening to themselves while teaching, and observing their students at the same time. This skill is dependent on having learned, as previously described, to resonate with the expressions and body language of students, while the preservice teacher listens to the sound of her own voice. In this way, the teacher can determine if the content being conveyed is genuine and actually connects with students. If not, the teacher has developed the skills through more preliminary contemplative practices to flexibly respond and to adjust what she is saying or doing. The embodied physical presence of the teacher also contributes to fuller verbal communication of content.

WAIT-TIME EXERCISES

If we revisit the Pedagogical Contemplative Teaching Competency—Creates pauses during instruction and transitions to encourage participation, self-care, and insight—we can see how the mainstream teaching strategy of wait time can be adapted to a contemplative approach. Traditionally, teachers use wait-time pauses after asking questions to elicit more participation and more considered responses from students. Wait-time exercises can be practiced during BA upper-level courses and during practice teaching. The preservice teacher is instructed to notice one inner experience that is prominent while waiting before calling on students. For example, the preservice teacher might be feeling distant from the class. In that case, a quick flash of self-compassion practice could reestablish a heartfelt connection with the students.

Wait time is particularly useful in teaching emergent bilingual learners. It is a strategy that can assist CLD students or students who need more time to process information to fully engage in the lesson. With CLD students, for example, the student hears the question in English and must first either translate the question into his or her first language or take the time to comprehend the question. Then the student needs to develop an answer, and, depending on which language the student is thinking in, she must then translate her answer into an utterance that the teacher and the class will understand. This process can take a student anywhere from 3 to 5 seconds (Grassi & Barker, 2010). In traditional teacher education, we talk to teachers about how uncomfortable it can be to engage in wait time when they are working with a group of 35 anxious learners who want to participate. Traditional strategies include having teachers count 5 seconds before calling on students, writing the question on the board so students have time to process the information, having students write their answer before they participate orally, and having students think–pair–share in small groups before producing an answer for the whole class.

That said, none of these strategies require teachers to look inside themselves when engaging students in wait time, nor do they give them strategies for waiting patiently. While they are pausing,

> contemplating teachers are taught to notice, non-judgmentally, their own thoughts, emotions, or sense experiences. . . . An infinite variety of experiences can occur to contemplative teachers during Wait Time. They could ponder the question they have just asked the class and notice if they have any predetermined or favored responses that they expect the students to offer. If so, they could appreciate those, let them go, and open to whatever the students may offer. (Brown, 2014, p. 277)

Preparing Contemplative Program Instructors for Preservice and Inservice Teachers

Preparing contemplative preservice teachers requires that they have sufficiently trained contemplative or mindful instructors to guide them. It is not enough to teach *about* mindful and/or contemplative practices and pedagogies. Nor is it enough to have an established personal mindfulness practice. The university instructor needs to embody contemplative competencies personally in the classroom, relate meaningfully with preservice teachers in and out of class, as well as manage class activities using contemplative pedagogy.

Finding ways to train contemplative or mindful teachers has been one of the greatest challenges in the field of mindfulness in education altogether. For example, when Patricia Jennings, Christa Turksma, and I (Richard C. Brown) were developing the CARE for Teachers program at the Garrison Institute, we struggled with how to train facilitators in order to scale up the program. What we found was that certain participants were repeating CARE year after year. Capitalizing on that, we invited some of them to trainings and to an apprenticeship-style approach to CARE program facilitation. Even though it was a slow and time-consuming process, this approach has yielded some excellent facilitators.

In the MA in Contemplative Education program at Naropa University, our approach to preparing program instructors had a similar apprenticeship focus. Particularly during our 3-week summer program, the following elements were employed, most of which have been carried over into the BA licensure program:

• *Co-teaching wherein both instructors are present for every class period.* For the BA licensure program co-teaching is not economically feasible. Whenever the instructor of record feels the need for support, I (Richard) participate in their courses to instruct the preservice students in selected foundational practices and bridge exercises.

• *Frequent faculty meetings at which teaching and learning were major topics of discussion.* We hold monthly contemplative curriculum meetings. I (Richard) also offer weekly office hours for BA faculty who may wish to discuss a range of issues, questions about their courses, or ways of working with their students.

• *Openness to having nonprogram faculty participants in our courses, which often led them teaching in the program.* As of now, this practice has not carried over into the BA licensure program.

• *Development of contemplative assessment rubrics with all-faculty participation.* We are continuing to adapt the rubrics developed in the MA for use in the BA licensure program.

These approaches require a great deal of generosity on the part of the instructors, who voluntarily spent more time in the classroom and in meetings, despite receiving inadequate compensation. It is their passion for the collegiality and personal fulfillment that comes from participating in relatively selfless learning communities that has made this approach very fruitful. Meaningful learning communities are deeply invigorating for all.

We feel strongly that every person involved in the Contemplative Teacher licensure program—instructors, cooperating teachers, supervising teachers, and students—should be well supported in learning contemplative strategies. For this reason, we support our instructors and students through the resources of the carefully sequenced contemplative bridge exercises illustrated in the chapter that are tailored to their particular syllabi. Instructors, students, cooperating teachers, and supervising teachers are also mentored by experienced contemplative faculty. Providing additional contemplative support is Naropa's CACE, which sponsors numerous contemplative pedagogy colloquia for all Naropa faculty throughout the academic year.

While we are in the beginning stages of this licensure program, we look forward to developing future teachers who are not only well versed and prepared in the state teacher quality standards, but also are contemplatively prepared and can incorporate contemplative practices that complement state standards into every facet of their classroom.

Conclusion

In our approach to contemplative education, the main focus is on an indirect, experiential process in mastering individual competencies or skills. We do not want to overtly teach any principles of contemplative education, preferring instead for them to arise in guided discussion from students' direct experiences with specific exercises, discussions, and classroom applications. Because the contemplative developmental process is multidimensional both on the inner and outer levels, it could easily become disintegrated and formulaic if we focused on singular outcomes.

Contemplative teaching is an ever-changing dance of multiple interrelated competencies. By engaging in contemplative activities, mindfulness, awareness, embodiment, and caring become infused in increasingly specific classroom teaching methods in individual classroom situations. We have found that over time, using contemplative methods produces sustainable and meaningful personal and community transformations in teaching and learning.

References

Ahmed, K., Trager, B., Rodwell, M., Foinding, L., & Lopez, C. (2017). A review of mindfulness research related to alleviating math and science anxiety. *Journal for Leadership and Instruction, 16*(2), 26–30.

Alexander, M. (2012). *The new Jim Crow: Mass incarceration in the age of colorblindness.* New York: New Press.

Brown, R. C. (1998–1999). The teacher as contemplative observer. *Educational Leadership, 56*(4), 70–73.

Brown, R. C. (2014). Transitions: Teaching from the spaces between. In O. Gunnlaugson, E. Sarath, C. Scott, & H. Bai (Eds.), *Contemplative learning and inquiry across disciplines* (pp. 271–286). Albany: State University of New York Press.

Brown, R. C., Simone, G., & Worley, L. (2016). Embodied presence: Contemplative teacher education. In K. Schonert-Reichel & R. Roeser (Eds.), *Handbook of mindfulness in education* (pp. 207–220). New York: Springer.

Grassi, E., & Barker, H. (2010). *Culturally and linguistically diverse exceptional students: Strategies for teaching and assessments.* Thousand Oaks, CA: SAGE.

Hanh, T. N. (2009). *Happiness.* Berkeley: Parallax Press.

Hayward, J. (1995). *Sacred world.* New York: Bantam Books.

Heitzeg, N. (2016). *The school to prison pipeline: Education, discipline, and racialized double standards.* Denver: Praeger.

Maynard, B., Solis, M., Miller, V., & Brendel, K. (2017). Mindfulness-based interventions for improving cognition, academic achievement, behavior, and socioemotional functioning of primary and secondary school students. *Campbell Systematic Reviews, 5*, 147.

Stuart, S. K., Collins, J., Toms, O., & Gwalla Ogisi, N. (2017). Mindfulness and an argument for Tier 1, Whole School Support. *International Journal of Whole Schooling, 13*(3), 14–27.

U.S. Department of Education. (2016). The state of racial diversity in the educator workforce. Retrieved April 17, 2018, from *www2.ed.gov/rschstat/eval/highered/racial-diversity/state-racial-diversity-workforce.pdf.*

Welwood, J. (1992). *Ordinary magic.* Boston: Shambhala.

Wiggins, G., & McTighe, J. (2005). *Understanding by design.* Alexandria, VA: ASCD.

CHAPTER 10

Being in School Transformation

Toward Equity and Social Justice

VELMA L. COBB

For we have, built into all of us, old blueprints of expectations and response, old structures of oppression, and these must be altered at the same time as we alter the living conditions which are a result of those structures.

—AUDRE LORDE

According to the Merriam-Webster dictionary, *transformation* is "a complete or major change in someone's or something's appearance, form, etc." Transformation speaks to an act or process of changing an original configuration into another. *Transformation* feels like the word of the moment, much like *reform* was the go-to word for the decade beginning in 2000. Regardless of the packaging—No Child Left Behind, Blueprint for Reform, Race to the Top, college- and career-ready standards (the Common Core State Standards), Socioeconomic Integration, for example—most of these reform efforts have lacked the comprehensiveness to be considered true transformation. I use the word *transformation* here to signal a movement toward social change in schools. Social change requires a change in educators themselves and in the system and organization of education.

I have been an educator for more than 40 years. I have lived through the many generations of equity in education reform and bring both a personal and professional perspective to the story of transformation. Each generation of reform has tried to fix the problems of schooling for poor students and students of color. Yet in 2018, the schooling a child receives continues to be predictive of race, ethnicity, language, socioeconomic status, gender, and zip code. Johnson, Uline, and Perez (2017, p. 1) note:

> In the United States, it is remarkably easy to predict school attendance rates, reading performance, course passage rates, performance on state achievement tests, school suspension rates, enrollment in advanced classes, graduation rates, college attendance rates, or almost any other important academic outcome simply by knowing five student variables: race/ethnicity, language background, family income, gender, and zip code. Huge gaps in achievement, associated with these variables, challenge our cities and states and pose significant threats to our social and economic *wellbeing.*

Historical Background

For 8 years (2008–2016), I directed the Touro College Equity Assistance Center (EAC), one of 10 EACs (now currently 4) belonging to the network of U.S, Department of Education-funded technical assistance centers. The EACs are the only technical assistance providers that have their origin in the Civil Rights Act of 1964, and their mission is to assist states, districts, and schools to ensure that all learners receive a high-quality education and achieve at a high standard, regardless of the differing variables they bring to the classroom. The term *equity-based excellence* best captures the goals of the EACs work (Scott, 2016).

The EACs identified six generations of civil rights and educational equity approaches in the pursuit of a culture of equity-based excellence. I will outline them briefly here, but see Scott (1990, 1995, and 2016) for a fuller discussion. Looking at these generations of civil rights and equity approaches gives us an evolutionary view of the trajectory of social justice in education and the sociopolitical context that reflects the viewpoints and mindsets that have shaped the story of learning and teaching. We need to understand the narrative of the past, be critically aware of the present, and be centered for a future that is currently being shaped by the moments in which we now live. The six generations identified by the EACs are as follows:

• *First generation: 1954–1964—Litigation,* starting with *Brown v. Board of Education of Topeka, Kansas.* The goal of this first generation was racial, physical desegregation.

• *Second generation: 1964–1983—Legislation,* starting with the passage of the Civil Rights Act of 1964, which redefined the civil rights landscape for the next 20 years. This generation was characterized by several pieces of legislation that prohibited discrimination against children of color and opened up greater access.

- *Third generation: 1983–1990—State-driven reform efforts,* starting with reports such as *A Nation at Risk* (National Commission on Excellence in Education, 1983) and other reports that refocused the civil rights conversation on issues beyond access alone.

- *Fourth generation: 1990–2000—State and national government reform efforts,* starting with a national governors' meeting on education, challenging the country to view the new century as the birth of educational excellence for all (Scott, 1995). The goal in this phase was to create new schools that work for diverse students and to produce educators who could meet the challenges of preparing all students for the 21st century.

- *Fifth generation: 2001–2011—No Child Left Behind Act* (NCLB) passage, starting with the educational and civil rights conversation, challenging public schools to be accountable for disaggregated student achievement outcomes (Scott, 2001). Systemic equity and the opportunity to learn became the focus, enabling all students to learn at high levels.

- *Sixth generation: 2012–Beyond.* NCLB shifted to the *Blueprint for Reform* (U.S. Department of Education, 2010), which challenged public schools to be more focused on a rigorous curriculum taught by highly qualified, effective teachers under the supervision of dynamic principal leadership.

Despite years of effort, equity-based excellence remains the goal, and the attainment of that goal continues to challenge this nation's districts and schools. The current moment tells us that race continues to be a polarizing force not only in education, but also across many more sectors of our lived existence. This moment tells us that individual and system change are paramount to transformational change.

Mindsets, Culture, and Transformation

This historical context is important because it brings to light the viewpoints and mindsets that shape the narrative from which we can generate what's possible. Cultural conditioning reflects our view of the world, and that view of the world shapes policy formation and implementation. The ability to step out of "habits of mind" can assist in problematizing the stories underlying the policy narratives we are perpetuating (Cobb, 2017).

Public education continues to struggle with educating the masses of children to achieve high academic performance. Efforts such as college- and career-ready standards (or the Common Core State Standards), new teacher and leadership assessments, and new student assessments have attempted to transform education via changes in organizational structures, policies, and procedures, and other external regulatory frameworks. Another avenue for change has consisted of efforts that address the knowledge, skills, and attitudes of the individuals who affect teaching and learning directly; namely teachers, educational leaders, parents, and even the students themselves. Still, educational inequities persist.

Scheetz and Senge (2016) write, "Something in the very word 'system' or 'systemic' consistently leads us astray—seeking some magical change 'out there' when the most intransigent aspects of the 'out there' are inseparable from our habits of thought and action 'in here.'" The internal habits of mind that shape how we define the problem of reform and craft what we do to address those problems are central to seeking another way to transform education. The emerging work in mindfulness and other conscious or contemplative practices in education and other fields has begun to uncover the internal work required for true, sustained, transformational change. Mindfulness and other conscious practices have the potential to address what Scheetz and Senge (2016) call the "inner nature of inequity" (Cobb, 2017). The use of these practices does not mean that the external structural or organizational systems-change efforts or the growth in knowledge, attitudes, and dispositions of key individuals in the education enterprise are not needed. Rather, I am suggesting that internal work provides the impetus for and the conduit through which the structures, procedures, and practices can ultimately be transformed. "Transformation begins with the individual" (Jennings, 2015).

In an interview (Cobb, 2017) with Kevin Kimashiro, former Dean of the School of Education at the University of San Francisco, he described this dilemma:

> "When we try to name the moment we're in, we impoverish our viewpoint and therefore limit ourselves to a problematic partial strategy if the way we name the moment isn't really connecting the dots between multiple things going on. . . . I think we need to be much more mindful of the dots that need to be connected to accommodate the multitude and diverse factors that make up the tapestry of our present dynamic and integrated landscapes. We need to be able to connect these dots in a much more sophisticated way; otherwise, we won't really be able to come up with strategies that respond to the moment."

Social change speaks to creating a natural coherence in the education enterprise. This coherence involves the interconnectedness of the personal and professional and of the organization and culture. The interconnectedness of the personal and professional speaks to the wholeness of the individual, an alignment of a person's cognitive, physical, emotional, and spiritual aspects. The interconnectedness of the organization and culture speaks to social and interactive conditions of the environment and the alignment of policies, structures, practices, and procedures. The social justice and contemplative practice fields offer a unique and greatly needed entry into transforming education (Petty, 2017). Education is a political act. It is personal and relational. The relational and political nature of education requires the inclusion of consciousness and social justice if an authentic transformation in how the masses of children are educated is to occur. This chapter invites a continued conversation about the juxtaposition of the personal and professional, about global interdependence, and about a broader view of internal consciousness building and external systems change.

Being versus Doing

Admittedly, the language of transformation tries to embed into system-reform efforts the ideas of relationships, collaboration, vision and meaning, voice, and reflection, but these ideas are considered supportive at best of the real work of "doing" reform or transformation. So as much as the literature on reform and transformation talks about the need to invest in these notions of "being," the push and pressure to "do" is dominant, leaving "being" by the wayside. Most system-reform efforts place "accountability" at the center of "fixing" public schools. The "being" elements—relationships, collaboration, vision and meaning, voice, and reflection—are nebulous and oftentimes are considered intangible. They speak to culture and context. These "being" change elements are most often not attended to in education, nor in other major sectors such as housing, finance, employment, health, environmental issues, or social justice. Neither is the intersection between these sectors attended to, though collectively, each impacts the other.

We identify these elements and offer educational workshops in hopes that individuals will take it upon themselves to better understand how they influence attitudes, behaviors, and viewpoints, while the organizational structures that reinforce, perpetuate, and reward inequities remain unchanged. Then we wonder why things remain the same. I have seen the structures, procedures, and practices that limit educational opportunity for all students; and I have watched individuals across the educational spectrum struggle to recognize and connect how their own assumptions, mindsets, and beliefs are complicit in the persistent and pervasive inequities in education (Cobb, 2017).

The Individual and Systems Change

Without inner change, there can be no outer change, without collective change, no change matters.

—ANGEL KYODO WILLIAMS, *Radical Dharma*

Seeing is not believing; believing is seeing! You see things, not as they are, but as you are.

—ERIC BUTTERWORTH, *Spiritual Economics*

Tal James, Executive Director of Movement Strategy Center, states:

> We cannot change social systems without transforming people and the
> way we are with each other, but neither can we wait for individuals to
> become their better selves without transforming the social systems that
> shape us. . . . Transformation is about bringing something new into exis-
> tence, not just rearranging what exists. It's about fundamentally altering
> relationships within and between people. (in Gass, 2014, p. 43)

The journey of individual and systems change is intractably linked. To
just change the system, as most of the education reform movements have
tried, falls short. To change individuals (leaders, teachers, students, and
parents) loses traction also because multiple systems constantly shape who
we are and the context in which we find ourselves. Staci Haines, Executive Director of Generative Somatics, describes what is needed this way:
"Individual transformation on its own does not create social change. But
social change without dealing with our individual selves leads to solutions
from our 'old shape' and not the liberating change that we need" (in Glass,
2014, p. 42).

Bob Anderson (1998), Founder and CEO of the Leadership Circle,
contends that most efforts to change are unsuccessful because key variables
are often ignored. He states that we often tackle the obvious and easy attributes of change, such as individual skills and behaviors and organizational
policies and procedures, but tend to shy away from tackling the "invisible,
insidious, emotionally wrenching" personal and cultural aspects (p. 6).

Anderson (1998) describes both internal and external domains of
change for individuals and the organization or collective. He uses the term
collective in reference to the organization's social dynamics of individual
interactions. Most leaders and change efforts focus only on the external
aspects of change for both individuals and the organization. In the field
of education and in most industries, individual external performance is
addressed through the acquisition of knowledge, skills, and behavioral
development via training and coaching. Likewise, at the external organizational level, change is addressed through revision of components such as
policies, procedures, and reporting structures. These external components,
both at the individual and organizational level, are isolated symptoms of
what's really going on, but are often treated as if they are the root causes
of the problem.

The individual internal domain involves an aspect of change that
addresses the mindset, values, and beliefs that lead to a change in consciousness. The organizational or collective internal domain involves an
organizational culture that is reflective of the hidden assumptions, myths,
stories, and unwritten rules that drive the day-to-day interactions (Anderson, 1998). Rarely do change efforts address the internal domains of the

individual or the organization, even though the internal and external domains are interdependent and affect the other and work inextricably together. Transformational change requires both internal and external changes in both individuals and in the organization itself.

With the increasing popularity of mindfulness, emotional intelligence, and other wellness supports, school staff are encouraged to seek personal development, but few schools (and businesses as well) have embedded this work as part of systemic change development. An individual's internal domain is that of consciousness, and refers to inner development. My use of the term "being" is in reference to this domain. True transformational change requires inner shifts in consciousness and culture to absorb changes in the identity of the individual and in the organization.

"Organizational change is not a question of skills and structure alone, but of identity and world-view" (Anderson, 1998, p. 6). Identity is one's self concept: how we see ourselves and through which we relate to the surrounding world. Likewise, the organization must also shift identities in the change process. If I, as a teacher, see myself as the person who knows and the orchestrator of learning in my classroom, learning about developing independent learners is helpful, but demonstrating that I can treat my students this way in my classroom requires a shift in consciousness of how I see myself as a teacher. This shift, in turn, will be reflected in how I redesign instruction and engage with students. My view of students as independent learners is reflected in all aspects of my practice, such as how I speak and interact with students, as well as in my mindset or views about teaching and learning. On the school's organizational or collective level, professional development can support my shift in consciousness by providing the external knowledge, skills, and behavioral expectations. The school might even revise some processes and procedures that encourage and provide opportunities for students as independent learners. Yet, the tone and expectations within the schools' culture can carry deeper meanings that contradict written statements or the view of students as independent learners.

Now a common occurrence in schools and in corporate America, culturally responsive sustaining workshops often focus on identifying and unearthing the implicit biases that are embedded in the assumptions, mindsets, and beliefs that are reflected in the behaviors and practices that perpetuate inequities. Only a few workshops are intentional in focusing on approaches that give principals and teachers the tools to sharpen and intervene in the thinking patterns that foster greater awareness, deep listening, presence, and self-management. Workshops typically name the neuroscience behind the patterns of behavior, the cultural influences that shape our worldview, and the sociopolitical contexts that reinforce and reward the status quo, with the hope that in naming the implicit biases, in building the knowledge base on culturally responsive pedagogy, and in acknowledging the existing sociopolitical landscape that folks will "do better" because they "know better." So we provide people with the knowledge and evidence at a cognitive level of what is happening, but allow them to put that knowledge into practice without additional support. Even when folks want to change, we need to recognize that change is hard work. Mindfulness and other contemplative practices assist in training the mind, interrupting thinking, and giving us greater presence to align who we want to be with actions we choose to take.

Jon Kabat-Zinn (1994), considered to be the guru of mindfulness, defines it as "paying attention in a particular way: on purpose, in the present moment, and non-judgmentally" (p. 4). His pioneering work offers mindfulness as a practical, systematic process of self-observation, self-inquiry, and action. Mind-based emotional wisdom is at the core of knowing oneself (Mackey & Sisodia, 2014; Tan, 2012). Marturano (2014) describes the cultivation of this way of knowing as "training the mind." Our experiences, behaviors, and even thoughts can change the structure and function of the brain (Davidson & Bagley, 2012). Moreover, these changes do not just benefit child growth and development, but can occur in the brain well into adulthood.

Meditation, yoga, and mindfulness are the most well-known contemplative practices. These practices and many others cultivate "an inner technology of knowing and thereby a technology of learning and pedagogy" (Hart, 2004). Increased attention and focus, better concentration, and social and emotional growth and development are some of the effects of these kinds of practices, which can make learning transformative. These practices create the space for us to observe or witness the patterns of our thinking. In noticing when we are not present, we are able to see more clearly when our mind is hijacked or triggered by our emotions. Contemplative practices sharpen our mind by giving us greater agility over what we attend to and focus on.

Creating the Future, Not Fixing the Present

> Education either functions as an instrument which is used to
> facilitate integration of the younger generation into the logic of
> the present system and bring about conformity or it becomes the
> practice of freedom, the means by which men and women deal
> critically and creatively with reality and discover how to participate
> in the transformation of their world.
> —PAOLO FREIRE, *Pedagogy of the Oppressed*

As we look at this movement of joining contemplative practices with social justice and equity, we basically are talking about transformative social change in education and in the world. As shown earlier, education has a long history of incremental, transitional, gradual, and developmental reform. Transformation is about profound change, such that what's on the other end of that change creates breakthroughs individually and at the collective and systems level.

The Wheel of Change offered by the Social Transformation Project (Gass, 2014, p. 19) is a conscious organizing framework that addresses the transformation of individuals, organizations, and society. This framework asserts that true, sustainable transformation involves three interdependent elements: (1) hearts and minds, (2) behavior, and (3) structures. Any of these elements can be an entry point to the work of equity-based excellence; however, all three elements must be addressed for true transformation and for transformation to be sustainable. Further, the optimum outcomes, which cannot be quantified, include the mental, cultural, and spiritual dimensions of being that are often overlooked (Petty & Dean, 2017).

Hearts and Minds

I believe that mindfulness and other contemplative practices provide the tools for the internal work in our hearts and minds that enable us individually and collectively to access thoughts, feelings, emotions, beliefs, and values. This is the awareness component of the internal work. These practices also assist in managing the stories that shape who we are and our views of the world. Through these stories, we shape our habits of mind and how we interpret the collective interactions and context in which we find ourselves. The internal work brings clarity to discern things as they are, not just what we want them to be. This clarity, ultimately, helps to better determine what's possible. "If we want to make change, we must change the way we think and feel" (Gass, 2014, p. 19).

Behavior

As stated earlier, being mindful is not enough. Yes, it is important to acknowledge our notions of being so that we might develop an awareness of self, of others, and of what is around us and the ability to be present to what is. Changing habits is equally important. Many mindfulness practices start with setting an intention. Intentions are purposeful acts that can be a guide for how we want to show up or be present (Jennings, 2015). The same intent can also guide the way we are present, the language we use in conversations with others, and the norms and agreements by which we relate to others.

Structures

The structures or systems that constitute our external environment are the third component of change. There is a tendency in the process of making change to start with structures, mistakenly identifying isolated problems as the gist of what's not working. Change then becomes programmatic and piecemeal, as if fixing isolated problems will fix the system that perpetuates and further ingrains the issue (Anderson, 1998). In education, as in all sectors, the manner in which we have conceived the structures, processes, practices, and cultures of the organizations that guide our work is a direct reflection of how we see and interact with the external world. At this time, for example, accountability has become synonymous with testing. Teaching is scripted. Instruction is geared toward the knowledge and skills that are reflected on standardized tests.

The Social Transformation Project (Gass, 2014, p. 21) offers nine principles that encompass the many features of transformative social change. As educators undergo the transformative changes that mindfulness can support, it is imperative that local schools and school districts also undertake change to create positive environments and cultures that not only allow but also foster a sense of being, strong relationships, a belief in equity and justice for all, the presence of compassion, and, dare I say it, love. The following principles work in tandem with one another and also acknowledge both the internal and external domains of change of the individual and the organization or collective:

1. Attend to the whole system.
2. Be the change.
3. It's about the "we."
4. Practice, practice, practice.
5. What we appreciate, appreciates.
6. Engage the heart.
7. Balance the yin and yang: focus and flow.
8. Connect to the source.
9. Go the distance—sustainability.

Attend to the Whole System

Anderson's (1998) internal and external domains of change regarding the identity of individuals and the organization must be front and center in the transformation process. To be effective, teachers must cultivate an inner and outer well-being in order to provide for the social– emotional demands of the classroom. Most of the time we prioritize the cognitive demands, making sure that teachers have acquired the appropriate content-area and pedagogical knowledge. Certainly this knowledge is important, but teachers' psychological, emotional, and spiritual well-being is as equally necessary. Mindfulness practice provides teachers the tools with which to develop inner well-being. With mindfulness, teachers are better able to be intentional, aware, and present for what is happening, have the ability to adjust attitudes, and manage the social context within the classroom and building (Jennings, 2015).

This whole-systems approach is what the Management Assistance Group calls a "thriving justice ecosystem" (Petty & Dean, 2017). Deep equity lies at the core, requiring the centering of inner and outer work equally. Schools will need to understand and address the "multiple, structural, institutional, interpersonal and individual/internal causes (both historic and current) and recognize the social construction of identity, power, and privilege over time" (Petty & Dean, 2017, p. 2). Although transformation begins with the individual, the social contextual environment provides a medium for either supporting or hindering change or development. The organization or system must attend to the underlying culture of purpose, meaning, and collective interactions, and not just tinker with external structures, processes, and procedures even though these elements might also dictate change. Meena Srinivasan (2014) likens bringing social-emotional learning and mindfulness to young people and adults without enriching the social–emotional learning and mindfulness of the structures and systems in which they find themselves to "putting a Band-Aid on a broken system." We are reminded of the interrelationship of the inner and the outer and of personal change and organizational change. Supporting the well-being of adults and children in schools also means creating a school culture that acknowledges and nourishes care and compassion.

Be the Change

"The process of transformational change must always model what it seeks to create" (Gass, 2014, p. 23). Mindfulness and other contemplative practices allow us to access our inner wisdom and nature, especially when faced with the many distractions and disruptions that will inevitably arise. Disruptions can mean new leadership; new national, state, or local policies; changing demographics; changing trends or market needs; and so forth. I have talked frequently in this chapter about "being," because who we are shapes what we create. Mindfulness asks us to be present in the moment with what is, nonjudgmentally. Teachers must be fully present with students to adequately address their needs. Leaders and teachers alike must hold the tensions and challenges of complexity and uncertainty, as they make countless decisions large and small with clarity and compassion (Brown & Olson, 2015). Practices such as centering the breath, deep listening, movement, and visualizations enable teachers to access their inner wisdom, resources, and strengths. Likewise, systems must have the agility to be flexible with the needs of both adults and students. Organizations that align procedures and processes with a clear purpose, foster open communication, and enable shared responsibility alongside accountability are transparent, inclusive, and courageously committed to confronting the persistence of race, sexism, homophobia, and other inequities. The culture supports personal and organizational/collectivist self-examination and healing. In the words of Rev. Dr. Martin Luther King, Jr.:

> Somehow we're caught in an inescapable network of mutuality tied in a single garment of destiny. Whatever affects one, affects all indirectly. For some strange reason, I can never be what I ought to be until you are what you ought to be. You can never be what you ought to be until I am what I ought to be. This is the interrelated structure of reality. (Gass, 2014)

It's about the "We"

"It can no longer be 'me' and 'them,' it must become Us" (Jensen, 2018, p. 5). The inner and outer change required for transformation in both individual teachers and the school as an organization involves trust, and trust requires emotional safety. Emotions are physiological reactions that evolved to assist in human physical survival, but today most threats to us are psychological, causing physical and emotional stress (Jennings, 2015). As individuals, we are all conditioned by experiences that shape perceptions, which feed our thoughts, emotions, and beliefs (King, 2015). Mindfulness practice enables greater awareness of the self, which includes assumptions and biases, and fosters the ability to perceive and separate the realities of the present moment from emotional triggers that stem from conditioning. The practice supports intention, attention, and focus, and managing responses in the social context of what is actually occurring (Jennings, 2015). In the classroom this means that teachers are able to access and trust their inner knowing to create a welcoming, nurturing, and compassionate space. Rather than using control and punishment as the only means of maintaining order, teachers have greater awareness of the classroom dynamics in real time and are able to booster students' capacity for self-regulation and increased prosocial behavior. There are no lone warriors, because we are all interconnected and interdependent on one another, operating within larger systems (Gass, 2014).

While transformation begins with the individual, true, sustained transformation necessitates a collective organizational approach as well. The interlocking nature of the individual and the system ensures movement. The Rockwell Leadership Institute defines leadership as "the ability to inspire and align others to successfully achieve common goals" (in Gass, 2014, p. 24). School transformation requires everyone involved to interact with one another and work together: administrators, teachers, other professional and nonprofessional staff, students, parents, and the community. Schools are the metaphorical "canary in the mine," most often reflecting the larger ills and trends of society and the nation at large. They are living organisms—complex and dynamic—comparable to an ecosystem of "fluid interrelationships and evolving interdependencies" (Thompson, 2005, p. 18). Transformative change within schools requires the development of shared ownership around a common purpose and vision. Additionally, the enterprise of education itself is intertwined with movements like Black Lives Matters and Me Too and with the shootings of Black males, mass school shootings, the opioid epidemic, and so forth. Education is not neutral. A movement for social transformation necessitates alignment with and among these voices. For far too long, education has seen itself as a neutral bystander in the larger sociopolitical context of which it is a part. Educators and education as a social institution can no longer be bystanders. The mindfulness, equity and excellence, and social justice movements are coalitions that can support the goals of school transformation. Individual change is important, but collective change is equally essential in education transformation. The "we" in this principle involves understanding the self not only in relationship to others, but also in relationship to the sociopolitical context. As Archbishop Desmond Tutu put it, "We can only be human together."

Practice, Practice, Practice

"Change the story and you change perception; change perception and you change the world" (Jean Houston). The brain is a remarkable organ, and the advances in neuroscience give us an opportunity to understand the social nature of the brain and the influence of environment on our worldview. This research speaks to a mind–body connection (Dickmann & Stanford-Blair, 2009; Marturano, 2014; Siegel, 2011). Dickmann and Stanford-Blair state "the brain is the body and the body is the brain. . . . What affects one affects the other" (p. 29). What we experience shapes our mind, and our mind shapes how we see and experience the world. The nature of the brain to create patterns of knowing enables us to respond quickly, and yet we can be swayed by this habitual pattern of knowing and ignore new informational nuances that can help us in seeing things in a new and unique way. This principle of "practice, practice, practice" in transformative social change reminds us that experiences and conditioning shape perception, including interpretations, judgments, feelings, fears, and preferences, and that perceptions are mental creations (King, 2018).

R.A.I.N. is one mindfulness practice that is used to address difficult emotions and reduce habitual knowing (King, 2018, p. 109). The acronym stands for Recognize, Allow, Investigate, and Nurture. I have borrowed King's adaptation of Nurture for the "N" here, rather than the original use of Nonidentification for the "N."

The "R" for Recognize involves noticing and naming what is happening without identifying with what's going on. The inquiry of noticing and naming is intended to open the space for seeing what is happening without the overlay of conditioned thoughts and emotions. The "A" for Allow refers to the ability to be with or see what is happening without forming assumptions, expectations, biases, for example, about it. Being with what is happening does not mean condoning or agreeing with it; rather is invites an openness to acknowledge things as they are. The "I" for Investigate involves being curious about and in tune with how what is happening in the moment is affecting oneself physically, emotionally, cognitively, and spiritually. Last, the "N" for Nurture involves asking what is needed to address the emotional stress of the situation. After recognizing, allowing, and investigating what is surfacing as a result of what's happening in the moment, nurturing is acceptance by letting go of wanting things to be different than what they are. The automaticity of our conditioning is so ingrained that practices like R.A.I.N. remind us to step outside of the conditioned default responses and be open to new possibilities and intentional in choosing new responses.

Mindfulness and other contemplative practices invite us to continually return to the larger richness of our true selves. The practices of care and compassion within a school culture invite us to see and be with the seasons of change and challenges within ourselves and also with what is around us.

What We Appreciate, Appreciates (Creating Positivity through Appreciation)

"In other words, focusing positive energy creates more positive energy" (Gass, 2014, p. 28). Although as educators we talk about assets, the narrative about education in general and urban education specifically is one of "fixing problems" that emphasizes what's wrong. We need to change that story. Developing a mind state of openness to the present moment requires that we recognize our personal scripts that reinforce our habitual patterns. Scripts are our stories, the stored emotional memories or conditioned responses that shape how we think, feel, and behave (Jennings, 2015). Many times these scripts are negative and distance us from experiencing the current moment fully. We play out these scripts not only in what we tell ourselves, but also in how we communicate and interact with others. Organizations also have scripts. Many times long-held memoires of what worked or didn't and what's possible and what isn't are so deeply embedded in organizations that any new attempts at change are met with an overwhelming reluctance. Much like personal scripts can limit individual choices and options of what's possible, the same can be true for organizations. Positive emotions are contagious and create a rich environment for learning. They open the space for a broader set of thoughts, perceptions, and responses (Jennings, 2015).

Valerie Brown and Olson (2015) identifies 10 elements of mindfulness attitudes that support greater appreciation of nurturing positivity

(1) Intention—to nurture capacity; (2) Beginner's Mind—a curiosity and wonder about what's happening; (3) Nonjudgment—impartial observance of what is; (4) Allowing and Openness—a softening approach to emotions; (5) Non-striving—not grasping for something different; (6) Equanimity—a sense of balance and centeredness; (7) Letting Be—acceptance of what is; (8) Self-reliance—trusting our intuitive gut and heart as well as our cognitive brain; (9) Balance—in the face of change, being evenhanded toward options; and last, (10) Self-compassion—kindness to oneself. These elements foster greater resilience and well-being of the self and build stronger relationships with others. The elements address Barbara Fredrickson and her colleagues' theory of "broaden and build" (in Jennings, 2015 p. 84)— the idea that broadening the emotional awareness and resources that individuals can access develops their capacity for positive thoughts, responses, and perceptions which, in turn, creates greater resilience.

Engage the Heart

"The transformative approach seeks to rebalance head with heart, reason with feeling" (Gass, 2014, p. 29). This rebalancing is an openness to not knowing and embracing questions, an openness to equity, and a generosity of spirit to ourselves and others. Love is the strongest positive emotion that connects us to another (Jennings, 2015). Research also points to the heart as a major center of intelligence, as is the cognitive brain (Gass, 2014). While our culture often shies away from emotions in general and love in particular in the professional realm, our emotions are always with us (Kabat-Zinn, 1994). The element of engaging the heart in school transformation enlists many of the other elements but stands on its own, because at the center of mindfulness, equity, and social justice is the interconnectedness of the personal and/or professional and the organization and/or collective discussed earlier in many ways.

"The human heart is the first home of democracy" (Terry Tempest Williams, in Palmer, 2011, p. 93). Palmer (2011) identifies Five Habits of the Heart. First, "we are all in this together" harks back to the illusion of individualism and advances the fact that we are dependent on and accountable to each other. Second, the "appreciation of otherness" recognizes that "us and them" doesn't have to mean "us versus them" and openness to the unfamiliar can be a masterful teacher. Third, the "capacity to hold tension creatively" reminds us that challenges to our thoughts, beliefs, and understandings offer opportunities for new insights and possibilities. Fourth, a "sense of voice and agency" offers connection to our truth but reminds us that truth is concomitant with action. Finally, the "capacity to create community" goes beyond that which we naturally resonate with as community; rather community can be crafted and recrafted for as many times as the personal and collective space demands.

Marturano (2014) describes the cultivation of this way of knowing as "training the mind." Contemplative practices cover a wide range of activities that aim to develop the "natural human capacity for knowing through silence, looking inward, pondering deeply, beholding, witnessing the contents of our consciousness. . . . " (Hart, 2004, p. 29). The idea is that in creating an opening of awareness to the self, there is also an opening of awareness to others and the world around us.

Balance the Yin and Yang: Focus and Flow

We all struggle with the notion of "not knowing." Even in acknowledging the complexity and ever-changing global nature of our educational world, the thought of not knowing is uncomfortable. As educators, I think this struggle is pervasive because we see knowing as being central to our profession. Our male-dominant culture is one that promotes and cultivates control, domination, and "power over." We privilege action. Taoist philosophy and other wisdom traditions recognize the existence of two energies that work in dynamic interaction with each other: yang—the active principle—and yin—the receptive principle (Gass, 2014). This balance of yin and yang parallels my earlier discussion of being and doing. The focus on action, yang energy, propels us forward, but must be tempered with the qualities of yin energy, stepping back to reflect, to see what is present without judgement. Yin allows us to focus and attend to what is present before us, to sit with uncertainty and to trust in the natural flow of life, and to not get caught up in how we want life to be.

"Transformational change is an ongoing dance of finding and living the right balance" (Gass, 2014, p. 32). What we know about creativity and innovation is a perfect example of the interplay of yin and yang. We have all had the experience of working on a problem and having the solution elude us, only to have it come to us when we least expect it, in the shower or while doing something totally unrelated. Neuroscience has allowed us to study the stages of creativity. Goleman (2013) describes these stages as three modes of focus: first, "selective attention," wherein we define and frame the challenge before us; second, "orienting," wherein we seek and immerse ourselves in ideas, data, information, and even past experiences that might provide input to solving the challenge; and finally, "open awareness," wherein we let go or pull back to allow space for our creative brain to make connections in new ways. Stepping back and being open to new possibilities is where creativity and innovations reside. "Being" and "doing" and the internal and external work in personal and organizational or collective change all have dimensions of balance. Individuals and organizations tend to have a bias for action over reflection, a fixation with knowing and being right, and a propensity to confuse activity with results.

Mindfulness practices, such as pausing and centering the breath, ask us to be still so that we can be open to learning new possibilities, to cultivating trust and faith in the self and others, and to allowing for the natural unfolding of life.

Connect to the Source

School transformation with a social justice lens requires an internal connection to a source that is larger than us and refuels and replenishes. Gass (2014, p. 35) describes the connection to a source in the following way.

> The transformative approach invites us to cultivate a connection to a source of meaning and energy beyond our personal needs, ambitions, and fears. The transformative process asks us profound questions, such as:
>
> - Who are we?
> - Why are we here?
> - What gives our life meaning?
> - At the end of our days, what would have been a life worth living?
> - From where do we draw strength?

Margaret Wheatley (2015) describes the connection as that "forgotten place," the human spirit. That deeper wellspring of strength asks educators to repeatedly ask the question "what is education?" We ask that question and know in our inner core that it is not test scores or meeting standards. The love of learning, fullness of growth, and curiosity of development are the answers that surface and keep us in the game. Parker Palmer (2000) furthers this idea of connection with the notion of vocation. He notes that the Latin word for vocation is voice, and states that first one has to listen to what life is calling you to be and do. Perhaps the hope is that through a greater connection and awareness of self we all might listen and find out what we are called to do, or our vocation. Scott Thompson (2005, p. 49) states, "The foundation for sustainable change in education involves three closely related essentials: trust, openness and ownership. Trust engenders openness, and openness invites connections, and connections stimulate the innovation that is essential to the whole system change in public education." We have to take ownership and responsibility for the change we want to occur. We have to be the change and the connection to the source; whatever we name or call that source, allows us to rediscover, renew, strengthen, and draw that which is our anchoring influence. Thompson refers to leaders having a spiritual presence that enables them to stay present in spite of the "noise" surrounding them. I take his notion of spiritual presence, not as reference to religion, but rather a centeredness of purpose and focus beyond the "noise," the "mental and emotional commotion" (p. 40) that surrounds leaders trying to advance change.

Go the Distance—Sustainability

"The principles and practices of individual and organizational sustainability must be integrated into all our transformational work. Sustainability cannot be an afterthought but must be baked in from the beginning" (Gass, 2014, p. 36). We can no longer operate in chronic crisis mode as if that is the norm. We cannot continue to be the firemen, whose main tasks are putting out fires. We must step forward to create the future, not just fix the present. The transformation of schools and education require a long-term commitment. On a personal level, there will be times when the magnitude of what's needed will overwhelm and frustrate even the most resourceful. Mindfulness practices, be they meditation, yoga, music, body movement, visualization, or some other contemplative exercise, are resources to assist us in returning to a touchpoint for rejuvenation, renewal, and replenishment.

Conclusion: Readiness for the Mindfulness Journey

> Whatever you do or dream you can do—begin it. Boldness has genius and power and magic in it.
> —JOHANN WOLFGANG VON GOETHE, *Faustus*

As educators, school transformation is tied to our inner transformation and vice versa. Our individual and collective practices will fortify us and give us the courage to move beyond the structural, procedural, and process reforms that tinker at the edges of what is needed to truly transform schools and the educational process. We must build relationships within the mindfulness community, recognizing, acknowledging, and holding space for traditional wisdom and other contemplative expressions. We must allow the wholeness of all voices within this evolutionary journey, rather than attempting, as is our usual stance, to define, codify, and limit the expansive possibilities of the inner work that will be needed. We must constantly check ourselves for assumptions, judgments, and unconscious bias and be curious and open to our tendency to bifurcate and limit our knowing and seeing of what is. We must work to balance our being with doing, the yin and yang, such that we are in flow with the universe. Last, we must be the change we want to see, take courage in doing what is right, and stay the course on this evolutionary journey.

References

Anderson, B. (1998). The spirit of leadership. Retrieved from *https://static1.square-space.com/static/58d59ba3e6f2e12e70f106d0/t/5a20d3ac8165f51b7d*.

Brown, V., & Olson, K. (2015). *The mindful school leader*. Thousand Oaks, CA: Corwin Press.

Cobb, V. (2017). The question about the question: Transforming educational policy from the inside out. Retrieved March 2018, from *www.contemplativemind. org/icea*.

Davidson, R. J., & Begley, S. (2012). *The emotional life of your brain*. New York: Hudson Street Press.

Dickmann, M. H., & Stanford-Blair, N. (2009). *Mindful leadership: A brain-based framework*. Thousand Oaks, CA: Corwin Press.

Gass, R. (2014). What is transformation?: How it advances social change. Retrieved April 21, 2018, from *http://stproject.org/resources/publications/what-is-transformation*.

Hart, T. (2004). Opening the contemplative mind in the classroom. *Journal of Transformative Education, 2*(1), 28–46.

Jennings, P. A. (2015). *Mindfulness for teachers: Simple skills for peace and productivity in the classroom*. New York: Norton.

Jensen, A. (2018, June 6). Revitalizing school community. Retrieved from *www.6seconds.org/2018/06/06/revitalizing-school-community-lessons-principals-office*.

Johnson, J., Uline, C., & Perez, L. (2017). *Leadership in America's best urban schools*. New York: Routledge.

Kabat-Zinn, J. (1994). *Wherever you go there you are: Mindfulness meditation in everyday life*. New York: Hyperion.

King, R. (2018). *Mindful of race: Transforming racism from the inside out*. Boulder, CO: Sounds True.

Mackey, J., & Sisodia, R. (2014). *Conscious capitalism: Liberating the heroic spirit of business*. Boston: Harvard Business School.

Marturano, J. (2014). *Finding the space to lead: A practical guide to mindful leadership*. New York: Bloomsbury Press.

National Commission on Excellence in Education (1983). A nation at risk: The imperative for educational reform. Retrieved from *www2.ed.gov/pubs/NatAtRisk/risk.html*.

Palmer, P. J. (2000). *Let your life speak: Listening for the voice of vocation*. San Francisco: Jossey-Bass.

Palmer, P. J. (2011). *Healing the heart of democracy*. San Francisco: Jossey-Bass.

Petty, S. (2017). Waking up to all of ourselves: Inner work, social justice & systems change. Retrieved March 2018, from *www.contemplativemind.org/icea*.

Petty, S., & Dean. A. (2017, April 13). Five elements of a thriving justice ecosystem: Pursuing deep equity. Retrieved April 22, 2018, from *https://nonprofitquarterly.org/2017/04/13/five-elements-of-a-thriving-justice-ecosystem-pursuing-deep-equity*.

Scheetz, M., & Senge, P. (2016). Systemic change and equity. Retrieved from *www. capacitybuildingnetwork.org/article3*.

Scott, B. (1990, September). In pursuit of equity: An idea whose time has come. *IDRA Newsletter, 17*(8), 9–12.

Scott, B. (1995, January). The fourth generation of desegregation and civil rights. *IDRA Newsletter, 22*(8), 9–12.

Scott, B. (2016). The regional Equity Assistance Centers—Fifty-years and counting: Forging Civil-Rights-based technical assistance to serve all students by building equity-centered capacity in public schools. Retrieved from *www.capacitybuildingnetwork.org/article7.*

Siegel, D. J. (2011). *Mindsight: The new science of personal transformation.* New York: Bantam Books.

Srinivasan, M. (2014). *Teach, breath, learn.* Berkeley, CA: Parallax Press.

Tan, C. (2012). *Search inside yourself: The unexpected path to achieving success, happiness (and world peace).* New York: Harper Collins.

Thompson, S. (2005). *Leading from the eye of the storm: Spirituality and public school improvement.* Lanham, MD: Rowman & Littlefield Education.

Wheatley, M. J. (2005). Foreword: The human spirit and school leadership. In S. Thompson, *Leading from the eye of the storm: Spirituality and public school improvement* (pp. ix–xiii). Lanham, MD: Rowman & Littlefield Education.

U.S. Department of Education. (2010). Blueprint for reform: The reauthorization of the Elementary and Secondary Education Act. Retrieved from *www2.ed.gov/policy/elsec/leg/blueprint/blueprint.pdf.*

Index

Note. *f* or *t* following a page number indicates a figure or table.